Understand Ethics

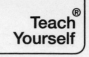

Understand Ethics

Mel Thompson

For UK order enquiries: please contact Bookpoint Ltd,
130 Milton Park, Abingdon, Oxon, OX14 4SB.
Telephone: +44 (0) 1235 827720. Fax: +44 (0) 1235 400454.
Lines are open 09.00–17.00, Monday to Saturday, with a 24-hour
message answering service. Details about our titles and how to order
are available at www.teachyourself.com

For USA order enquiries: please contact McGraw-Hill Customer
Services, PO Box 545, Blacklick, OH 43004-0545, USA.
Telephone: 1-800-722-4726. Fax: 1-614-755-5645.

For Canada order enquiries: please contact
McGraw-Hill Ryerson Ltd, 300 Water St, Whitby,
Ontario, L1N 9B6, Canada. Telephone: 905 430 5000.
Fax: 905 430 5020.

Long renowned as the authoritative source for self-guided
learning – with more than 50 million copies sold worldwide –
the Teach Yourself series includes over 500 titles in the fields of
languages, crafts, hobbies, business, computing and education.

British Library Cataloguing in Publication Data: a catalogue record for
this title is available from the British Library.

Library of Congress Catalog Card Number: on file.

First published in UK 1994 by Hodder Education,
338 Euston Road, London, NW1 3BH.

First published in US 1994 by The McGraw-Hill Companies, Inc.

This edition published 2010.

Previously published as *Teach Yourself Ethics*

The Teach Yourself name is a registered trade mark of Hodder Headline.

Typeset by MPS Limited, A Macmillan Company.

Printed in Great Britain for Hodder Education, a division of Hodder
Headline, 338 Euston Road, London, NW1 3BH, by Cox & Wyman
Ltd, Reading, Berkshire RG1 8EX.

The publisher has used its best endeavours to ensure that the URLs for
external websites referred to in this book are correct and active at the
time of going to press. However, the publisher and the author have
no responsibility for the websites and can make no guarantee that a
site will remain live or that the content will remain relevant, decent or
appropriate.

Hodder Headline's policy is to use papers that are natural, renewable
and recyclable products and made from wood grown in sustainable
forests. The logging and manufacturing processes are expected to
conform to the environmental regulations of the country of origin.

Impression number   10 9 8 7 6 5 4 3
Year   2014 2013 2012 2011 2010

Contents

Meet the author

Welcome to *Understand Ethics*!

It seems to me that our personal lives are shaped by two kinds of things: the circumstances in which we find ourselves and the choices we make. About the former we can often do little; but the latter ... well, that's where ethics comes in. There's nothing more immediately relevant than thinking about issues of good and bad, right and wrong, and making choices that reflect them. Being able to state our views clearly and justify them rationally when it comes to moral questions, is a great way of sorting out the values by which we wish to live, and an aid to personal integrity and a sense of purpose.

And if you are ever tempted to think that ethics is irrelevant, just open a newspaper.

Mel Thompson, 2010

Only got a minute?

Ethics, or 'moral philosophy' is about thinking through issues of right or wrong. It examines the moral choices that people make, what they are based on and how they may be justified.

Ethics can be divided into two elements: ethical theory and applied ethics. 'Ethical theory' asks whether morality should be based on a rational interpretation of nature, anticipated results, personal development or the needs of society, and also examines questions about the status of moral language, free will and so on. 'Applied ethics' applies such theories to various aspects of life: medical ethics, issues of war and peace, life or death, environmental ethics, animal rights, business ethics, etc.

Of course, morality only makes sense if people are free to choose what to do, so we need to examine the extent to which our circumstances – our background, environment, economic position, emotional state – determine us and can justify, and explain, our actions.

Can there be absolute standards of right or wrong, or is everything culturally and socially conditioned? This is key in a multi-cultural environment, where the values on which ethical choices are made may vary between cultural groups.

Ethics links to questions about law and justice, and also to religion; religions offer their followers a particular view of life and a set of values by which to live – both of which have a direct impact on moral questions.

No rational human being can escape moral responsibility, for refusing to even consider whether something is right or wrong is itself a moral choice; only infants, psychopaths and the unconscious are beyond considering such things. Ethics is about life and what we should make of it!

5 Only got five minutes?

'Descriptive ethics' simply looks at how people behave, without trying to tease out whether it is right or wrong to do such things. It deals with facts, not values or judgements. Once you ask if something is right or wrong, you have entered the realm of 'normative ethics': dealing with the norms or principles of action. It is important to recognize the distinction between facts and values, because facts alone do not make a sound ethical argument. The fact that something is socially acceptable does not, in itself, make it right. As the eighteenth-century Scottish philosopher David Hume once said, you cannot derive an 'ought' from an 'is'.

Some argue that we are conditioned by our background and by all that has happened to us, such that each action is completely determined by our past. If that is the case, should anyone be blamed for anything they do? Opposing such determinism is the fact that people believe themselves to be free and responsible – they sense that they have 'free will'.

Given that we experience moral choice, and that we want to comment on the rights or wrongs of what other people do, we need to establish some rational way of deciding such things. The history of ethics provides us with a number of different approaches.

From the thinkers of Ancient Greece – particularly Aristotle – come theories that attempt to decide morality on the basis of the essence or purpose of human life, and on the qualities that constitute the 'good life'. These developed into the 'natural law' and the 'virtue ethics' approaches to moral questions.

The most widely used approach to deciding ethical questions today is 'utilitarianism', which argues that the right thing to do is that which offers the greatest benefit to the greatest number of people involved.

Immanuel Kant sought to devise general principles, based on pure practical reason, to determine whether something was right, irrespective of its consequences. So, for example, it would be wrong to lie because, if everyone were free to lie or break promises, it would make nonsense of the whole idea of truth. He also argued that you should always treat others as ends and never as means. These general principles seem straightforward and clear, but are they practical?

Some have argued that people genuinely seek the good in and for others and that, faced with suffering, feel a natural desire to help. Hume believed that reason takes second place in assessing what we want to do: emotions set our personal agenda. Kant claimed that nobody could be said to be good unless they have a genuinely 'good will'.

There is an entirely separate approach to examining the ethics that apply to society, through the 'social contract'. Governments and laws reflect what people perceive to be in their own best interests.

Of course, most people now live in societies that are multi-cultural, and even where one culture predominates locally, the ubiquitous influence of the media means that everyone is aware of a range of views and cultures. It is therefore tempting to say that all moral arguments, and the values on which they are based, are relative to the particular society from which they have come. But what follows from that? Should you therefore take a relativist line, and allow that anything is okay provided that the local society approves of it?

Ethics is far from easy. Faced with two equally convincing arguments, how do you decide which is right? There is no simple answer to that question – if there were, the world's issues would quickly be resolved. Rather, the process of ethical argument requires hard work and ruthless honesty.

10 Only got ten minutes?

Still wondering whether the study of ethics is relevant to your life? This summary will look at some practical questions and issues to which a study of ethics might be useful.

So let's take a look at the news, selecting just one newspaper, *The Guardian* on one day, Saturday 7 November 2009. This day was not selected on the grounds that it was particularly interesting or different from any other, it just happened to be when I was writing this section of the book, and it was just my usual newspaper. There is no room here to unpack each of the issues raised, nor to give all the details that would be needed for a serious ethical consideration of them; this is simply to set the agenda.

'Culture of impunity' at police unit

This front-page item highlighted the very small percentage of complains about a police squad, many of which alleged 'oppressive behaviour', that were upheld, and said that Scotland Yard faced calls for an 'ethical audit'.

Moral issues here concern the responsibility of those whose duty it is to protect the public, the right of an individual to have a complaint taken seriously, and what (in the real-life conditions of police work) constitutes 'oppressive behaviour'.

Fears of backlash against US Muslims after shooting spree

Following the shooting dead of 13 and injuring 28 by a Muslim soldier at Fort Hood, it was feared that there might be increased hostility towards the Muslim community as a whole. US President Barack Obama and others appealed for people to be patient and not to jump to conclusions about the motive for the killings.

How far does a person's religious or ethnic background influence what they do? It is also important to consider the mental stress that might lead someone to become a mass murderer, and whether any such killer could be of 'sound mind' and therefore morally responsible.

Row over private care in NHS to flare again
Where a health service has limited funds, it is tempting to allow those patients who wish to pay for treatment to do so. The British government agreed to review the way in which the amount of income generated from private sources had been capped.

Should an individual be free to pay for treatment or services within a nationalized service? Some argue that the whole point of a health service is that it should be free at point of delivery, and that all people should be treated equally. Should money should count when it comes to health care? Or is it unfair on those who cannot pay?

Stop corruption or else, Brown warns Karsai
Acknowledging that the government in Afghanistan seems unable to prevent corruption, questions were asked about whether it was fit for purpose.

How should a government be judged? Can there be an international standard? If so, what should be done about the many governments that fall below it, whether through incompetence or the deliberate repression of their people? Should the international community interfere in the internal workings of a sovereign state?

Groups condemn plan to throw turkeys off tower
Animal welfare groups opposed the plan to throw 50 turkeys off a 100 foot high tower, to see whether or not they could fly. The person organizing the pre-Christmas stunt is reported to have said 'It's not cruel because turkeys are supposed to be able to fly like all birds, so if they can, then what's the problem?'

Recently, ethics has become much more aware of the issue of our treatment of other species. Should animals have rights? What happens when animal rights conflict with human needs?

Climate talks end with threats of summit walkout
Negotiations ahead of the Copenhagen climate change summit
in December 2009 were stuck over the issue of how much money
richer countries would provide to help the developing world limit
its carbon emissions, as well as the extent to which they would
commit to cut their own emissions.

How do you establish fairness? This is a key feature of ethics as
well as political philosophy.

Civil unrest has a role, says Gore
Al Gore, a former US presidential candidate, warned that,
unless dramatic action was taken, there was likely to be a rise in
civil disobedience targeted against fossil fuel polluters. In justifying
non-violent law-breaking, he is reported to have said that 'Civil
disobedience has an honourable history, and when the urgency
and moral clarity cross a certain threshold, then I think that civil
disobedience is quite understandable, and it has a role to play.'

Laws are made by agreement, and in a democracy they should be
able to be changed if a majority want it. Is moral conviction, or a
perception of a greater good, sufficient to allow (or even require)
law-breaking?

Student dares to criticize Khamenei to his face
A 25-year-old maths student, speaking at the end of a meeting
between the supreme ruler of Iran, Ayatollah Ali Khamenei, and
scientists, launched an unprecedented criticism of the state media,
and in particular for the fact that no criticism of Khamenei seemed
to be allowed. The supreme leader responded calmly and agreed
that it was right for people to be able to criticize him.

Freedom of speech needs to be balanced against the danger of
allowing people to incite hatred on grounds of race or religion,
or to promote terrorism.

Wall Street gets H1N1 vaccines while hospitals face shortage
Three major financial institutions in New York were among
the first to take delivery of swine flu vaccines, in spite of a

general shortage, having been among the first employers to apply for them.

How does the natural right to look after oneself relate to moral questions about helping those most in need? Is it possible or realistic to accept equal consideration of yourself, your close family, your friends and strangers?

11 bodies and counting... angry families ask why police ignored their pleas

An article suggested that racial prejudice hampered the investigation into what had happened to missing black women in the area around the house in which their bodies were found. In particular, the impression was given that the attempt to find those who were black, or who had drug problems, was regarded as less urgent that for whites from more affluent areas.

This is quite a complex issue, because it may not simply be a matter of radical prejudice, but one of the patterns of behaviour and experience of disappearances in the past. Can you treat everyone as an individual? Should you attempt to do so? How do you avoid social and racial stereotyping? And is such stereotyping a moral fault, or just a lack of imagination or education?

Obama promises fresh help as jobless rate in US hits 10 per cent

A government can stimulate the economy by public spending, tax cuts and by the adjustment of monetary policy. This article looks to government to help the unemployed.

Should society as a whole, in the form of a government, intervene in economic matters? Should everything be left to free markets? Is it natural and inevitable that some will suffer while others succeed? And what responsibility do we all have for those who suffer?

And in the obituary column...

An obituary of Winifred Tumin, who had spend many years involved with the reform of charity management, commented: 'Her close colleagues speak of her blazing sense of justice and her fearless readiness to fight injustice.'

In many spheres of life – as here in the charity sector – there are qualities that make for good ethical judgement. These include a clearly thought out sense of what it right, of what basic justice requires, and an ability to stand back from accepted norms and authorities and to be fearless in challenging them.

By hook or by crook

An article in the 'Work' section describes the techniques used to get prospective job applicants to pay out money for a 'CV rewrite'.

This raises questions about business ethics. Is it right to promise more help than you might realistically be expected to deliver? If you were in the medical profession, might it not seem right to offer treatment even if the hope of recovery were slight? What then is the moral difference between the two situations?

These are just some of the issues raised in one newspaper. To study ethics – looking at ethical theories and how they may be applied to practical issues – sharpens the mental sensitivity to almost everything that appears in the news. Can there be a more important subject to study?

1

Introduction: the art of living

'What should I do?'
'How do I know what is right?'

These basic questions are the starting point for ethical debate, for ethics is about moral choices. It is about the values that lie behind them, the reasons people give for them and the language they use to describe them. It is about innocence and guilt, right and wrong, and what it means to live a good or bad life. It is about the dilemmas of life, death, sex, violence and money. It explores human virtues and vices, rights and duties.

To be interested in ethics is to be interested in life! Each day we are bombarded with news of personal choices and their consequences, from the sexual proclivities of the famous, to the violence and tragedy of war; and from the sight of those who are starving in an otherwise prosperous world, to the casual vandalism and petty crime of inner city streets. The explanations given for these things may vary, from elaborate justifications in terms of a political or economic ideology, to the general complaint that traditional values have vanished. We cannot escape from moral issues, even if we are lucky enough to find that our own lives are untouched by painful decisions or tinges of guilt.

Babies are lucky. They feel hungry, or dirty, or wet, and just scream until someone figures out what is wrong and gives them what they need. They do not have the intellectual ability to question how they got into their particular mess, or the steps they need to take to get out of it. They are not morally responsible.

One essential difference between a baby and a mature adult is that the adult recognizes when there is a problem to be overcome, or a difficult choice to be made, takes action and then accepts responsibility. **Ethics is the rational discussion of that process.**

In this book we shall be looking at a variety of ethical arguments, from Aquinas to Nietzsche, Machiavelli to Hobbes, and Bentham to Kant, testing them out as we apply them to a whole range of moral issues. But first we need to explore just what it is that makes something moral or immoral.

What makes something moral?

Many choices are a straightforward matter of personal preference, and the actions that spring from them are neither moral nor immoral. They only become the subject of moral debate because of the intentions behind them, their results, and the values – of society or of the individual – that they reflect.

Example

Someone asks you 'Shall I wear red or blue?' This is not a moral question and, unless they are going to a political rally, your answer will reflect no more than a preference for one colour rather than another.

BUT – What if the person who asks you is about to take a walk that will lead him or her across a field in which you know there is a particularly unfriendly bull? (Assuming that the bull is not colour blind and hates red!)

The answer now becomes a matter of moral choice. Shall I, out of hatred or mischief, suggest red? If the person is injured or killed, am I to blame? Is the bull guilty, or am I?

If the bull cannot help but charge when it sees red, can it be blamed for doing what comes naturally? On the other hand, if I have a compulsion to cause mischief, which makes it emotionally impossible for me to suggest the safer colour, can I use the same argument to claim my own innocence? If not, then what degree of freedom (psychological, emotional, physical) renders me morally responsible? And are we free, anyway, if every factor is fully taken into account? A close friend, seeing the glint in my eye as my lips frame the word 'red', might comment 'I just knew you'd say that!'

What if I know the bull is in the field, but refuse to suggest which colour the person should wear? Do I bear any moral responsibility for the consequences of withholding that information? Does it make any difference if I secretly hope that they will be hurt, or if I am indifferent? Am I less guilty by taking a passive rather than an active part in the decision?

This example shows that a key question for ethics is that of freedom. If we are not free to choose what we do, we cannot be held morally responsible for our actions.

Our freedom to choose is often limited by the choices of others, and our moral responsibility is therefore proportional to the degree to which our choice is significant. In this case, I take greater responsibility, because the bull was not free to choose whether or not to charge. Where freedom is shared more equally, a person's contribution can be seen positively ('aiding and abetting') or negatively ('contributory negligence').

Actions can be divided into three categories:

▶ **moral** – *if they reflect a person's values and those of society*
▶ **immoral** – *if they go against a person's (or society's) values*
▶ **amoral** – *if they do not reflect choices based on values or social norms.*

Insight

Of course, an individual may think that something is moral even if the rest of society thinks it immoral. Doing something immoral is not the same thing as breaking the law. Actions can be moral but illegal, or immoral but legal.

Whether you think an action is moral or immoral will depend on your values and the ethical arguments you use to decide what is right. How many actions or choices are moral and how many relegated to the general 'amoral' category, will depend on your moral sensitivity, the range of values to which you consciously subscribe, and whether you belong to a society which operates by definite rules and values.

Example

When faced with a restaurant menu, a newly convinced vegetarian with a residual passion for meat will have a greater moral dilemma than a cheerful omnivore. A hungry Jew or Muslim will have added problems if faced with nothing but pork, and for some Buddhists, Hindus and Jains, eating meat may go against their most basic principle of not harming other creatures.

▶ A crucial moral question for one person may be of negligible significance to another.

Issues that are morally significant usually have to do with relationships, agreements between parties, intentions and possible outcomes. The moral status of an action may therefore depend less on what actually happens than on the intention of the person who performs it and the appropriateness of what is done.

Example

A masked stranger makes you lie on a table, drugs you into unconsciousness, takes out a sharp knife and slices into your naked body. Is the action moral, immoral or amoral?

At this point you might well want to know if the person with the knife is a competent surgeon or a student of the Marquis de Sade!

A description of the action itself is not necessarily the best guide to its moral consequences. You might therefore ask:

- Is this a qualified surgeon?
- Have I consented to this operation?
- Is it likely to benefit me?
- Have the implications of it been explained to me?
- If the person is not a surgeon, do I want him or her to continue? (It might, after all, be an emergency, and an unqualified surgeon might be better than none.)
- What are his or her motives for doing this operation? (Money? Genuine altruism?)
- If for motives other than these (e.g. sexual gratification), would I still want him or her to continue, if I believed that it would benefit me?

Facts alone do not decide whether something is right or wrong: 'People are dying of starvation' is not a moral statement. But if you add '... and you are doing nothing to help', then it becomes a moral issue if the person addressed is in a position to help, but does not do so.

Nuclear power ...

A headline, highlighting a report published in March 2006 into the future of nuclear power generation in Britain, read:

'Nuclear power is dangerous, expensive and unwanted.'

This may look like a moral statement, but it is not. It simply records an interpretation of facts that have been investigated. In order to turn it into an ethical argument about whether it is 'right' to go ahead with a new generation of nuclear reactors, one would need to say whether, and on what grounds, the danger and cost were worthwhile – a life-saving operation can be dangerous and costly, but people do not say that it is therefore wrong to carry it

(Contd)

out! Whether it is wanted or not depends on the views of those consulted and the alternatives available – and that, in itself, does not make an ethical argument.

In other words, for an issue or an action to be described as moral, it needs to take into consideration human choices and intentions and the values that lie behind them.

Insight

Simply presenting facts, however important they may be, is not the same thing as framing an ethical argument.

What is the point of ethics?

In practical terms, the study of ethics can offer two things. First of all, it helps one to appreciate the moral choices that people make, and to evaluate the justification they give for those choices. But secondly, it involves a reflective sharpening of one's own moral awareness – a conscious examination of values and principles, of how these have influenced one's life, and (more importantly) of how they can be used to shape the future.

You already know far more about ethics than you might realize, for although 'Ethics' is a branch of philosophy with a long history of debates, its own special terminology and standard arguments, it is based on principles which, consciously or unconsciously, people use all the time in deciding what to do. You do not have to know the term 'utilitarian' in order to see the sense in wanting to choose what promises to give the greatest benefit to the greatest number of people. Therefore, although this book will outline ethical theories and the terms used in ethical debate, they will be examined in the context of actual dilemmas. Some moral choices are clear-cut; others are more problematic. It is by looking at the problematic ones that we start to appreciate the issues involved in ethical debate.

A situation

In August 2009, Ali Mohmed al-Megrahi was released from prison in Scotland on compassionate grounds and allowed to return to his native Libya, since he was suffering from prostate cancer and was thought to have only three months to live. He had been convicted in 2001 of the 1988 bombing of a Pan Am airliner over Lockerbie in which 270 people died, but had always protested his innocence and was preparing to appeal again against his sentence.

The Scottish justice secretary made it clear that al-Megrahi was released on humanitarian grounds, not as part of any political deal, and that he was, in any case, under sentence of death from 'a higher power' (in other words, God). It was argued that one should show mercy even to those who showed no mercy themselves. At a press conference, the justice secretary said:

The perpetuation of an atrocity and outrage cannot and should not be a basis for losing sight of who we are, the values we seek to uphold, and the faith and beliefs by which we seek to live. Mr al-Megrahi did not show his victims any comfort or compassion. [But] compassion and mercy are about upholding the beliefs we seek to live by, remaining true to our values as a people, no matter the severity of the provocation or the atrocity perpetuated.

For these reasons alone, it is my decision that Mr al-Megrahi be released on compassionate grounds and allowed to return to Libya to die.

Al-Megrahi's release was opposed by the British and American governments and by many who had lost relatives in the bombing. One relative in the US said that it was 'utterly despicable' to show him any compassion.

(Contd)

There are several interlocking moral issues here:

▶ Is it right to show mercy to someone guilty of such a crime? Some argued that retribution demanded that he should die in prison.

▶ It was never clear who was behind the bombing, whether or not it was ordered by the Libyan (or other) government, and what part al-Megrahi played in the overall plot – he certainly could not have acted alone, even if guilty. How secure was his conviction?

▶ If al-Megrahi had been acting under orders, should he take full responsibility for what was done? Is his situation any different from an agent or soldier who kills under orders from his government?

▶ Shortly before the Lockerbie bombing, an Airbus A300, flying in Iranian airspace with 290 people on board, was shot down by a US guided missile cruiser, sailing within Iranian territorial waters, which mistook it for a fighter aircraft. In 1996, the US agreed to pay $61.8 million in compensation to Iran for those killed. Is it possible that the Pan Am bombing was a response to this – an act which (even if the result of a mistake) could be regarded as a sign of a recklessly proactive use of force?

▶ If it was, does that lessen the guilt of whoever ordered the Lockerbie bombing?

In 2009 it was revealed that, far from being a modest employee of the airline, Megrahi held £1.8 million in a Swiss bank account. It was argued that he was handling the money in order to break international sanctions against Libya and buy aircraft parts. There is no evidence available to explain the money or its intended use. A British member of parliament, hearing about the bank account, said 'Far from being the wrong man, this suggests Megrahi was an international co-ordinator of terrorism for Libya.'

This is an example of evidence being used to reach a premature conclusion about guilt or innocence. Evidence that might be used to prove the breaking of sanctions is here attached to the terrorism accusation.

There is nothing simple about the ethical issues here. Moral choices, political and legal process, and the sense of outrage at loss of life blend into a situation where care is needed to ascertain exactly which, and to what extent, any one person is responsible for what happens.

In practice, ethics tends to start by observing the moral choices people make and the reasons they give for them. From these it produces theories about what is, or should be, the basis for saying that something is morally right or wrong. It then returns to consider actual situations, to see whether the theories help to make sense of the moral issues and lead conclusions that make sense logically and practically.

Insight

This procedure is similar to that used by science, where hypotheses are framed as a result of observations and then tested out against subsequent evidence to see if they are adequate. But, whereas science seeks to explain reality, ethics seeks to change and influence it, with commitment rather than scientific objectivity.

What price integrity?

Maturity is about taking responsibility for your own life and acting in a way that reflects your own values. And a key feature of maturity is personal integrity – applying basic values to the decision-making process, and therefore living in a way that allows your personality to be expressed in what you do. But what price integrity? One of the hazards of taking ethics seriously, and of trying to live up to personal values, is that one may have to take the consequences, and that may not lead to the most comfortable or hassle-free life. What of those who risk their own lives in order to save others? Those who publicly expose corruption? Those who campaign for human rights in a country where they are systematically denied?

There is always a temptation to compromise principles for the sake of an easy life, but often it is a matter of scale. If a moderately well-off person is offered a quick, risk-free way of making £10 through some morally dubious scheme, he or she might well refuse. But what if the same scheme involved millions of pounds? If it promised to benefit not just that person but many other people as well? When the stakes are very high, integrity (and the morality that it entails) becomes expensive!

Example

Let us look at an example connected with the two great motivators: sex and money. If you were to be offered £50 to have sex with someone you do not particularly like, you could afford to take a moral line (e.g. that, as a matter of principle, you will only have sex with someone you like, and that you will certainly not set aside that principle, and therefore your integrity, for the sum of £50). You therefore decline the offer.

But what if you were desperate and hungry? What if you were on the streets (literally) with no means of support? Compared with the need for food, shelter and £50, sex might be regarded as an inconvenient necessity of survival. You could argue that your integrity requires that your own survival, and perhaps that of others who depend on you, should take precedence over your sexual preferences. There are many places where prostitution is undertaken for just such reasons. How does that change the moral nature of the act?

Or change the scale of rewards on offer:

There is someone who has fallen in love with you, but you do not find him or her attractive. On the other hand, he or she is wealthy. This relationship will provide you with all that you have ever dreamed of. Might it not be worth a little pretence? Might you not feel that you really could 'fake it' – for years if necessary – for the sake of all that? Might it not be possible, you argue, justifying your decision, that you will eventually get to like this wealthy partner?

The crucial test, however, is the choice between integrity and survival; to choose death rather than loss of integrity is the basic question behind every martyrdom, from Socrates, through centuries of religious persecution, to those who agree to give testimony against criminals or terrorists, knowing that they risk their lives doing so.

Rights and responsibilities

So far we have been looking at how individual moral choices reflect ideas about right and wrong, but there is another side to ethics. Much discussion in ethics is about the rights that a person should have – in other words, what they can reasonably expect society to do for them, and what they are expected to contribute to society in return. These are embodied in, for example, the United Nations Universal Declaration of Human Rights. We assume that, in a civilized society, people will be treated in a way that respects their basic needs (as in the American Constitution) for life, liberty and the pursuit of happiness. Where there are gross violations of these basic rights, we may recoil in horror. We say, 'It should not be allowed!' but are then forced to recognize that there may be nobody able to enforce those standards – that torture, execution or genocide is allowed in that place. Innocent people are allowed to be killed. Society does not act to impose a moral standard, either because it cannot, or because it will not.

Looking at society as a whole, we can ask:

▶ *What rights should you have?*
▶ *What responsibilities should you accept?*
▶ *Do you have a duty to fulfil a certain role in society?*

In other words, what can we expect of other people, and what can they expect of us? What is it that makes a society 'civilized'?

Not all rules imposed by society are necessarily moral. In the UK, a person is required drive on the left-hand side of the road. In the United States, the same person is required to drive on the right. That is a social convention, so obeying it is not a matter of morality. Social etiquette and convenience are not the same thing as social morality, even though they can influence behaviour. They only become the subject of moral debate when they concern matters of value, and imply general views about the purpose and nature of human life.

For reflection

In Kigali, Rwanda, on 24 April 1998, 22 people found guilty of genocide in the 1994 civil war were executed. Tied to posts in a football field, hoods were placed over their heads and 'targets' tied around their chests. Masked police ran from one to the next, pumping bullets into the targets, followed by another policeman with a pistol who gave the coups de grace at point blank range. This was watched by a crowd of many thousands, including women and children, who cheered as justice was seen to be done. Many of those watching had suffered and been bereaved as a result of the earlier civil war.

This took place in spite of calls for clemency, and was condemned by the United Nations, the European Union, the Vatican and human rights groups.

▶ Issues are never simple. How do you deal with the aftermath of genocide? Is there a place for retribution? What responsibility does the international community have to attempt to prevent the atrocities of civil war in the first place? How, in the confusion of a bloodbath, do you establish the sort of evidence needed for a fair trial? Exactly how do these executions differ legally and morally from those

carried out on convicted criminals in the United States and
elsewhere?

▶ Faced with the horror of what human beings can do to one
another, instant or emotionally charged responses are seldom
adequate. We need to assess the whole situation and look
logically at the moral principles involved.

In asking these questions, we have already started the process of
ethical debate; we have asked about laws and rights and about the
expected consequences of actions; we may sense instinctively that
certain things are wrong, no matter what the circumstances, and
seek to justify that conviction.

The art of living

A work of art is something created, by inspiration, by intuition, by
a sense of balance, by a thoughtful use of the materials available.
It offers more than a simple view of canvas, paint, stone or whatever
else has been used. It may be minimalist, saying something through
its very simplicity. It may be rich in symbolism or colour or form,
complex and challenging. But whatever it is, a work of art is the
deliberate product of a mind. It is an attempt to 'say something',
to express meaning, or value, or hope.

Ethics is about the art of living – seeing our life as the material
out of which, through the choices we make, we are gradually
constructing a work of art. We are more than flesh, bones and
mortgages. We cannot be defined by our financial, work, social
or political status. We are not simply consumers. We are not
automata, programmed by genetic, environmental and social
factors. We have feelings, intuitions, dreams, ambitions.

But what has this to do with a more usual list of moral issues?

▶ *Should I have an abortion?*
▶ *Should I help these people to die if they are in pain?*
▶ *Should I join the army or be a pacifist?*
▶ *Should I take advantage of someone else's financial miscalculation?*

You may choose to think through all these things (and this book will encourage you to do just that), but if you are faced with one of these choices, especially if the stakes are very high, your choice may not be based on rational thought alone. It will be based, in all probability, on the cumulative effect of many other choices that you have made over the years. Fundamentally, it will be based on what your life is actually trying to 'say'. It will be based on the image you have of yourself and your (perhaps unconscious) convictions about life.

This introduction has presented what we might call the 'existential' aspect of ethics – looking at the way in which our moral choices reflect who we are and what we want to become. That is a very personal approach to the subject and not one that everyone would favour, but it is useful in reminding us that ethics links to fundamental questions about the value and meaning of human life. Unless we have a sense of what human life is for, or why it has value for us, ethics can become simply a matter of pragmatic calculation. It is the values which lie behind ethical arguments that link them to the broader philosophical and religious questions. You can certainly study ethics without taking this personal approach – looking at agreements and obligations, or applying utilitarian principles, for example – but, for most people, ethics remains a matter of personal commitment to take moral dilemmas seriously.

THINGS TO REMEMBER

From this chapter, remember that ...

▶ *ethics is concerned with the rational justification of moral judgements*

▶ *ethics can be applied to almost all aspects of life*

▶ *ethics examines the process of making choices and taking responsibility*

▶ *moral questions concern conscious human decisions and intentions*

▶ *morality presupposes and requires free will*

▶ *actions can be categorized as moral, immoral and amoral*

▶ *moral significance goes beyond the facts of a situation*

▶ *ethics reflects questions about maturity and integrity*

▶ *ethics considers agreed rights and responsibilities*

▶ *an existential approach to ethics looks at the way in which people give shape and meaning to their lives.*

2

Free to choose?

In this chapter you will learn:

- *to explore how much freedom we need to make sense of morality*
- *how reductionism challenges moral arguments*
- *how philosophers have tackled the issue of freedom and determinism.*

What kind of freedom?

Nobody is completely free to do anything that he or she may wish. Freedom is limited in different ways:

▶ *I may decide that I would like to launch myself into the air, spread my arms and fly. I may have dreamed of doing so. I may have a passion for Superman films, and feel certain that in some way it should be possible. But my physical body is, and will always be, incapable of unaided flight. To overcome that limitation, I must resort to technology.*

▶ *I may wish to be a famous and highly talented artist, musician or gymnast, but my freedom is again limited. It may not be physically impossible for me to achieve these things, but it requires such a level of experience, training and natural ability, that my chances of achieving what I want are severely restricted.*

▶ *I may wish to go to London and parade myself naked before Buckingham Palace. There is no physical limitation to inhibit me and no great skill required, but I am likely to be arrested if I do so.*

These are examples of limitation to actual freedom. Whether by physical laws, natural abilities, or legal or social restraints, we are all limited in what we can do.

If I am to make a moral choice, I must be free to do, or not to do, the thing in question. It cannot be morally wrong of me not to fly, because I am unable to do so. On the other hand, walking about naked in public could become a moral issue – if it were argued that I would give offence by doing so – because it would be something that I had chosen to do and could have refused to do had I considered it wrong.

Determinism

Science is based on the observation of natural events and their causes, and from the resulting information is able to develop theories by which events may be predicted.

You look up and say 'I think it is going to rain.' You do not thereby imply that the weather has a personality, and that you guess that it has decided to enjoy a little precipitation. Rather, you make a comment based on the clouds, wind, dampness in the air, and on your observation of similar things leading to rain on previous occasions.

▶ *The falling of rain is determined absolutely by certain atmospheric conditions.*
▶ *The fact that you may be inaccurate in predicting those conditions, and therefore the coming of rain, does not detract from the fundamentally determined nature of that event.*

> ▶ *Given certain conditions, it will rain; without them, it will not: the weather is determined. Its absolute prediction is theoretically possible, even if practically difficult.*

The prediction of rain is possible because it is recognized that all physical phenomena are causally connected. Everything from the weather to the electrical impulses within human brains can be explained in terms of physical laws. This is **determinism.**

From the rise of modern science in the seventeenth century to the early part of the twentieth century, it could be said with some certainty that science was mechanistic. The whole world was seen as a machine, knowledge of which would enable mankind to predict and control the action of individual things. Even the process of evolution, as set out by Darwin, had a mechanistic and **determinist** basis. With the theory of natural selection, we have a clear example of the way in which change is forced forward through the operation of an impersonal law; that only those who survive to adulthood are able to breed, and it is they, rather than others of the species, who pass on their characteristics to future generations.

Although, in the general run of things, science still appears to be largely determinist, some philosophers have made much of the fact that in quantum mechanics, for example, things at a sub-atomic level happen in a random way. Overall trends can be seen, but the action of individual particles cannot be predicted. But that does not imply that, at the level at which humans engage, the whole world is indeterminate – that is limited to the world of particle physics.

Insight

At that sub-atomic level, the very act of observing some phenomena causes them to change, so it is not possible to formulate and test out physical laws with quite the crude certainty that prevailed in the nineteenth century. That does not discredit the general rule that events are determined by pre-existing causes and conditions.

Nevertheless, overall, including the spheres of sociology and psychology (which explore issues that are morally significant), science has retained a largely determinist viewpoint. There is a general acceptance that all events (including human action) may be explained in terms of prior events, which are considered to have caused them. And in the case of human action, this may be explained (at least to some extent) in terms of the effect of environment or upbringing on the individual, along with all the other physical constraints that limit our action.

Example

A car swerves across the road and collides with a tree, killing the driver.

Why did the car swerve? Did a tyre burst? If so, how worn was it? Was there a fault in its manufacture? Was there a steering fault in the car? If so, was there a design fault? (Accidents in which the harm done is made worse through a design fault can lead to the manufacturer being prosecuted, as having contributed to that overall harm.)

What if you trace everything back, from the skill of the driver, to the food that he or she has been eating (was the driver faint? sick? drunk?), to whether the tree should have been planted so close to the road? The driver may have had control over some of these things, but not over others. Yet everything that has ever happened contributes in some way to each event. Is anyone to blame? What if the road had not been built? What if cars had not been invented?

If we had total knowledge, everything would be seen to fit a seamless pattern of cause and effect. But those experiencing that event (the driver before dying; those who knew him, or witnessed the crash) will see it differently. They may wish that other decisions had been made. They may feel guilty, saying 'if only…'. There is an inescapable sense that events are influenced by human choice. Without that sense, the issue of moral responsibility would not arise.

We may be socially or psychologically predisposed to act in a certain way, as a result of upbringing or environment. Our genetic make-up may give a predisposition to violence, depression, schizophrenia or our particular sexual orientation. Does that imply that we take no responsibility for these things?

If a direct causal link could be shown, then the case for determinism in these areas of life would be strengthened. On the other hand, whereas physical traits (e.g. the colour of one's eyes) are 100 per cent due to heredity, studies of twins have suggested that behavioural factors, such as homosexuality, can have a heredity factor as low as 31 per cent. This illustrates what common sense would suggest, that there are other factors as well as our genes that influence our behaviour. This does not, however, disprove a claim that everything is determined. It merely shows that no one factor alone can be shown to determine the final result, but taken together they do so, each contributing something to the determinist equation.

Example

With advances in genetics, it has become widely recognized that many features of life, from sexual orientation to the predisposition to certain illnesses, could be detected via one's DNA. Thus, for example, insurance companies or mortgage lenders could require a genetic test to assess a person's likely future health. But what are the implications of such information?
Take homosexuality as an example:

▶ If homosexuality is genetically determined, would that imply that one's sexual preferences are not a matter for moral debate?
▶ For those who are anxious about their sexual orientation, it may alleviate a sense of guilt, instilled by some traditional social or religious opposition to homosexuality, for it is difficult to see how a person can be blamed for his or her genetic constitution.
▶ If a simple blood test could show homosexual orientation, and if that test could be carried out on a foetus early in pregnancy, would that be a sufficient reason for abortion if the parents felt that they did not want homosexual offspring? If so, on what moral grounds?

> ▶ If varieties of behaviour (whether sexual or otherwise) are due
> to genes, should all forms of behaviour be accepted as of equal
> value? If not, then on what basis do you hold that some forms of
> behaviour are right and others wrong?
>
> Even if genetic determinism were proved, that would not in itself
> remove all these moral issues.

Insight

In the third of the points in the box above, the moral issue is
not whether homosexuality is right or wrong, but whether
it would ever be right for parents to choose – on the basis of
their own moral views – whether their child should or should
not be born.

These things may influence our freedom, but not necessarily the
freedom of our will (which we shall examine further on page 32).
We may *believe* we are free to choose, even if the psychologist,
sociologist or behavioural geneticist claims to know better.

Reductionism

Reductionism is a philosophical rather than an ethical problem, but
it is relevant because it claims to render moral language, and the
whole idea of personal freedom, meaningless.

I raise my arm, reaching out to pick up a pen. What is actually
happening?

▶ *The muscles contract due to a chemical change.*
▶ *That chemical change is brought about through stimuli
passing through nerve cells.*
▶ *The tiny electrical impulses in the nerves originate in the brain.*
▶ *The brain contains many millions of tiny circuits. For every
movement of the body and thought passing through the mind,
there is the corresponding electrical impulse in the brain.*

If you pass an electric charge across my brain, I will twitch my muscles involuntarily. If the blood supply to part of the brain is cut off, those brain cells will die, and as a result parts of my body will cease to operate normally (as happens when someone has a cerebral thrombosis). I may not be aware that the damage is in my brain; all I will know is that my leg will not work.

Now this leads a **reductionist** to claim that the thoughts we have are 'nothing but' electrical impulses. Freedom is therefore an illusion in two ways: firstly, it is theoretically possible to predict any choice; secondly, choice is actually nothing but a set of electrical impulses that follow the laws of physics. Against this one could argue that such reductionism is like saying that a book is but a collection of letters printed on paper, or that a painting is nothing but spots of pigment on canvas. Whatever physical analysis a reductionist may offer, my experience of the book or of the painting is of something *more than* their material bases.

For moral choice (and therefore ethics) to make any sense, I have to believe that a person is *more than* determined electrical impulses. Yet there is nothing I can do that does not also involve the operation of my brain and, however many life-support systems I may be plugged into, once my brain is dead I am, in a physical sense at least, no more.

Insight

If a person accepts that all physical processes are causally determined, and that all personal choices and moral decisions can be reduced to electrical impulses in the brain, then ethics is meaningless. Our apparent freedom is an illusion caused by our failure to perceive the significance of brain activity.

A reductionist view also drains moral language of any valid meaning. A philosophical movement called **logical positivism**, which was influential in the early part of the twentieth century, took the view that statements were meaningful only if they were true by definition, or if they could be shown to be true by observation. 'Two plus two equals four' is true because it is a matter of mathematical definition. The statement 'There is a tree in the garden' they took to mean 'if you were to look out into the garden, you would see a tree' – it is therefore meaningful because there is evidence (actual or potential) to prove it true or false. But the statement 'It is wrong to kill' is neither a definition, nor could you find anything in the world 'out there' corresponding to the word 'wrong'. On this test, morality is meaningless, because it is based neither on logic nor on evidence.

Insight

The *only* valid form of ethics for a reductionist is **descriptive ethics** – saying what in fact happens in different societies, since that can be checked and confirmed by observation.

Notice why it is important to think clearly about reductionist and determinist claims:

▶ *A determinist says that all decisions are the result of prior factors. If determinism is true, we are not free to choose what to do. We therefore deserve neither praise nor blame for our actions. We do not have to know all the causes to take a determinist view – we just have to believe that there are sufficient causes.*

▶ *A reductionist claims that all mental operations are in fact electrical impulses in the brain. On that basis, they are part of the physical world and subject to determinism.*

▶ *We cannot be told that we ought to do something, unless we can do it. Without an adequate measure of freedom, morality makes no sense.*

Freedom and the State

In the discussion so far, we have been looking in a rather abstract way at whether or not a person is free to decide how to act. But in practical terms, even if we feel that we are free, we are actually constrained by the legal and social rules of the society within which we live.

If we are caught breaking a law, we are punished. If we are not caught, we may still feel guilty. Freedom is not simply a matter of biology, but of social and political life. If a person joins in a demonstration in favour of greater freedom, he or she is unlikely to be concerned about whether there can be a scientific explanation for each muscular action as he or she walks forward; but more likely to be campaigning for social or political freedom and restoration to the individual, of choices presently prohibited by some authority.

But should every individual be free to choose exactly how he or she should live? In any particular country, people need to decide whether they will all drive on the right or the left, otherwise there will be chaos on the roads. Common sense dictates that an individual should not have the freedom to drive on the other side. But should everyone automatically have a right to take part in the democratic process to select a government? The answer to this is not so clear, because the results are less obvious.

Plato, for example, (in *The Republic* book IX) argued that most ordinary people did not have a strongly rational nature, and therefore needed to be constrained in what they did by being ruled by those who were naturally more rational. Philosophers alone, he thought, would have sufficient detachment to be able to legislate for the good of society as a whole. In that book, Plato presents the different arguments in the form of a debate between individuals. One of these, Thrasymachus, argues that laws are always made in the interests of the ruling class, and Glaucon comments that basically everyone would like to act from purely selfish motives, although all would suffer as a result of the ensuing chaos. Both of these views of human and social motives find echoes throughout the history of ethics.

Insight

If most people live selfishly, social anarchy may result – therefore, some argue, you need established principles of right and wrong, to which people are required to give their allegiance. We shall examine this again in Chapter 7.

Mill: *On Liberty*

One of the key arguments about freedom was presented by the nineteenth-century philosopher J.S. Mill in his book *On Liberty*. He argued that, in all conduct that is 'self regarding' (in other words, whatever concerns yourself alone), there should be absolute liberty. The only limitation on liberty was what he termed the 'harm' principle, namely that you should do nothing that causes harm to another person. And, of course, it follows that you should allow everyone else the same degree of freedom that you seek for yourself.

The implication of this is that, if whatever you do concerns only yourself (or other consenting adults) you should be free to do it, **even if you harm yourself in the process**. The only point at which the law should step in, or you should be criticized morally, is if your actions – or words, or thoughts – cause harm to others.

The context of Mill's argument was that he wanted everyone to be able to develop themselves to their maximum potential, and not be stunted by having to conform to the norms of others. He saw freedom as an essential requirement for that.

How much freedom does morality need?

▶ *It does not need us to be absolutely free.*
▶ *It does not even need us to be free of things that influence our moral choice (indeed, the more sensitive a person is, the more he or she is aware of such influences).*

However, morality requires that:

▶ *Whatever may happen in terms of the mechanical side of life, we experience ourselves as free agents who can make genuine choices.*

▶ *Even if I admit the existence of external moral pressure to conform to some rule, I am acting morally only if I am in a position to think about and either conform to or reject the pressures on me.*

▶ *Other people, observing my behaviour, may come to conclusions about my personality and general attitude towards life. Having done so, they may predict accurately what I will do in any given circumstance. That element of prediction, however accurate, does not in itself prevent me from experiencing myself as making a free choice.*

FREE WILL

It is important to make the distinction between freedom in general and freedom of the will. I may look at various options, and think that I am free to choose between them. Someone who knows me well may, on hearing my decision, say 'I just knew you would choose to do that!' Is it possible for my will to be free, for it to be possible for me to weigh up all the factors involved and come to a genuinely free choice, and yet for someone else to be able to predict accurately what I will do? (And it will not be any use changing my mind at the last minute, or acting out of character, because those things too could be predicted.)

There is something intensely irritating about people saying that they know exactly what you will freely choose to do. This is because, in the moment of choice, we experience freedom. Robots and computers may be totally predictable, but most humans are convinced that they themselves are not.

Consider the following cases of murder:

1 *A thief shoots and kills a bank clerk in the course of a raid.*
2 *A husband or wife kills his or her partner after years of provocation and unhappiness.*
3 *A young man rapes and kills a girl whom he has not met before, on account of his particularly violent sexual urges.*
4 *A psychopath, unwisely released from a secure hospital to live in the community, kills someone for no apparent reason, does not attempt to conceal the crime, and shows no remorse when apprehended and charged with murder.*

All four have killed another human being. But are they all equally guilty in a moral sense? Do any of them have genuine grounds for having the charge of murder reduced to that of manslaughter, for example?

1 *It is assumed that the bank robber freely chooses to carry a weapon. Even if the actual shot were the result of being startled by a sudden movement, for example, that does not detract significantly from the general view that his act was murder, because he exercised freedom of the will in deciding to carry a loaded weapon.*
2 *With domestic murder, there may be a significant element of provocation. In that case, especially if the murder takes place in the course of a heated argument, it might be argued that the victim contributed to the situation that brought about the crime, or that (if sufficiently provoked) the murder took place while the person concerned was temporarily deranged. He or she might be charged with manslaughter on the grounds of diminished responsibility.*
3 *The issue in the case of the sexual murder is one of the freedom of the murderer to decide whether or not to act on his sexual impulses. If it can be shown that the condition is such that the person is not in control of himself or herself in certain situations, then psychiatric reports would be relevant evidence to bring before the court.*
4 *The psychopath is not in control of his or her actions, and does not respond to the normal inhibitions and rational constraints that apply to those who are sane.*

Two situations

A woman suffering from schizophrenia stabbed and killed a worker in the hostel into which she had moved on discharge from hospital. She was found not guilty of murder, on grounds of insanity. She claimed to believe that her victim was the anti-Christ.

In another case, a plea of manslaughter was accepted because 'his responsibility at the time of the killing was substantially impaired as a result of schizophrenic illness and/or psychopathic personality disorder' but that 'that mental state was likely to have been compounded by abuse of crack cocaine and alcohol'.

In the first of these, the plea for insanity seems straightforward, but in the second, there is the additional factor of having taken drugs.

▶ Does this mean that the person is morally responsible because taking drugs (as opposed to his illness) was a freely chosen act?
▶ Is it reasonable to argue that someone with that degree of mental disturbance is able to take responsibility for choosing whether or not to take drugs?

In each case, the law accepted a charge of manslaughter. But is there any moral responsibility here? Does it lie with the killer, or with the society that allows killers to be in a situation where their lack of normal restraint can lead to such harm? In what sense was either of them free?

The psychopath is certainly not free to choose how to act. But what of the person with an uncontrollable sexual urge? Or the provoked wife? In each case we have to examine personal, psychological and social factors.

Suppose it is shown that there is more vandalism in areas of high unemployment. Does that imply that those who are unemployed are less able to choose freely what they do? Are social pressures enough to justify actions, that can be regarded by other people as morally wrong?

In extreme situations, the pressure on a person is so great, that he or she feels that all freedom to choose what to do has been taken away. Unlike the psychopath, he or she is fully aware of the implications of what is done, but the need to act in that particular way is overwhelming. This is loss of freedom, but not freedom of the will. An extreme example of this is where death is the only alternative to a particular course of action.

Examples

Survivors of a plane crash in the Andes realize that they will die unless they get food. The only possibility is to eat the flesh of those of their number who have already died. Some refuse, and die. Others, reluctantly, eat the flesh, and many of them survive. The fact that some of them are able to make the choice not to eat, shows that the survivors can still exercise freedom of the will.

► If the only option is death, freedom is severely limited.
► In these circumstances, can cannibalism be regarded as a morally acceptable choice?

In 2004, photographs were published showing the abuse of Iraqi prisoners by their US guards in Abu Grahib prison. One feature of the abuse was forcing men to perform actions of which they would feel ashamed. In such cases, the prisoner loses his freedom to act as he wishes, but not his free will. The fact that he can feel humiliation and guilt shows that he is acting against his will, and yet feels responsible for what he has actually done. In other words, the person feels guilty at having been forced to behave in a particular way, even if the only alternative was to accept whatever was threatened if he did not obey.

(Contd)

Interestingly, in such situations there may be a mismatch between what is observed and what is experienced. From the external point of view, the humiliated prisoner is innocent and a victim, since he was forced to act against his will. From the point of view of the person experiencing it, however, there may be a sense of guilt at having given in to the pressure to obey.

One particularly interesting example of the way in which freedom can be limited is that of blackmail or hostage taking.

In the case of blackmail, there may well be three different moral situations involved:

▶ *The blackmailer is trying to limit the freedom of his or her victim, which, in itself, is a moral (most would say 'immoral') act.*
▶ *The person blackmailed may be required to do something that he or she regards as morally wrong.*
▶ *But the person blackmailed may also act out of fear that some other action from his or her past will be exposed if he or she does not comply with the blackmailer's demands – the acceptance of responsibility for this creates the third moral dilemma.*

Hence, the blackmail victim has three choices:

▶ *To admit to whatever past action the blackmailer is threatening to expose.*
▶ *Go public on the blackmail, which may also involve an admission of the action for which he or she is being blackmailed.*
▶ *Do what the blackmailer says.*

Where hostage taking or blackmail affect the lives of others, the pressure to conform to the blackmailer's demands may be even greater, as in the following situation.

A situation

The manager of a supermarket is attacked in his home by thieves who demand that he takes money from his own supermarket and delivers it to them. His wife and two children are held. He is told that they will be harmed if he fails to carry out the orders he has been given.

▶ As he drives to the supermarket that morning, is he free to choose what he will do?
▶ Should he be morally blamed for taking the money and handing it over?
▶ If he informs the police and his wife or children are harmed as a result, who is to blame for that harm? Does he share the blame with the thieves who actually carried it out, on the grounds that he could have prevented it by following their instructions?

In February 2006, a robbery at the Securitas Depot in Kent, in which thieves made off with over £50 million in banknotes, posed exactly the same moral dilemma for the security manager, who was threatened at gunpoint and told that his wife and son, who were being held by the thieves, would be at risk if he did not co-operate. In the end, the robbery went ahead and no one was harmed physically. No blame of any sort attached to the manager, as it was recognized that, with his wife and son held, he was not free to do other than as ordered.

Blackmail, whether of an emotional or physical variety, is the attempt to change what a person would be expected to do according to his or her own free will. A person who is being blackmailed is still free to choose whether or not to conform to the blackmailer's demands, but now there are radical new factors to take into account.

In the case given above, if there had been no threat, the supermarket manager would have been in a position to balance the benefit of having a large sum of money against the likelihood of being caught stealing from his shop, and his sense of honesty and loyalty to his company. In such circumstances, he would probably choose not to steal, which is what happened on every other day as he went to work. However, if the choice is between the death of wife and children on the one hand, and stealing from the company on the other, then – even if he were to be caught, blamed and given a long prison sentence – he might judge it the right thing to do.

Insight
What is being taken away from the supermarket manager in this instance is the freedom to act without duress – not free will as such. The choice is therefore still a moral one.

A situation

After years of what was described in court as 'constant abuse, withdrawal of sexual relations and suggestions that he was not a real man and could not provide a proper home' a Cambridgeshire man battered his wife to death and buried her body in the garden. During his trial in December 1998, it was pointed out that her abuse and ridicule had destroyed his self-esteem, affected his health, and caused him to attempt suicide twice. On the night before the murder, he was said to have suffered a 'torrent of abuse'. He pleaded manslaughter on grounds of diminished responsibility, and was sentenced to six years imprisonment.

▶ In such a situation, to what extent can the husband be considered 'free' at the point at which he killed his wife?

Overall, we need to be aware that nobody is completely free, for we all act within physical, emotional, social, legal or political constraints. On the other hand, such constraints still leave scope for freedom of the will; if we make choices, if we decide whether or not to obey a rule, we are exercising what feels like personal freedom. The key question is whether that experience of freedom is real or illusory. And if it is illusory – if it can be shown that everything is determined and explicable – does that take away all personal responsibility?

THINGS TO REMEMBER

From this chapter, remember that ...

▶ *an individual's freedom may be limited by physical circumstances, natural abilities or legal restraints*

▶ *determinism argues that every event is explained by prior causes*

▶ *we can never know the sum total of causes for an event*

▶ *reductionism is the view that mental acts (i.e. moral choices) are nothing but brain activity*

▶ *Mill argued for the maximum liberty, as long as it was compatible with not harming other people*

▶ *there is a difference between absolute freedom and free will*

▶ *whereas freedom is observed, free will is experienced*

▶ *moral and legal responsibility requires a sufficient degree of freedom*

▶ *blackmail is the attempt to subvert free will*

▶ *'diminished responsibility' implies the inability to act freely.*

3

....

What do we mean?

In this chapter you will learn:
- *about the three different kinds of ethical language*
- *some key terms used in ethical language.*
- *four basic theories about ethical language.*

Three kinds of language

To make moral statements, or to argue about them in ethical debate, we have to use language, and much of philosophical debate about ethics in the twentieth century was concerned with the meaning of moral statements, and whether it is possible to show that they are either true or false. So, once we have decided that we are free to make moral choices and to talk about them, we need to address the problem of the sort of language that we will be using to do so.

In ethics, three different kinds of language are used. We need to · distinguish them carefully, and know which we are using at any one time, if we are not to become confused.

DESCRIPTIVE ETHICS

This is the most straightforward form of ethics. It consists of descriptions of the way in which people live, and the moral choices they make. It simply presents facts. Two simple examples of descriptive ethics follow.

> **Most car crime is carried out by young men in areas of high unemployment.**

The actual information may be correct or incorrect. It can be checked by referring to police records and employment statistics. But notice that the statement does not make any moral claim about youth and crime, nor does it say whether unemployment is a good or bad thing. It does not even make (although it may be taken to imply) a connection between crime and unemployment.

> **Muslim men may marry up to four wives, provided that they are able to provide for them and treat them equally.**

Again, this makes no moral judgement, nor does it enquire whether it is possible to treat wives equally. It simply states the fact about what is permitted within a certain religious and cultural setting.

Insight
The danger with descriptive ethics is that it may imply moral judgements by the way in which information is presented, without actually explaining the basis on which those judgements are made.

NORMATIVE ETHICS

Ethics is concerned with ideas about what is right, about justice, about how people should live. It examines the choices people make, and the values and reasoning that lie behind them. This is sometimes called 'substantive' or 'normative' ethics. Almost all moral argument, when it is concerned with the rights or wrongs of particular issues, is of this kind.

> **It is always wrong to steal.**

This is a normative statement. It can be challenged by using another normative statement, e.g. 'No, I think it is right to steal on some occasions.' What you cannot do is challenge a normative statement by using a descriptive one. So a person who responds by saying 'but everyone around here steals if they get a chance' is not actually countering the claim that it is wrong to steal. Everyone may do something, but that does not make it right.

Descriptive ethics is about facts, **normative ethics** is about values. Both are needed, but it is essential to realize that you cannot argue directly from the one to the other: **you cannot get an 'ought' from an 'is'.**

Insight

The attempt to do this was termed the 'naturalistic fallacy' by G.E. Moore in his influential book *Principia Ethica* (1903), and had been pointed out earlier by David Hume – see page 66.

META-ETHICS

It is also possible to stand back from moral statements and ask:

▶ *What does it mean to say that something is right or wrong?*
▶ *Are there any objective criteria by which I can assess moral statements?*
▶ *What is moral language? Is it a statement about facts of any kind?*
▶ *Does a moral statement simply express a person's wishes or hopes about what should happen?*
▶ *In what sense can a moral statement be said to be either true or false?*

Questions like these are not concerned with the content of moral discourse, but with its meaning. This fits in very closely with much twentieth century philosophy, which explored the nature of language and the way in which statements can be shown to be true or false. Looking at moral statements in this way is called **meta-ethics**.

For a person coming to a study of ethics primarily in order to examine moral issues (rather than treating it as a branch of philosophy), there are two questions that might be asked of meta-ethical theories:

▶ *Does this theory ring true to my experience of making moral statements?*
▶ *Does it actually help me to decide if something is right or wrong?*

Insight
A theory may be correct in terms of the logic of its argument, but for the practical business of looking at ethical issues, the key questions are: Is it plausible? Is it usable?

In this chapter we will look at the meaning of some important moral words – some definitions of which were given by the ancient Greek philosophers, and which have been part of ethics ever since. But we shall also look at a number of meta-ethical theories. Although meta-ethics is a recent arrival on the philosophical scene, it is worth considering it now so that, as we look at ethical theories of the past, we may assess them in terms of meaning, as well as in terms of their moral conclusions.

Notice that each kind of ethical language has its dangers:

▶ *The danger of descriptive ethics is that facts will be mistaken for values.*
▶ *The danger of normative ethics is that, in arguing that something is right or wrong, one may end up preaching rather than informing, recommending one particular course of action rather than setting out all the possibilities, consequences and values, and then allowing a person to make an informed and thoughtful choice.*
▶ *The danger of meta-ethics is that one may become so obsessed with the issue of meaning that it becomes impossible to offer any practical guidance for the difficult choices that people have to make.*

Defining key terms

Moral language uses certain words, without which normative ethics would not make sense. One of these is the word **ought** – expressing a sense of moral obligation. We shall see in Chapter 6 that this is fundamental to the experience of moral choice. Another is **justice** – examining the rights of individuals in society and the way in which they 'ought' to treat one another. Justice has been an important concept in social ethics since the ancient Greeks, and we shall look at it in Chapter 8, as part of our consideration of law and order.

The most basic word, however, is **good**. An action is judged 'right' or 'wrong' depending on whether or not it is a 'good' or 'bad' thing to do. Before we can talk about moral values we need to know what we mean by this term. Actions cannot be right or wrong unless we know what we mean by goodness. But can it be defined?

You could try to define 'good' in absolute terms (that something is good in itself) or in relative terms (that it is good in its particular context). You can also define it in terms of what it can achieve – so an action is 'good' (and right) if the results of that action are 'good'. This would be a utilitarian assessment, as we shall see later. But we are still using the word 'good' and are therefore no nearer a definition.

Aristotle argued that something was 'good' if it fulfilled its purpose. On this theory, a good knife is one that cuts well; a good plant is one that grows strong and healthy. This formed the basis of what is called the **natural law** approach to ethics. According to this, everything has a natural purpose in life, and actions are right or wrong depending on whether or not they contribute to the fulfilling of that purpose.

A religious believer may say that 'good' is what God approves, and take a particular revelation (e.g. the Bible) as the norm for understanding goodness. Another may take a particular experience, or the life of a religious leader, as the starting point for understanding the 'good' life. The meaning of the word good will therefore depend, in part, on the source of the values that are called 'good', and that is not something on which everyone will automatically agree. It is a key feature of the **intuitionist** theory of ethics that 'good' cannot be defined (see page 41).

There are two important distinctions to be made when defining key words – and particularly the word 'good'. Your definition can be **subjective** or **objective** (based on your own personal preferences, or based on external, social or legal facts). It can also be **relative** or **absolute** (depending on individual or cultural circumstances, or something that should apply to everyone everywhere).

Insight

If your view of what 'good' means is subjective, it will also tend to be relative. The idea that there is a single absolute good, requires a more objective viewpoint – based on observation or pure logic.

Some theories

Ethics is concerned with what moral language means, what it does, and how it may be verified. We shall therefore look briefly at some theories about moral language. But first, before we can say anything about goodness, we have to decide whether or not we can actually know what goodness is.

INTUITING WHAT IS GOOD

In 1903, G.E. Moore published *Principia Ethica*. In it he argued that goodness could not be defined, because it was unlike any other quality. In other words, if you try to say 'Something is good if …' you will never find a definition that does not reduce and limit the idea of goodness, and therefore make it inapplicable to other things.

He therefore came to the view that to say something is 'good' is rather like saying that it is 'yellow'. You cannot define a colour, you simply point to it and say 'That is what I mean by yellow.' Try defining yellow for the benefit of someone who has never seen that colour – it cannot be done!

We know that something is 'good' by intuition – it is self-evident. We can define an action as being 'right' if it leads to a 'good' result. We can argue rationally about many moral problems – deciding which of various options will lead to the 'good' – but we cannot define that basic idea in itself.

Everyone does in fact understand the question 'Is this good?' When he thinks of it, his state of mind is different from what it would be, were he asked 'Is this pleasant, or desired, or approved?' It has a distinct meaning for him, even though he may not recognize in what respect it is distinct. Whenever he thinks of 'intrinsic value' or 'intrinsic worth', or says that a thing 'ought to exist', he has before his mind the unique object – the unique property of things – which I mean by 'good'.

(from *Principia Ethica*, chapter 1)

Although Moore himself did not use the term, this approach became known as **intuitionism** and was later developed particularly by W.D. Ross (in *The Right and the Good*, 1930, and *Foundations of Ethics*, 1939) and by H.A. Prichard (*Moral Obligation*, 1937). Prichard argued, for example, that the idea of 'duty' was not definable. Our obligations to other people are self-evident.

Now there would seem to be a major objection to the claim that we all intuit what is good. If what is good, and my duty, are self-evident, how is it that I can find myself in a quandary? Life is seldom straightforward, and I may find myself at a loss to know what I should do. Indeed, if people were never uncertain about what they should do, there would be no ethical debate at all!

Ross overcome this difficulty by suggesting that I know what my duty is, but that sometimes one duty conflicts with another, and a choice therefore has to be made. Ethical dilemmas are therefore the result of such conflicting duties.

Insight

It seems to me that there are times when people genuinely do not know what would be the right thing to do. Particularly in a multi-cultural environment, where there is no single ethical tradition, people may not have clear intuitions about such matters.

A situation

Children have to be taught how to behave. A baby simply screams until it gets satisfaction; a growing child learns what is socially acceptable, and curbs its needs. Later in life, the adult appears to have an innate sense of right and wrong.

▶ If this is so, at what point does a person develop that innate sense?
▶ And how can you tell if that sense of right and wrong is not just the product of early training, now permanently enshrined in the unconscious?

Moore accepted that, in practical terms, one might judge an action according to its predicted results – trying to do what maximizes good in the world – but he differs from utilitarianism (see Chapter 5) in that **he will not allow that this assessment of results** *defines* **what is meant by 'good'.**

EMOTIVISM

In the early part of the twentieth century there developed an approach to language that is generally known as **logical positivism.**

It was an attempt to break down language into its simplest components and examine their meaning. This movement, inspired by the early work of Wittgenstein (as seen in his *Tractatus Logico Philosophicus*), is represented by the Vienna Circle of philosophers (including, for example, Carnap and Schlick) and became widely known through the publication in 1936 of A.J. Ayer's controversial book *Language Truth and Logic*.

The details of this approach need not detain us, except to say that it held that all meaningful propositions could be divided into two categories – **tautologies** (statements that are true by definition, e.g. all bachelors are unmarried) and **empirical statements of fact**, verified by observation. If a statement was not a tautology, and could not be shown to relate to externally perceived facts, then it was said to be meaningless. Now, on that basis, moral statements are meaningless, as they are neither statements of fact nor definitions. If my saying that you 'should' do something is neither a statement of fact nor a tautology, what is it? One answer to this is termed **emotivism**.

Ayer suggested that a moral statement is a kind of command:

> *The exhortations to moral virtue are not propositions at all, but ejaculations or commands which are designed to provoke the reader to action of a certain sort. Accordingly, they do not belong to any branch of philosophy or science.*

For Ayer, moral judgements expressed the feelings of the speaker. Carnap (a member of the Vienna Circle) also thought that moral statements were commands (if I say 'This is the right thing to do, I really mean 'do this!') while Schlick thought that they were rules. Bertrand Russell argued that differences in values (and therefore differences in the moral statements that are based on them) are not a matter of facts, but of taste.

C.L. Stevenson, in *Ethics and Language*, 1947, claimed that, once you strip the supposed facts away from moral statements, they are revealed for what they really are: expressions of a person's own preferences and emotions. **To say that something is right is really just another way of saying that I approve of it.** Stevenson therefore argued that 'good' was a **persuasive definition**. He was less concerned with what moral statements meant in themselves, and more with what they were for. **A statement has an emotive meaning if it is intended to produce a response in the person who hears it.**

There are two main criticisms of this approach:

▶ *A moral argument is not really judged according to the response it evokes, but on whether its claims are valid. Morality is not just about emotions, but may be discussed rationally.*
▶ *To claim something is right or wrong is to make a policy statement. If I claim my moral judgements are universal (they should apply to everyone) they cannot be based on feelings, for I cannot say what others should feel, nor can I know what I will feel on other occasions.*

Insight

To put it crudely, the emotive theory reduces morality to a set of cheers or boos, sounded off in response to experiences that are liked or disliked. Some people may indeed make moral statements on that basis, but it does not do justice to the rational character of moral arguments.

PRESCRIPTIVISM

Whereas the **emotivist** asks what sort of effect a moral statement aims to have, a **prescriptivist** is more concerned about what is happening when someone actually makes a moral statement.

R.M. Hare (in *The Language of Morals*, 1952, and *Freedom and Reason*, 1963) is the best-known representative of this approach. He asks about what a moral statement is meant to do, and concludes that a moral statement is 'prescribing' a course of action – recommending that something should be done, rather than just expressing the feelings of the speaker.

This may sound similar in practice to a **command,** but there is a difference. If I see someone about to steal a car and I shout out 'Stop that!' I am referring to that single incident. I am not suggesting that stopping doing things is a general principle on which I expect the person to base his life! On the other hand, if I say 'It is wrong to steal!' I am giving a piece of advice that can apply to future situations as well.

Nevertheless, prescribing and giving commands have something important in common: they both relate the content of what is said to the response that saying it is intended to evoke. Now this is certainly true of all commands, but is it true of all moral statements? I may discuss moral issues related to something that happened in the past. I may say, for example, that I believe the extermination of millions of Jews and others under the Nazi regime was absolutely wrong. That is a moral statement. But it is not directly suggesting that anyone with whom I am discussing that issue is actually in a position to respond to it in practical terms. I am not recommending a course of action. I am merely commenting on the way in which a certain action conforms to or goes against fundamental values that I hold.

An important point made by Hare is that moral statements should be **universalizable.** We shall consider this again in Chapter 6, when we look at the philosopher Kant. For now we need note only that this underlines the distinction between a command and a prescriptive statement. The **prescriptive statement** is making a general point; one that could be applied to situations in the past and the future, and to other people, as well as to the person to whom it is addressed.

A situation – the Bentley case

In 1952, Christopher Craig and Derek Bentley, following a break-in at a confectionery warehouse in South London, were cornered on the roof of the building by police. Bentley, having already been

(Contd)

caught, called out to Craig (who was carrying a gun and being pursued by a police officer) 'Let him have it, Chris.' Craig shot and killed the officer.

The words used by Bentley were ambiguous. They could have been taken to mean that Craig should hand over the weapon, or that he should shoot. The court decided the latter, and Bentley was therefore found guilty of murder along with Craig. Craig, being only 16 at the time, was given a prison sentence. Bentley, who was 19 but had a mental age of only 11, was hanged in January 1953.

In July 1998, after a long campaign by his family, the Lord Chief Justice Bingham ruled that Bentley had not received 'that fair trial which is the birthright of every British citizen', and he was officially cleared of murder.

Quite apart from the issue of capital punishment, the Bentley case raises many ethical points:

▶ To what extent should someone be responsible for the actions of another, if it is judged that he or she incited that person to act?
▶ Should a person with a mental age of 11 be deemed responsible under the law? But, if so, of what could an 11-year-old be held responsible?
▶ In the heat of the moment, many things might be said or done that, on reflection, are unwise. Should Bentley's shout be considered something he freely chose to do, or simply a reaction to the situation he found himself in?

But notice that Bentley was considered to have 'prescribed' a course of action in saying 'let him have it'. He was therefore deemed responsible for what followed. The problem with the case lay in the ambiguity of what was prescribed. If that is so, we may ask:

▶ Is a person who makes a moral statement responsible for actions taken by those who accept it as something 'prescribed' for them to do?

This issue was raised again during a court case in London in early 2006 in which a radical Muslim cleric was accused of inciting acts of terrorism, and in legislation proposed by the UK government to limit criticism of religious groups that could be taken to incite hatred or violence. But notice:

▶ In such situations we have to distinguish between what is said and the intention of the speaker to 'prescribe' a course of action.
▶ The problem is that intention is subjective. If a speaker, whose words have provoked violence, claims that it was not his or her intention to do so, on what grounds can that claim to contradicted?

NATURALISM AND METAPHYSICAL ETHICS

Reading Plato's *Republic*, or Aristotle's *Nicomachean Ethics*, we get the very definite idea that, in spite of the various views that are put forward and examined, there is ultimately a rational basis for the idea of goodness and justice – arising from the nature of human life, or the needs of a society to organize itself in a harmonious way.

The implication of this is that there is an objective basis for ethics. On the other hand, some of the theories put forward in this chapter may suggest that there is no objective truth in ethics, but that everything centres on the wishes or feelings of the person who makes the moral statement. This 'ethical subjectivism' may seem appropriate for a society that has no single religious, social, political or cultural base, for people differ from one another so greatly that it is unlikely that they would share the same values, or choose to act in the same way.

However, when it comes to moral issues, people try to persuade others about how they should behave. They argue as though there were some objective truth about which different people could in principle agree.

> **Insight**
>
> If right and wrong depend only on personal and individual tastes, there seems little point in discussing moral issues at all, for one could never reach a conclusion, or get beyond simply comparing preferences.

This situation gives rise to two other theories about ethical language. **Naturalistic ethics** is the term used for the attempt to explain a set of moral terms from the facts of human life. It is the positive side of what G.E. Moore criticized as the 'naturalistic fallacy' – the attempt to derive an 'ought' from an 'is'. To be fair, those who propose a modern naturalistic ethic (e.g. Richard Norman in *The Moral Philosophers*, 1983) do so on the basis of observed social relationships and in a way that gets round the simple application of Moore's criticism. But naturalistic ethics still seems to 'reduce' moral language to the task of giving pieces of social information.

By contrast, **metaphysical ethics** insists that morality should be valued in itself, and should be related to our understanding of the world and of our place within it. It points out that moral choices are related to our general understanding of life, and the value that we find in it: in other words, to our 'metaphysics'.

An interesting exposition of this approach was given by Iris Murdoch in her book *Metaphysics and a Guide to Morals* (Penguin, 1994), where she points out that the moral choices people make in times of crisis are based on the values that they gradually build up in their habitual way of dealing with the world. Hence, we should not separate off the moment of moral choice from the rest of our experience of life and our interpretation of it. We make ourselves what we are, and our choices follow from that.

Summary of theories

▶ **Intuitionism** – one just instinctively knows when something is right!

▶ **Emotivism** – one uses moral statements to express feelings, and influence the feelings of others.

▶ **Prescriptivism** – one uses moral statements to 'prescribe' a general course of action.

▶ **Naturalism** – relating moral statements to particular features of the world and of social relationships.

▶ **Metaphysical ethics** – relating moral statements to a general understanding of the world, its meaning and its values.

Now it is clear that, when we use moral language, we may be doing a combination of some or all of these things. We may speak about something being 'good' without knowing how to define what we mean by that word. We may speak out because we want to express our emotions. We may want to recommend a course of action. We may also feel convinced that there are objective grounds for saying that something is right or wrong.

It is important to be aware of these meta-ethical theories so that we recognize the basis on which we are using moral language – and hopefully save a great deal of misunderstanding and arguing at cross-purposes.

These theories suggest that we can take either a subjective approach to ethics (it expresses my feelings, my intuitions about what is right, or my prescribed course of action), or an objective approach (there are features of the world and of human beings that make this particular action right and that one wrong). In general, the more subjective approaches will produce criteria that are personal and individual. The more objective ones will produce criteria that are able to be applied universally.

'Is' and 'ought'

We have already mentioned G.E. Moore's 'naturalistic fallacy' argument that you cannot get an 'ought' from an 'is'. This reflected a position taken much earlier by the eighteenth-century philosopher David Hume. He pointed out that those who write on religion or morality tend to slip from matters of fact to matters of value:

> *In every system of morality, which I have hitherto met with, I have always remarked, that the author proceeds for some time in the ordinary way of reasoning, and establishes the being of a God, or makes observations concerning human affairs; when of a sudden I am surprised to find, that instead of the usual copulations of propositions, is and is not, I meet with no proposition that is not connected with an ought, or an ought not. This change is imperceptible; but is, however of the last consequence. For as this ought, or ought not, expresses some new relation or affirmation, it is necessary that is should be observed and explained; and at the same time that a reason should be given, for what seems altogether inconceivable, how this new relation can be a deduction from others, which are entirely different from it.*

A Treatise on Human Nature, 1738

Hume, here as elsewhere, delights in debunking traditional religious and moral arguments. But he highlights a feature of moral argument that is absolutely crucial, and which links with our discussion of the nature of religious language.

The logical positivists argued that moral statements were meaningless, since they were neither tautologies nor matters that could be proved true or false with reference to evidence. We looked at the reactions to this claim – principally in pointing to the emotive and prescriptive approaches to understanding what moral language was about. In effect, the logical positivists were restating Hume's point. Although based on facts, moral language goes beyond them. In the crudest sense this is simply the 'just because everyone else does it, does not make it right' argument.

To what extent, then, can moral judgements be based on facts? If facts have to be interpreted, or if something more is needed before we can move from saying 'is' to saying 'ought', then we need to make clear what that extra is. This issue is illustrated most clearly by the 'natural law' approach to ethics, to which we now turn.

THINGS TO REMEMBER

From this chapter, remember that ...

▶ *'descriptive ethics' describes how people behave, without reference to right or wrong*

▶ *'normative ethics' is about whether actions are right or wrong*

▶ *'meta-ethics' is about the meaning and significance of ethical language*

▶ *Moore argued that 'good' could be known, but not defined*

▶ *intuitionism sees 'good' as always self-evident*

▶ *emotivism sees 'good' as what is approved of*

▶ *prescriptivism sees ethical language as recommending a course of action*

▶ *naturalistic ethics try to relate morality to objective features of life*

▶ *metaphysical ethics relates morality to an overall view about what life is for*

▶ *you cannot derive an 'ought' from an 'is' (the naturalistic fallacy).*

4

....

Is it natural?

In this chapter you will learn:
- *about the origins and basis of natural law*
- *about challenges to the natural law approach*
- *to consider whether people are naturally good or bad.*

So far we have looked at whether or not we are free to decide how to act, and what it means to make a moral statement. But moral statements, even if they are expressing a personal preference or recommending a course of action, make claims about 'right' and 'wrong'. If moral issues cannot be settled simply by checking facts, what other rational or objective basis can there be to argue that something is 'right' or 'wrong'?

In the chapters that follow, we shall look at attempts to find a basis for moral judgements: to justify them in terms of the expected results of an action, the experience of a sense of 'ought', the desire for personal growth or the needs of society. But first, we shall examine a theory which claims that everything is created to a particular design and for a particular purpose, and that fulfilling that purpose is the 'good' to which everything aims. It is called the theory of **natural law**.

The natural law approach was developed by Thomas Aquinas in the thirteenth century, and became a central feature of Catholic moral thinking. To find its roots, however, we need to go back to the fourth century BCE and the philosophy of Aristotle.

Does it have a 'final cause'?

Aristotle distinguished between efficient causes and final causes: an **efficient cause** is what gets things done, a **final cause** is the purpose or intended end product. A child grows up to be an adult. Aristotle would say that an efficient cause of the child's growth is food and drink, but the final cause is the adult into which the child is growing. Similarly, if I take a piece of wood and carve it into a statue, the efficient cause is the knife that I use, but the final cause is the image that I seek to create.

On this theory, everything (both every object and every action) has some final meaning and purpose (its 'final cause') – its essential nature and place within the overall scheme of things – and this is what determines its 'good'.

Insight

This is not 'natural' in the sense of being based on what we observe in nature, rather it is nature *as interpreted by human reason*. Everything is judged good, if it does what reason understands to be its purpose and essence.

There are other important themes in Aristotle's ethics, including the idea of achieving a balance between the extremes of excess and deficiency, but the 'natural law' theory is based on his idea of final causes.

Aquinas used Aristotle's ideas to argue that the world was created by God, and that everything should therefore have God's ultimate purpose as its final 'end' or 'good'. To understand God's will for it, and therefore what is 'right' for it, you only have to look at the purpose for which it has been made. A good knife is one that cuts well: that is what it is designed to do. But how do you decide what is a good human life?

Aquinas argued that everything had its proper 'end', as part of God's providential ordering of the world, but humankind was special in that it was also given reason and freedom. Humans could therefore understand and choose whether or not to follow their proper 'end'. This he called 'natural law' – the rational understanding and following of God's final purpose.

Let us take an example that has been important within Catholic moral thought.

Example

Consider the act of heterosexual intercourse. (Sadly, we need to consider its 'final cause', although its 'efficient causes' tend to be more entertaining.)

▶ Its natural purpose is to fertilize an egg, which in turn will be nurtured within a womb to produce another human being. This process helps to maintain the human species.
▶ Given the physical contortions involved, it is difficult to imagine how copulation could occur by random chance in the course of normal social life! Sexual attraction and arousal is therefore the means that nature has supplied for achieving this particular end.
▶ Sexual arousal and the act of penetration are therefore the 'efficient cause', while the production of a new human being is the 'final cause' of the sexual act.

However, if it is only the final cause that determines right and wrong, then strictly speaking, in terms of sex:

▶ intercourse between members of the same sex is wrong (because it cannot result in conception)
▶ intercourse with those who are outside the age range for childbearing is wrong (for the same reason)
▶ anal and oral intercourse and masturbation are wrong (for the same reason)
▶ any attempt to frustrate the process of conception is wrong, because it tries to separate off the sexual act from its natural purpose.

(Contd)

In traditional Catholic teaching it is therefore wrong to practise contraception. Each sexual act should include the possibility of conception. Pope Paul VI's encyclical letter *Humanae Vitae* (1968) expressed it in this way:

'The Church ... in urging men to the observance of the precepts of the natural law, which it interprets by its constant doctrine, teaches as absolutely required that any use whatsoever of marriage must retain its natural potential to procreate human life.'

Sex within the 'safe period' of the woman's ovulatory cycle is generally permitted in Catholic moral teaching because the failure to conceive at that time is part of nature's limitation, rather than the result of a direct attempt to do something unnatural. The same applies to those who are past childbearing age, on the grounds that, by a miracle, conception might take place.

This example shows that 'natural law', unlike most other theories we will consider, gives the possibility of producing a clearly defined rule that can then be applied universally. An action is right or wrong in itself, without reference to all its possible consequences (e.g. an act of sex might result in the birth of a child who grows up to be a mass murderer; but that does not make the sexual act morally wrong, only regrettable!).

You may not always know what the results of your actions will be. You are therefore only responsible for the immediate consequences of your action, not for any secondary and unintended effects. This is sometimes called the **law of double effect**. It can be a surprisingly useful theory for those who wish to practise contraception without going against 'natural law', because if a woman suffers from painful or irregular periods, a doctor may prescribe 'contraceptive' pills in order to regulate her cycle. The fact that the hormone in the pills acts as a contraceptive is a secondary effect, and is not the intention of the original prescription. 'Natural law' morality is maintained: the doctor is right in his prescription, because it has the intended effect of regulating the cycle and relieving discomfort; the woman is right in having sex while taking the pill, because the pill is not a deliberate attempt to frustrate conception.

Insight

The issues presented here are not intended to undermine the principle of natural law, but to illustrate the problem of trying to find a single objective rule to cover a situation that may have many complex layers of meaning and intention.

Natural law requires an 'act analysis' approach to moral argument – it breaks the situation down into the various acts involved and tries to establish the moral significance of each. In practice, a couple may have sex for many different physical and emotional reasons, but the natural law approach does not generally allow for these to be taken into account.

By contrast, the approach to the issue of contraception taken by other religious groups – along with most secular moral thinkers – is more likely to be based on the expected results. It takes into account factors like the ability of the couple to provide for any children they may conceive. Globally, contraception may be promoted because of population problems in areas of poverty – again, the claim that contraception is 'good' is based on the anticipated result of too many children and an inability to give them what they need. Because there are many factors to be weighed, if issues of right and wrong are based on expected results, the decision about contraception is then generally left to the conscience of the individuals concerned. With natural law, however, there is a tendency to go for a clear right/wrong judgement.

Example

AIDS has had a devastating effect on the population of parts of Africa. But a rumour spread, allegedly by those who were opposed to the use of contraception on religious and 'natural law' grounds, that condoms did not prevent the spread of AIDS, and should not be used.

(Contd)

Two separate issues are raised by this:

1 There is a 'double effect' problem here. Is the condom used to prevent the spread of AIDS, but with a secondary and unintentional effect of preventing conception?
2 There can be few clearer examples of the difference between judging an action according to expected results (preventing the spread of AIDS), and as an act in itself (the frustration of the 'natural' purpose of sex).

However, the matter is never straightforward. It could be argued, for example, that the availability of condoms encourages promiscuity and thereby – on the assumption that they will not always be used properly or responsibly – the spread of AIDS. But to take that line is already to have accepted the principle that morality is determined by results – exactly what those in favour of the use of condoms are arguing.

Some features of 'natural law'

- *The term 'natural law' should not be used simply to refer to the laws of nature, which form the basis of science. It is the result of applying reason to what happens in nature.*
- *As traditionally presented, the 'natural law' theory of ethics is based on the idea that God creates everything with a particular purpose in mind, and that people are therefore required to understand it and act accordingly. Hence, its authority tends to be religious.*
- *'Natural law' can be examined quite apart from its religions interpretation, as a rational theory relating behaviour to the basic features of human life, its place within the world, and the basic requirements for its survival.*
- *It has the advantage that, once a 'final cause' is established, it may be applied to all people at all times. A natural law theory need take little account of prevailing social attitudes.*

> *It is not based on personal preferences, nor of guessing what the results of an action might be in terms of the happiness or otherwise of those involved – it is simply based on an examination of rational purpose. Potentially, it is a very 'clear cut' ethical theory.*

Natural law supports other general views of moral behaviour. Aquinas (in *Summa Theologiae*) presented the four cardinal virtues – prudence, justice, fortitude and temperance (which had been used as a basis for morality by the Stoics) – as fundamental qualities of the moral life. The opposite of these virtues are the seven capital vices (often called the 'seven deadly sins'), which are pride, avarice, lust, envy, gluttony, anger and sloth. From a traditional standpoint of belief in God, one might say that the former allow a human being to fulfil his or her potential as a human being as intended by God, whereas the latter frustrate that intention.

But the issue of what is 'natural' is wider than Aquinas' theory, for 'natural law' is essentially about finding the rational principles on which the world is made and which may therefore guide action. But many actions that may be described as natural are irrational and destructive, so further questions to be asked.

How do you decide what is 'natural'?

Science bases its 'laws of nature' on observation, and they claim to be no more than an interpretation of the best available evidence. If something is observed that does not fit in with an established law, then either the observation is inaccurate, or another (as yet unknown) law has unexpectedly come into operation. Our understanding of the way in which nature works is therefore constantly being modified.

If this also applies to 'natural law' as an ethical theory, then we cannot establish fixed criteria for right and wrong – which was the aim of Aquinas and others who followed this line of thought – because our concept of what is natural, and therefore of 'final causes', will always be open to modification.

> ## Insight
>
> In other words, natural law is about what life *should* be like, given a rational and purposeful creation, but that may not be what life is *actually* like.

Example

It is natural for someone who is seriously ill to die. Does that mean that one should not interfere with the natural course of a disease by giving medicine?

In the natural world, the strongest animals often mate with as many sexual partners as they can, fighting off weaker rivals. Should there be selective breeding among humans? Is monogamy unnatural?

These examples suggest that there is no easy way to establish the 'final cause' that will enable us to say with certainty that we know exactly what every thing or action is for, or what part it has to play in an overall purposeful scheme of the universe.

The idea that the universe as a whole has a purpose and direction, and that it (and everything in it) has been created for a specific reason, is not a matter for scientific examination, but for religious belief. Those without such belief will not necessarily see a rationally justified 'final cause'. Indeed, one of the main arguments against belief in God has been the apparent pointlessness of suffering. Once pointlessness replaces purpose as a general view of the natural world, then the 'natural law' argument starts to break down.

Moral statements cannot be established by the observation of facts; you cannot argue from what 'is' to what 'ought to be' the case.

When you record facts, you do just that; facts are neutral in terms of ethics. Once you make a moral statement, however, you bring in values and wishes, you recommend that something should be done, or you express feelings. These things are over and above the facts to which they are applied.

At first sight, the 'natural law' argument seems to argue from something that 'is' (the nature of the world) to what 'ought' to be done. It does this on the basis of belief in a creator God who guarantees that things have a purpose which suits their nature, and to which they can freely respond in a positive and creative way.

There are other ways of trying to link 'ought' and 'is'. In Eastern philosophy, the idea of **karma** – that actions have consequences that cumulatively influence the future – relates the state of the world to moral choices. But this gives only a 'hypothetical' command (in other words, one that says 'If you want to achieve X, then you must do Y'), not an absolute moral command.

Insight

To get an absolute command (or 'categorical imperative', as we shall see later) you have to presuppose someone who gives that command. Within the natural law theory, as it has developed since the time of Aquinas, that 'someone' is God. This gives its moral pronouncements an authority that may not be justified by the logic on which the argument is based.

Applying 'natural law'

It is one thing to have universal principles, another to apply them to individual cases. This is often referred to as a 'deductive' method of moral argument – one that starts with general rules and then deduces the morality of a particular situation from them. This process may also be called **casuistry**.

Casuistry is often regarded as a pejorative term (implying that the principle is applied in an unfeeling, contrived, or irrelevant way), but the process of applying rules or principles to individual cases is found in all branches of ethics and law, and is very much a common sense approach.

We have already looked at the natural law approach to matters of sex and contraception, so let us continue that theme:

A situation

Two adults of the same sex are attracted to one another. They wish to express that attraction physically, to live together with the same legal and social support that they would receive as a heterosexual couple, to adopt children, and to bring them up in a family home. Is what they wish to do morally right?

▶ Until the 1967 Sexual Offences Act, homosexual acts between consenting male adults were regarded as crimes in Britain. They were then made legal for those who had reached the age of 21 (as opposed to heterosexual acts, which are legal from the age of 16). In some Muslim countries, following strict Shari'ah laws, homosexuality is punishable by death. By contrast, in Classical Greece, homosexual love was widely practised, and socially acceptable. There is therefore no universally held view about homosexuality and its place in society.
▶ Since homosexuality involves what used to be called 'unnatural acts', it is a particularly suitable situation against which to test 'natural law' as an ethical theory.

This is how a 'natural law' argument might view that homosexual partnership:

▶ According to natural law, the purpose of sex is procreation. Since homosexual acts cannot lead to conception, they are 'unnatural' and therefore wrong.

- On this basis, heterosexual acts within a stable relationship (i.e. one that will enable children to be nurtured) or celibacy are the only morally acceptable sexual choices.
- Because of this, there is no moral objection, according to natural law principles, to the couple living together, or feeling attracted towards one another. The only objection is to any physical sexual acts that may take place between them.
- Because they cannot form a 'natural' family group, a natural law argument would suggest that homosexual couples should not be allowed to adopt children, who 'naturally' thrive only with the benefit of both mother and father role models.

Against this line of argument:

- One might argue that the presence of sexual organs in a human being implies that he or she is designed for sexual activity and the conception of children – in which case, celibacy is as unnatural as homosexuality, since it is a denial of the complete natural function of procreation. If this is established, then it is illogical to accept a celibate partnership between those who are sexually attracted.
- Some people are naturally attracted by members of the same sex. They experience their feelings as completely natural. Any difficulties that arise are the result of social conditioning, not nature.
- Sexuality can be said to achieve three ends:
    1 physical pleasure
    2 the deepening of a relationship
    3 the conception of children
  Only the third end is precluded by homosexual relationships. But is not the search for pleasure and for deep relationships as natural as the conception of children? If a marriage is known to be infertile, are heterosexual acts between its partners therefore immoral simply because conception is impossible?
- Marriage is a social function, and promiscuity can be practised equally by homosexuals and heterosexuals. The fact that homosexual couples cannot marry does not preclude deep and permanent relationships.

(Contd)

> ► If a homosexual couple form a stable relationship, they may be able to offer children a home that is, at the very least, as valuable to their upbringing as one in which there is either a single parent, or a heterosexual couple with a bad relationship. Hence, it would seem illogical to discriminate in this matter.
>
> The introduction of civil partnerships in the UK, in December 2005, was recognition that stable homosexual relationships deserved the same legal and financial protection enjoyed by heterosexual couples who marry.

In pointing out some of the ways in which the 'natural law' view of the homosexual couple's situation might be challenged, it is not intended to undermine the principle of natural law as such, but to show that there are some areas of morality – particularly where relationships are concerned – where it is difficult to consider morality mainly in terms of specific actions.

Insight

Although in this section we focus on Aristotle's contribution to the 'natural law' approach to ethics, there is another important aspect to his ethics: paying attention. The virtuous person is one who pays thoughtful attention to everything that he or she does, acting thoughtfully. Thoughtful attention to food, for example, will avoid either starvation or gluttony, but will tend to eat moderately – an example of Aristotle's famous 'mean' between extremes. That's an essential part of the ethical life; simply to pay attention to what we are doing and why we are doing it.

Are we naturally good or bad?

The philosopher Thomas Hobbes (1588–1679), in his book *Leviathan*, saw the life of man in a natural state as 'solitary, poor, nasty, brutish and short'. He took the view that, left to their own devices, people are naturally greedy. They want freedom, but also power (which included riches, reputation, success, nobility and eloquence – all that might give one person an advantage over others), and the inevitable result of this is that they would struggle against one another in order to gain it. In such a society, everyone is judged by his or her power:

The value, or WORTH of a man, is as of all other things, his price; that is to say, so much as would be given for the use of his power: and therefore is not absolute, but a thing dependent on the need and judgement of another.

Unbridled competition, allied to seeing everyone in terms of his or her power, may lead to social anarchy. Hobbes therefore argued that it was in the self-interest of all, for people to set aside their claim to total power in order that they might live peacefully with others, for otherwise there will be constant danger of losing everything. In effect, he came down to a form of the 'golden rule' – do as you would be done to. He applied reason to human society, pointing out what was needed for society to function – but recognized that, without reason, people would be in a state of self-destructive greed and anarchy.

Such anarchy would not have been tolerated for long by Niccolo Machiavelli (1469–1527), who (in *The Prince*) argues that a ruler must know how to use his power and needs to be feared as well as respected by his people. His views on political power, and the measures that a person should be prepared to employ in order to gain and maintain it, suggest that in a natural state, humankind is ruthless and competitive. Both Hobbes and Machiavelli see natural life as essentially a struggle for power and survival.

By contrast, Jean-Jacques Rousseau (1712–78) thought that people were born essentially good – as was everything that came directly from nature. He argued that, if the conditions are right, people will flourish and be morally good. Human nature is fine in itself; the trouble is with the way in which society is organized. If temptation is put in people's way, a certain number of them are going to fall for it. This way of thinking led many twentieth century socialists to assume that, once the dictatorship of the proletariat arrived, a just society would be established and all would be well. It also finds expression in the caricature of the social worker who, defending a criminal, lays all the blame on the circumstances of his or her upbringing, thereby diminishing moral responsibility.

Another example of this positive attitude to the natural is Henry David Thoreau (1817–62). In *Walden*, or *Life in the Woods*, he saw God within all nature and everything as therefore inherently good. He argued that people spent too much time worrying about earning a living, and seeking for things they do not really need – leading lives of 'quiet desperation'. By contrast, he sought a far simpler and more natural way of living.

We shall be looking at some of these thinkers again later. For now we need only recognize that human life is complex, and that it is seldom possible to see what it would be like without the constraints of society. Opinion is divided:

▶ *Are human beings fundamentally ruthless and savage, restrained and tamed by society, but liable at times to revert to their 'natural' behaviour?*
▶ *Or are human beings fundamentally good and caring, made antisocial and brutalized by society, but, given the right environment, capable of reverting to their gentler nature?*

Points for reflection

▶ Looking at the items in any newspaper, consider whether you believe humankind to be more 'Hobbes' or more 'Rousseau' (to use an extreme form: more 'savages tamed by society' or more 'angels corrupted by society').
▶ What do these views suggest about punishment and reform?
▶ Should society have more rules or fewer?

- ▶ Should morality be left to the conscience of the individual, or imposed by society?
- ▶ Aristotle saw reason as the distinctive human quality. Was he right?
- ▶ John Stuart Mill (whose ethics we will look at in Chapter 4) pointed out that most of the things people are punished for doing (e.g. murder, rape) are common occurrences in nature. Should ethics be seen therefore as a distinctively human step away from the natural order?
- ▶ Watch a cat 'play' with a mouse.

So far in this chapter we have moved from a formal and rational view of nature – the natural law argument of Aquinas and others – to a brief look at the more general question of naturalism in ethics. But in modern times, such questions have acquired a new context, for it is impossible to consider human nature – or nature in general – without taking evolution into account. We no longer think of fixed entities, but of directions of change.

Evolution, change and the natural law

If the whole world is in a state of constant change; if galaxies are moving outwards towards an unknown future; if stars are born and die, and planets spinning around them are vulnerable to their death and many other cosmic accidents; if life on planet Earth is a recent phenomenon and subject to a process of evolution – how can the purpose or goal of anything be fixed?

Darwin's theory of natural selection is not part of ethics. It is a scientific theory, based on the observation of species. It argues that those best adapted to their environment will prosper and multiply. Species that fail to adapt will eventually decline and vanish. It does not say that this *ought* to happen; it just observes what *actually* happens, and then seeks to provide a theory to explain it.

It is tempting, however, to create a morality based on evolution. Henri Bergson (1859–1941), in his book *Creative Evolution*, felt that you should act in a way that enables you to follow the stream of evolutionary life in the direction of the future, that you should do nothing to impede the progress of evolution. Herbert Spencer (1820–1903), in *The Principles of Ethics*, came to the view that the good is what gives pleasure. But he also considered 'the survival of the fittest' and was prepared to say that misfits, weaklings or those who are stupid should be left to their fate, and should not be allowed to impede the rise and progress of those who are more able.

In a way (although he did not link it specifically with evolution) this reflects the attitude of Friedrich Nietzsche (see Chapter 7), who spoke of slave morality and master morality, and felt that Christianity and democracy were holding back human progress by allowing too much consideration to be given to the weak at the expense of the strong, encouraging the attitude of 'slaves' rather than that of 'masters'.

Notice how very different this approach, which considers the development of individuals and species as a 'good' to be achieved, is from that of 'natural law'. In the latter, you look at particular actions and judge if they are right or wrong in themselves. Any theory of personal or global development – of evolution, in other words – looks at each decision and action in the light of the direction of evolution and change. What will this action allow me to become? What effect will this action have on the future of humankind? Such ethics is dynamic and forward looking – and it is based on results, not on the intrinsic value.

The natural law approach is based on the idea that reason can interpret the essence, purpose and 'final cause' of things. We need to consider whether this is compatible with a world viewed from the perspective of evolution and change.

For reflection

Is morality the result of deliberately going against our basic instincts, as suggested by Richard Dawkins at the end of *The Selfish Gene*: 'We alone on earth can rebel against the tyranny of the selfish replicators'? Or is some sense of morality genetically programmed into us? Research on the behaviour of apes suggests that there may be the basics of morality – in the attitude of groups to individuals, and the support given by one individual ape to another. So, for example, animals that fight can 'make up' afterwards. Is this programmed into them in order to help the species survive in a competitive environment?

Looking at the development and survival of species in the wild, one important factor is communication and co-operation – hunting in packs, for example, or warning others of approaching danger. This at least opens up the possibility that morality, in more complex animals, is a survival mechanism and therefore perfectly 'natural'.

Insight

A key feature of natural law is that it attempts to relate issues of right and wrong to our overall understanding and interpretation of life. It argues, in effect, that our moral choices should not be simply random, nor based on our personal interests, nor even on our emotional responses or existential commitments, but on a rational interpretation of the inherent value and purpose of things. However much we may question how it works in practice, there can be no doubt that its approach is not one to be dismissed lightly.

THINGS TO REMEMBER

From this chapter, remember that...

▶ *natural law is* **not** *the same as the observation of what happens in nature*

▶ *natural law is based on nature as interpreted by human reason*

▶ *Aristotle distinguished between efficient and final causes*

▶ *the fulfilment of a final cause or purpose, rationally understood, is good*

▶ *'the law of double effect' argues that you are only responsible for the immediate consequences of your action, nor for secondary or unintended consequences*

▶ *natural law, as presented by Aquinas, is based on the belief in God as creator and therefore giver of meaning and purpose*

▶ *the application of rules to a particular situation is termed casuistry, and is not necessarily a bad thing*

▶ *opinion is divided about whether human beings are naturally good*

▶ *some thinkers have attempted to base morality on the perceived direction of evolutionary advance*

▶ *natural law seeks to relate morality to an overall understanding of life, rationally interpreted.*

5

Looking for results

In this chapter you will learn:
- *about egoism and hedonism*
- *the three main kinds of utilitarian arguments*
- *about criticisms of utilitarianism.*

Egoistic hedonism

EGOISM

Egoism is the view that, whatever we may claim, we actually do only those things that we believe will benefit ourselves.

One could claim that – whether they accept it or not – people in fact act in their own best interests. A psychologist could argue, for example, that even those who appear to do things for the sake of others are in fact pleasing themselves in doing so. They may enjoy helping others, or they may delight in being thought of as kind and unselfish. Deep down they have a need to give themselves to others, a need to bolster their own sense of goodness by doing so, perhaps to cover some unacknowledged guilt. One could, therefore, be utterly unselfish for utterly selfish motives.

The jibe that the unselfish person is a 'do-gooder' may imply this form of egoism. If I say of someone that they are 'too good to be true' it may imply the sense that, at some level, people naturally display selfish tendencies, and the apparent absence of them is suspicious.

On the other hand, we need to keep in mind that the aim of religion is often given as the breaking down of fundamental human selfishness; that people in their natural state are selfish, but that, through spiritual practices, they can genuinely overcome this. St Augustine (354–430) believed that all people had an evil impulse, as a direct result of the Fall of Adam, and that they could be restrained only by the coercive power of the state and the laws of the Church.

Hobbes (in *Leviathan*) argued that people are motivated by the desire for gain, security and their own glory. But others (e.g. Rousseau) have seen a natural state as one in which there is a desire to co-operate and feel pity towards others. In either case, this is in general a statement about what 'is' rather than about what 'ought' to be – and is therefore more a comment on the background or starting point for ethics than a conclusion about how people should act.

> ### Insight
> Whether people are naturally selfish, and whether – through religion, therapy, rehabilitation programmes or the like – this selfishness can be overcome, is a matter for personal judgement. The key question is: Is it rational or right to act always in one's own interest?

An **ethical egoist** is someone who claims that everybody should pursue his or her own best interest. Here, selfishness is a policy, not a fact to be regretted. Few thinkers have argued in favour of selfishness as an ideal, but argue that, as it is what actually motivates people, it should be taken into account. Perhaps the most obvious example of this is Machiavelli (1469–1527), who claimed that people will do what is right only under compulsion and that generally, given the chance, they will do what is in their own interest. Ambition, and the desire to gain power, is what really motivates people. But Machiavelli was not strictly an ethical egoist, for he did not say that one could define what was right or wrong by reference to self-interest – only that, in the practical business of politics, in order to maintain the integrity and success of the state, a prince must be prepared to do what appears to be evil. He says, for example, that you should not keep promises if that goes against your own self-interest, or if the reason for making the promise in the first place has now changed. This, of course, leads to a sceptical view about the possibility of any objectively established moral values (and we shall therefore need to look at Machiavelli again in Chapter 10, where we will be considering scepticism and relativism).

According to an egoist ethic, the one obligation on an individual is to do that which benefits himself or herself. There is no moral responsibility to help others; you do so only if it pleases you to do so, and therefore you do it for your own benefit. On this basis, personal success in life is the basic motivation for actions and can therefore be used as their justification.

Example

If you are a genuine egoist and recommend that attitude to others, they are likely to develop themselves in a way that threatens you. Egoism is a benefit to you as long as others do not adopt it.

A manager, interviewing two candidates for the post of his immediate subordinate, recognizes that one of them will do the job adequately, and the other is likely to be brilliant at it. Which should he appoint?

If he is an egoist, the manager will certainly appoint the less able candidate, on the grounds that the brilliant one will progress to the point that he will take over the manager's own job. The task of an egoist is to restrain the development of those whose rise will threaten him, and utilize the powers of those who will not.

HEDONISM

Hedonism is the term used to describe an attitude that makes happiness the goal of life. Epicurus founded the school of philosophy in Athens in 307/6 BCE that was named after him. He held that the judgements we make are based on our feelings of pleasure or pain. But this is not simple sensuality, for Epicureans held that intellectual enjoyment was a pleasure worth seeking. Nor did the Epicureans indulge themselves, but lived quite simply. They held that mental pleasure was better than physical, and that fulfilment of the mind was superior to the pleasures of the body. The main goal for Epicureans was to have peace of mind.

So hedonism is not always a matter of crude or immediate enjoyment. An athlete may take up training to run a race, and may suffer in doing so, but overall the experience of the training and the race may be positive, something worthwhile, in spite of the work involved.

It is difficult to be a radically honest egoistic hedonist. You are not free to be unselfish, for you cannot argue against the claim of unconscious motivation – that all human responses, however apparently altruistic, are ultimately based on selfishness. You also have to suffer the conviction that every apparently helpful person, who is apparently trying to do something for you, is in fact doing something for himself or herself; you are simply being made the occasion of that person's happiness.

Example

I'll carry it myself and hope you feel guilty!

I shall feel pleased to have denied you the opportunity of helping. I am acting in my own best interest, and an aching back is a small price to pay for the satisfaction of having cheated a do-gooder out of selfishly doing good!

Maximizing happiness may require a consideration of the long-term effects of actions. So, for example, if I come across a vulnerable old person in a dark alley with a bulging handbag that is spilling over with banknotes, the prospect of a quick snatch might, in the short term, give me considerable pleasure. In the long term, it has to be weighed against the likelihood of being caught and punished by law for the action, or by my own conscience at having caused another person to suffer – or even, if I live to be old, the fear of walking down dark alleys while carrying all the wealth I have accumulated by such actions in the past.

We could argue, therefore, that there is short-term selfishness – 'I want that now!' – as well as long-term selfishness – 'I will enjoy life more if I follow these principles.' But in the latter case selfishness may actually be something that benefits others. In this case 'selfishness' does not refer so much to the expected outcome but to the motivation. Thus a person may be selfish by intention, but actually end up with unhappiness, because what is sought may bring only illusory happiness.

Example

▶ That extra drink before you drive may taste good, and may supply the happiness and sense of global harmony and universal insight that comes with mild intoxication. In the longer term, however, it may be a very short-lived happiness that is soon to be regretted.

▶ The sexual urge can be hard to resist – it promises intense happiness of regrettably short duration. That condomless moment of passion needs to be weighed against the risk of HIV infection or pregnancy. Refusing to have unprotected sex is not a rejection of happiness but a deferment of happiness – preferring the security of health (with the prospect of future sexual encounters) over immediate gratification.

If – taking a hedonist view – it is our duty to pursue our own happiness, what follows is largely decided by how we define happiness, and whether we take a short- or long-term view of how it is best achieved.

Egoistic hedonism may be self-defeating, as in the old joke in which a masochist encounters a sadist. Thinking that this could be the start of a really useful relationship, the masochist cries 'Hurt me!', but the sadist (being a sadist) replies 'No!' – an example of deferred pleasure!

Both Plato and Aristotle held the view that it is in a person's own best interest to act rightly. In this case, pleasure comes from doing good. But this is rather different from saying that pleasure is the same thing as goodness. They both argued for an objective idea of goodness, and then showed that following it would be beneficial.

However much it may be used to illustrate the way in which people sometimes act, egoistic hedonism is very difficult to sustain as an ethic to be shared with others, or to account for the experience of moral choice, conscience and the like. Nevertheless, in making a moral choice, it is natural that a person should hope that happiness, or benefit of some sort, will come from making the right decision. Consequences or results cannot be ignored – but the assessment of them generally takes other people (or the situation as a whole) into account, and not just the benefit of the person making the choice. This therefore leads naturally into the ethical theory called utilitarianism.

Utilitarianism

Jeremy Bentham (1748–1832) argued for the **Principle of Utility**, by which he meant that an action should be judged according to the results it achieved. This approach to ethics is called **utilitarianism**. It has been one of the most influential of ethical theories, and the one most widely used in ordinary 'common sense' decisions.

Bentham argued that an action should be judged according to its ability to offer happiness or benefit to everyone involved, or to avoid unhappiness and pain. He thought that all should be treated equally, and did not consider one form of happiness to be more important than another, although he took such things as the intensity and duration of happiness into account.

In his book *Utilitarianism*, John Stuart Mill (1806–73) further developed this theory, allowing that the effect of rules should also be taken into account, where their observance would benefit society as a whole. He also denied that all forms of happiness were of equal status, distinguishing higher (e.g. intellectual or cultural) and lower (e.g. sensual) pleasures.

In its simplest form, utilitarianism states that, in any situation where there is a moral choice, **the right thing to do is that which is likely to produce the greatest happiness for the greatest number of people** – a formula that had been proposed in 1725 by Francis Hutcheson (1694–1746) as a way of assessing political regimes, the best nation being that which produced the most happiness, or benefit, for the most people.

This seems a very straightforward approach to ethical decisions. But it raises two important points:

1 **How do you evaluate the results of an action?**
   ▷ *Is happiness or benefit to be judged entirely by the individuals concerned, or is there some more objective way of assessing it?*
   ▷ *In other words, what are your criteria for saying that a result is 'good'?*

Example

In December 2009, there was a debate in the UK about whether there should be minimum price for a unit of alcohol, in an attempt to discourage the growth in consumption and consequent increase in alcohol-related illness and death. Against this, it was argued that it is wrong to punish a responsible majority because of the foolishness of a minority. Some blamed the extension of licensing

(Contd)

hours, others criticized supermarkets for offering cheap drink. But supermarkets work in a competitive environment, and the increase in licensing hours was intended to bring about more civilized drinking and avoid a rush before 'closing time'.

In these and many other situations, action is taken on the basis of a predicted result which may prove to be quite false. Longer opening hours or an increase in the cost of alcohol may or may not change drinking habits. You may fix one problem only to create another, or offer benefits to some at the cost of harming others.

The same issue faces those who give aid to the developing world. The aim is generally to lift people out of poverty and starvation and to allow them to maintain themselves. The danger is that some forms of aid (e.g. agriculture that depends on machinery or chemicals) may create a situation where they depend entirely on the donor country for their livelihood. Equally, those who switch from subsistence farming to producing cash crops are then dependent on the market – and if that fails, they have nothing to fall back on.

The aim may indeed be to produce the greatest benefit for the greatest number, but there can be many different routes to that end, and deciding between them may not be easy.

2 **What if the results of an action are ambiguous?**
   ▷ *How do you balance the unhappiness caused to one person against the happiness of many?*
   ▷ *Is immediate happiness the criterion, or is it the longer-term benefit?*

For example, some would recommend that young offenders should be given a prison sentence, in the hope that it would encourage them to reform and thus not re-offend. This could imply that – although it is not experienced as such – the punishment may be regarded as increasing the happiness of the offender in the long term, as well as offering added happiness to those in society that he or she will not offend against in the future.

> ▶ *By what criteria do you judge what leads to happiness in this case? If you act against someone's wishes, claiming that it is 'really' for their greater happiness, you presumably do so on the basis of your idea of what constitutes the good life. On what is that idea based?*

The smiling headmaster of old who brandished a cane saying 'It's for your own good!' may have believed just that. But could it be proved? More and more evidence could be brought, and yet there would never be certainty. Some would point to occasions of genuine reform, others to establishing a cult of brutality.

But how far can you go with the assessment of what is good for society as a whole? Can a utilitarian assessment be used to justify resorting to warfare to settle disputes between nations?

The Falklands War

In 1982, the UK went to war with Argentina over the invasion by the latter of the Falkland Islands in the South Atlantic. The war was costly, both in terms of the men killed on both sides, and in terms of the weapons and ships destroyed, and the resulting cost of maintaining troops on the islands. As a result of it the Argentine invasion was repelled, and the Islands returned to British rule.

From a straightforward utilitarian position one might argue that it would be better to allow the Falklands to be taken over, rather than suffer such loss of life.

On the other hand, Margaret Thatcher, the British Prime Minister at the time, made clear that the decision to go to war was based on the absolute right to defend British sovereignty. This was a principle itself worth defending, apparently regardless of the cost involved.

Yet underlying this principle was another argument, this time a utilitarian one – if the UK decided that, because of the small

(Contd)

numbers of islanders affected, it was not worth defending the Falklands, then all other small dependencies would feel insecure.

Notice that what we have here is a utilitarian backing for the imposition of a general principle – not a utilitarian assessment of a particular situation in isolation. This is important because it points towards a variation of the utilitarian argument – 'rule utilitarianism' – to which we shall turn in a moment.

Similar questions could be asked of the war on Iraq in 2003. Both sides in the debate that took place before the war, and which continued long afterwards, use what amount to basically utilitarian arguments. On the one hand, there are those who point to the number of those killed in the war and its chaotic aftermath; others point to the number who may well have died under the continuation of Saddam's rule.

The argument about weapons of mass destruction was fundamentally utilitarian, namely that there was a threat being posed which suggested a future harm that outweighed the damage that a war would inflict. Those criticizing the war in retrospect might point to an increase in violence, suicide bombings and so on. The fact that assessments of the result of the war were so far wide of the mark, compared with what actually happened, illustrates just how difficult it is to get a decisive moral argument based on anticipated results.

Forms of utilitarianism

ACT UTILITARIANISM

Act utilitarianism looks for the results of an individual act in order to assess whether that act is right or wrong. In this form, utilitarianism accepts no general rules except the rule that one should seek the greatest happiness (or benefit – remember this is not a matter of emotions but of welfare) of the greatest number.

This offers no way of deciding between conflicting views as to what constitutes the greatest benefit. It also comes up against many of the problems of assessing results that we have outlined and illustrated above.

Act utilitarianism requires an assessment about pain or happiness that is related to each individual action. But the perceived results of an action may be explicable only in terms of social convention, not in terms of actual pain inflicted. People may choose to suffer – it is their happiness – but this may not be perceived by the external observer.

Example

You observe a scene of extreme suffering. A crowd of people hobbling, shuffling and obviously in pain run between lines of onlookers. You observe their exhaustion, and learn that they have run 26 miles and, in doing so, have suffered blisters, cramp and other aches and pains. Suppose you see one of them, at the limit of his or her endurance, slow to a walking pace, but the crowd of onlookers shouts that he or she should continue running.

Such action could be regarded as cruelty on a mass scale, yet thousands of people the world over will choose to go through just such an ordeal, pushing themselves to the limit. Voluntary suffering may be idiotic, but it is not immoral unless, by accepting it, genuine harm is done to others. A person who is determined to run a marathon in spite of medical warnings to the contrary, risks his or her life and all the suffering that their death could cause their family, so that might be regarded as immoral. Otherwise, running a marathon is an example of the acceptance of pain for no obvious result (other than that of personal satisfaction).

Pleasure and pain are therefore to be set in a social context, and may be misunderstood. It might be possible, for example,

(Contd)

RULE UTILITARIANISM

This rather more sophisticated approach to utilitarianism was put forward by John Stuart Mill, as follows.

▶ *Intellectual pleasures should be preferred to immediate physical pleasures, and that one should assess the quality of the pleasure anticipated as well as the quantity. (In this he followed the Epicurean tradition.)*
▶ *People may sacrifice themselves (e.g. losing their life in the attempt to save others), but that such sacrifice is not of value in itself, only in terms of what it achieved.*

He took an important step in allowing a utilitarian assessment to take into account those rules that benefit society as a whole. So, for example, the rule that it is wrong to take innocent human life is of general benefit to society, and should therefore not be broken, even if, in a particular case, killing an innocent person might seem to benefit other people. Thus the utilitarian can use general rules and principles, on the grounds that those principles have themselves been framed on utilitarian grounds.

Insight

This is the basis (as in the example of the Falklands War, given above) for saying that one should uphold the right of national sovereignty because this principle, applied universally, would benefit humanity as a whole.

As it has developed, those who take this line of argument have divided between:

▶ *strong rule utilitarians, who hold that one should not break one of these general rules to fit individual situations, and*

▶ *weak rule utilitarians, who would allow the pleasure or pain involved in a particular situation to take precedence over the general rule, while still allowing the general rule and its benefits to be taken into consideration.*

Fluoride in water

Fluoride, a substance found naturally in water supplies in some places, is good for teeth. Hence it would seem that a utilitarian argument should be in favour of introducing fluoride into water everywhere, so that all may benefit. However, fluorides (compounds of fluorine) are toxic if taken in sufficient quantity. There might be some straightforward balancing of benefit over risk, therefore.

However, it can also be argued that people should be free to decide whether or not they accept treatment, and that it is generally wrong to impose a remedy, even if it is known to be of benefit. A strong rule utilitarian argument might therefore oppose the universal introduction of fluoride (on the grounds that it would go against the beneficial rule that people should be free to choose) whereas a weak rule utilitarian argument would try to achieve a balance between known benefits and the modest loss of personal freedom of choice.

PREFERENCE UTILITARIANISM

Preference utilitariarism says that you should take into account the preferences of the person concerned in each case, unless those preferences are outweighed by the preferences of other people. In other words, this form allows people to say what for them constitutes pleasure or pain. It does not allow one person to impose his or her own criterion of pleasure on others, nor to make a utilitarian assessment on that basis.

Preference utilitarianism has become probably the most widely used ethical theory in areas of applied and professional ethics, largely due to the work of Peter Singer, whose books (especially *Practical Ethics*, published in 1979) have been immensely influential. Singer's work has been widely criticized by those seeking a traditional and absolutist approach. His basic principle is that one should seek an 'equal consideration of interests'. That does not mean that all have equal rights or should be treated equally, but that each should be treated in a way that is appropriate. Consideration will be given to the interests of animals, for example, but not by treating them as though they were people. Equally, someone who has been brain damaged and is in a persistent vegetative state does not have interests identical to those of someone who is conscious.

Singer's work

Peter Singer's work on ethics goes far beyond a simply case for preference utilitarianism. He argues, for example, that there are two things that make life worthwhile: the reduction in the amount of pain in the universe; and commitment to a cause that is beyond oneself. These, which provide a starting point for the ethical life, bring a sense of fulfilment and meaning. In other words, life becomes meaningful if you try to make the world a better place.

It is clear that utilitarian arguments can help you decide how best to put your ethical commitment into practice; they help you choose between options. But they don't, in themselves, give you a commitment to live the ethical life – you could, after all, always say 'Why bother?' even when faced with a convincing utilitarian argument for sharing wealth. Singer's work in ethics is challenging, in that it goes beyond simple utilitarianism, and touches the fundamental question about what it means to live an ethical life.

Utilitarianism works in a way that is the opposite to that of natural law: natural law starts with theories about the nature of the world and the purpose in life. From those general theories, it looks at each and every action and object and asks about its purpose. Once that is known, it claims that the right thing to do is that which fulfils the natural purpose, and the wrong thing is that which frustrates it. You start from principles, and apply them to individual situations.

With utilitarianism, the opposite is the case. You start with the pain or pleasure involved in individual situations and then take into account the wider pain or pleasure involved by the application of general rules, or the preferences of the people involved. The starting point, however, is with the immediate situation.

What the two approaches have in common is their desire to find some external, objective criterion (whether the pleasure or pain involved, or the purpose to be fulfilled) by which to show that an action is right or wrong.

In theory, using either of these approaches, it should be possible to present a case for morality which is convincing to other people, for it can be set out and demonstrated.

The limitation of the utilitarian approach, as we have seen, is that there is never enough evidence to provide certainty. It is always possible that the future will not turn out as we expect, and that our intention to maximize benefit will actually increase harm.

Insight

A utilitarian has to take a guess on the future, based on the best evidence available. But like any scientist, he or she must always be aware that predicting the future can never offer certainty.

General criticisms of utilitarianism

Society is complex. It does not consist of uniform people, all wanting the same things or expressing the same preferences. There will always be conflict of interests, divergence of views. Utilitarianism has taken this into account to a certain extent by allowing for 'preferences' to be expressed, rather than imposing on others what we consider to be for their greatest happiness. Nevertheless, the final decision is made in the interests of the majority, thus making it difficult to justify action on behalf of an individual or minority group. Any sense of social justice seems to demand that there should be cases where the majority freely give up something to their benefit for the sake of a minority or an individual.

Example

Sometimes, as a result of an appeal on television, the attention of a whole nation is focused on the plight of an individual. This is made especially poignant if the individual is a child desperate for a life-saving operation, or a local hero who is injured in the course of helping others. In these circumstances, offers of help are given that are out of all proportion to what would be allocated on a strictly utilitarian assessment of need.

- ▶ Are these the result of emotional indulgence rather than rational assessment of need?
- ▶ If so, is it wrong to give help to an individual in these circumstances?

A narrowly utilitarian assessment may preclude action being taken on behalf of an individual, on the grounds that it is not in the interests of the majority that so much relief should be expended on a single person. On the other hand, if the majority are presented with the facts in a way that engages them emotionally, they may well freely give up something (generally money, offered to the needy cause) in order that the individual may benefit. In this case, although the end result is an unequal sharing of resources, the preference of a majority of those involved – that they wish to give money – is satisfied. On strictly utilitarian terms, it would be wrong only if the preferences of the donors were outweighed by the preferences of those opposed to the donations being given. As always, the utilitarian assessment remains inconclusive.

Utilitarianism deflects our attention from the personal convictions and values that lie at the heart of moral choices, and makes the decision one that requires external assessment and calculation. But moral responses are not always a matter of conforming to what is reasonable, but of following convictions about what is 'right' even if it does not obviously lead to an increase in happiness.

Insight

Caricaturing a strict utilitarian, this criticism suggests that, as far as moral agency goes, utilitarianism turns the creative artist into a bureaucrat! In fact, of course, as we have seen in Singer's case, most ethical thinkers who use utilitarian arguments use them to establish the optimum course of action, given their prior moral commitments.

Often, when a moral choice has to be made, there is no time to calculate who will benefit and by how much. One has to act without knowing all the consequences. In such situations, my choice of action, often spontaneous, is based on convictions, not calculations.

A situation

A mother, walking along a river bank, hears a shout from behind her and turns to see her child topple off a bicycle into the raging

(Contd)

torrent. She plunges into the water, but is swept to her death, along with her child.

A utilitarian, confronted with information about the woman's remaining five, now motherless, children, and her work as a doctor, saving the lives of many, might say that she should not, on balance, have plunged into the water.

But is it possible, in all honesty, to say that she was not acting morally in attempting that hopeless rescue? And who, listening to the oration at such a person's funeral, would not wish, if put to a similar test, to have similar courage?

I am not arguing that a person who did not attempt the rescue could not perfectly well have justified his or her decision to stand by and watch the child drown. Indeed, it might take great courage to do that. But is it the only morally correct option?

Perhaps a situation that illustrates this in its starkest form is given in William Styron's novel *Sophie's Choice*. It explores the guilt of a woman, living in the USA, who had survived a Nazi concentration camp. Gradually the source of her terrible sense of guilt is revealed: she was held in the camp with her two children and was told that one could be saved but the other would be sent to die. But she must choose which: if not, both would die. She made the choice – knowing that, by doing so, she has condemned the other. She is haunted by that choice.

▶ From a utilitarian point of view, she did the right thing. To have refused to make a choice would have made it certain that both children would die.
▶ Equally, she is not to blame, because she did not actually choose that either child should die – she was not directly the agent of their deaths.
▶ But is it possible to live with such a choice? Does a utilitarian justification make the decision any more bearable?

There would seem to be two major limitations to the utilitarian standpoint:

1 *Utilitarianism, because it focuses on results, which are external to the person making the moral choice, does not adequately take into account the motive for making a choice – and yet it is motivation which would seem to be important in the assessment of whether a person was behaving in a moral way.*
2 *Utilitarianism does not explain why people sometimes feel that there are moral rules that should not be broken, irrespective of the consequences. This is a feature of moral dilemmas, and it is one to which we shall turn in the next chapter.*

There is one final thing to be said about utilitarianism. It is a popular approach, which appears to offer clear-cut ways of assessing what is right. The problem is that life is seldom so straightforward. Few would argue that utilitarianism is not a valuable rule of thumb for assessing what a reasonable person might choose to do. The question is whether (taken in isolation from all the other reasons why people choose to do one thing rather than another) it is adequate as an ethical theory. Human motivation is subtle, and people may justify their actions by reference to ideology, religion, ambition, personal need and so on. It is seldom simply a matter of weighing up the likely results and then making a choice – although such assessment may be a useful tool for a subsequent justification of a choice made instinctively, or from confused motivation.

Insight

However valuable and straightforward to apply, utilitarianism does not always have the last word when it comes to moral decision-making, even if it provides a check on other moral theories, by forcing people to face the consequences of their actions.

THINGS TO REMEMBER

From this chapter, remember that...

▶ *an egoist sees all action as done for personal benefit*

▶ *an ethical egoist thinks that it is **right** always to act to benefit oneself*

▶ *hedonism makes happiness the goal of life*

▶ *act utilitarianism judges an action according to its benefit for those involved*

▶ *rule utilitarianism takes into account the overall benefit of obeying rules*

▶ *preference utilitarianism considers the wishes of those involved, rather than imposing an external measure of benefit on them*

▶ *a narrowly defined utilitarianism will tend to benefit the majority rather than defend the individual*

▶ *we can never know all the consequences of an action*

▶ *utilitarianism may not sufficiently account for moral choices that do not yield measurable benefits*

▶ *utilitarianism works in conjunction with prior moral commitments.*

6

....

The experience of moral choice

In this chapter you will learn:

- *about conscience*
- *about arguing from the experience of moral choice*
- *about the Kantian approach to ethics.*

In Chapters 4 and 5 we examined two ways in which it is possible to justify moral claims – the first with reference to 'natural law', and the second based on the expected results. Both of these seek an external, objective basis for moral claims, examined rationally.

But there can be quite a different approach: to start not with reason, but with experience. What does it mean for us to experience a sense of right and wrong, to have a conscience, or a conviction that one particular line of action is the right thing to do, quite apart from any expected consequences it may have?

Conscience

Conscience is an inner conviction that something is right or wrong, and in ethical debate people sometimes ask whether they should obey moral rules, or whether they should rather obey their conscience. But conscience itself is a strange phenomenon. Clearly, it is not the result of a logical argument, and in some ways it is more like an emotion. A person's conscience may be troubled even if they have tried to follow ethical guidelines, or have fulfilled the expectations of other people or society. So what part can and does conscience play within ethics?

In a religious discussion, conscience may be thought of as the 'voice of God', speaking within the individual. If so, then it is a personal and internalized version of 'natural law', relating moral choice to fundamental features of the world (seen in religious terms as God's creation).

In a secular discussion, conscience is likely to be seen as the natural sensitivity to ethical issues – perhaps even as an unconscious way in which people apply moral principles to the particular situations they face. It is also possible to argue that there is a biological basis for conscience; in other words, that we are genetically programmed by emotions that promote the survival of our tribe or species.

The difficulty with both religious and secular approaches is that conscience, simply because it is experienced rather than being the result of a logic process, is not open to debate or rational challenge. You are unlikely to be argued into or out of having a conscience about something. Hence, conscience seems to have its own authority, and as such it cuts across other ethical principles and arguments.

LOGICAL REQUIREMENTS FOR CONSCIENCE

For the experience of conscience to make any sense, it seems to require two things:

▶ *freedom*
▶ *knowledge of the good.*

If you are not free to decide what to do, then you cannot be blamed for what happens. Morality implies freedom and a mind capable of understanding the significance of that freedom. That is logical, but it applies equally to conscience, for conscience is only experienced in the context of free moral choice.

Conscience also implies some innate knowledge of what is 'good'. Without that, it is difficult to make any sense of conscience, since having a conscience about something implies that there is something we 'should' do (or should have done, if we have a guilty conscience) – which implies that we know what the right thing is.

THREE DIFFERENT APPROACHES

Three thinkers are particularly interesting as a starting point for considering the nature of conscience: Aquinas, Butler and Freud.

Aquinas, dovetailing philosophy and Christian doctrine, considered conscience to be the requirements of God's law written within the heart. Thus, even those who do not understand Christian teaching have a natural sense of right and wrong, given directly by God. Naturally enough, Aquinas recognized that a person might have their moral judgement clouded by passion, ignorance or habits, and he noted that different societies had different views of what was right or wrong. Hence, although he says that you should always follow your conscience, he accepts that you might not understand the relevant moral principle, or appreciate that it applies to your particular situation. Hence your conscience is fallible and may lead you astray.

For reflection

If it is possible for your conscience to lead you astray, is it ever wise to follow conscience rather than reason, where they suggest different courses of action?

Joseph Butler (1692–1752) recognized that people were influenced by the need for self-preservation as well as a natural benevolence towards others. In fact, rather like Plato, he saw the human self as something of a hierarchy. Whereas for Plato, reason was to control the active passions as well as the baser needs, for Butler, priority was given to the conscience, which had the function of sorting out the conflicting claims of self-love and benevolence, thus promoting virtue by ensuring the right balance between the needs of the self and the good of others.

Insight

Butler echoes what is known as the 'moral sense' tradition – associated with philosophers like Francis Hutcheson and David Hume, and part of the background for the development of utilitarianism – that human nature has a built-in moral sense, and that it is only natural to feel concern for the sufferings of others.

A very different approach to conscience can be found in the psychological explanations given by Freud. He associated conscience with a sense of guilt, arguing that, through our early upbringing, we learn values that continue to influence our moral awareness and conscience later in life. Thus conscience is an aspect of what he called the *super-ego*. Since it is based on early experiences, it becomes an unconscious expression of the wishes of parents or other adults in that early period. As such, it may be very powerful is shaping one's personal choices, but it is difficult to accept it as a significant factor in a rational ethical discussion, for it is not based on any inherent sense of right or wrong, nor is it logical.

INNATE OR ACQUIRED?

A key question for conscience is whether it is innate or acquired. We may experience it as **innate**, but if Freud is right about its origins, then it is really **acquired** from our parents in our early years, and its authority is one that they continue to impose on us. If Aquinas is right, however, conscience is an essential part of being human – deeply innate and linked to the idea of a creator God and a rationally comprehensible creation.

Notice however that, even if Freud is right, it is the *moral principles* that are acquired, not the conscience itself. Conscience appears more like a *skill* or *faculty* than a set of rules. It is the unconscious ability to recognize moral significance. As a skill, then, it may well be innate and this is suggested by the fact that those who appear to have absolutely no conscience at all are regarded as psychopaths: there is something 'wrong' with them, they are not normal. It is normal to have a conscience.

Insight

That leaves open the question of why conscience is more developed in some people that in others, and upbringing may have a part to play in this.

The categorical imperative

Whether through conscience or through thinking about right and wrong, the experience of moral choice comes in the form of a sense that there is something I 'ought' to do regardless of the consequences. This is sometimes called a **categorical imperative**. Notice this distinction:

▶ A **hypothetical imperative** *takes the form 'If you want to achieve X then do Y.'*
▶ A **categorical imperative** *takes the form 'You should do Y.' It is absolute, having no conditions attached to it.*

The thinker most associated with this 'categorical imperative' is Immanuel Kant (1724–1804). Being an eighteenth-century German Protestant, he was very much concerned with the sense of duty. You do your duty (what you understand to be right) without regard to consequences. His main work on this is *Groundwork of the Metaphysics of Morals* (1785).

Kant held that the categories we use to understand the world – categories like space, time and causality – are not to be found in the data of our experience but are imposed on our experience by our own minds. We cannot prove that everything has a cause, but our minds automatically look for causes. **The mind plays an active part in shaping and ordering experience; it is not merely a passive recipient of what is 'out there'.** This is sometimes referred to as Kant's 'Copernican Revolution': just as Copernicus showed that the Earth revolved round the Sun, and not vice versa, so Kant showed that our minds determine the way in which we experience things.

In the same way, Kant argued that we would never be able to show conclusively that a certain action was right or wrong by reference to its expected results, because we would never have enough evidence, and might disagree about how to interpret it. The starting point for morals cannot therefore be something 'out there' among the data interpreted by our senses, but should be the actual experience of moral obligation – the feeling that there is something we 'ought' to do.

Insight

In other words, you do not first find out what is 'right' and then feel that you ought to do it; rather, that which you feel you ought to do is what you mean by 'right'.

Kant argued that to do your duty you have to exclude two other considerations: effects (or results) and inclinations. If you decide to do something, expecting that you will benefit by it, that is not a moral choice. Equally, if you decide to do something because you enjoy doing it, that is not a moral choice either. Kant also rejected external moral authority where it conflicted with personal moral conviction. Unthinking obedience is not a valid moral position – **one should act out of a personal sense of what is right.** His starting point is the 'good will', aided by the pure practical reason.

Kant therefore sought to set out in the general principles of morality, the absolute and rational requirements of the *categorical imperative* (the unconditioned 'ought'), which might be applied to all moral issues. What is more, he sought to do this 'a priori' – based on reason alone, not on the evidence about how people actually behave or the results of their actions. There are three main forms of his categorical imperative:

1 *Act only on that maxim (or principle) which you can, at the same time, wish to make a universal law.*
2 *Act in such a way as to treat people as ends and never as means.*
3 *Act as though a legislating member of the kingdom of ends.*

The implication of the first, and major, form is that I should only do something if I am prepared for everyone else to be free to act according to that same moral principle. This does not mean that I can only do something if I imagine everyone else doing it as well (that might well cause practical chaos), but I must be prepared for everyone else to follow the same logical principle. I should not consider myself to be a unique or special case.

Notice what this does not tell you. It does not tell you what the content of your moral decision should be; it does not say that this or that action is always right or wrong. Rather it provides a general principle – our willingness to see the basis of our action become a universal law.

There is a general question to ask of a theory such as Kant's: is it possible to give a general rule that can be applied to each and every particular act, or is it essential to know the particular purpose and context of that act, before deciding on its moral status?

Example

Breaking a promise
Is it ever morally right to make a promise knowing that one has no intention of keeping it? If I consider, at the moment when I make a promise, that I shall be free to break it, then – according to

(Contd)

Kant's first form of the categorical imperative – I should be willing everyone else to be free to make and break their promises. But Kant argues that this would make nonsense of the whole idea of making a promise, and it is therefore illogical to say that it is right to make a promise that one does not intend to keep.

So let us explore this idea further in relation to the question of whether it is ever right to commit suicide, another example that Kant himself used.

Kant argued that, if a person in desperate circumstances considers shortening his life in order to avoid future suffering, he does so on the basis of self-love. But that same self-love is what sustains life in the first place. To shorten life therefore involves self-contradiction, and hence it would be wrong.

But is that necessarily the case?

No two people are exactly the same, and nobody can know exactly the scale and quality of another person's suffering. Is it realistic to offer a general moral principle for suicide? If I were suffering from a serious and incurable illness, I might wish that everyone, if they were ever in this situation, should be morally justified in choosing to end their life. It might be quite possible to hold the view that no healthy person should commit suicide, but that someone in terminal pain should be allowed to do so. The self-love that Kant finds contradictory, need not be so, provided that it is an affirmation of tolerable life, not intolerable suffering.

The second form of the categorical imperative follows from the first. If you are prepared to universalize the principles on which you act, it implies that you are prepared to consider everyone else as an autonomous moral agent, also free to act on their freely chosen maxims. And that, of course, implies that they should be treated as ends in themselves, never as means to your own end. This aspect of Kant meets with almost universal approval. Most people would see any treatment of people as though they were 'things', disposable or merely there for our own personal convenience, as fundamentally wrong. Relationships in which one person exploits another are generally regarded as morally wrong, whatever the particular circumstances.

Insight

Recognition of the right of each person to be treated as a full, autonomous human agent is fundamental to Kant, but is also implied by the other ethical arguments considered in this book.

The third form follows from the second. Kant argues that you should always imagine yourself as being in the position of someone who is responsible for legislating for a society in which everyone is to be treated as an 'end', an autonomous individual. What is the right thing to do in such a society?

Notice that Kant sees the important touchstones as rationality (can you justify it in a rational way?) and universality (can you apply it to everyone?). The implication of this is that each individual constructs, and takes responsibility for, his or her own set of moral values, based on **duty** and the **good will**.

This is very different from the natural law or utilitarian approaches, and sometimes their priorities conflict, as in the following situation.

The cost of truth

You are held by a terrorist gang, who demand to know the whereabouts of a close friend or relative whom they clearly wish to kill. You know that the person concerned is in hiding. Do you tell the truth and admit that you know where they are, or do you tell a lie, either by giving the wrong location, or by saying that you do not know where they are?

Here the dilemma is between anticipating the harm that will be done if you tell the truth and your friend is killed, and the general moral principle that you should tell the truth.

(Contd)

You might want to argue that anyone, confronted similarly by the prospect of the death of an innocent person, should lie. In this case, although the rule about telling the truth could be universalized, so also could the rule about doing anything necessary in order to prevent innocent suffering.

The dilemma is caused by a clash between a utilitarian assessment (that telling the truth will end up causing suffering) and obeying a general principle of truth telling, established rationally.

Kant also suggested that, if you respond to an unconditional moral 'ought', doing so presupposes three things, which he termed the postulates of the pure practical reason:

- **God** – *because there must be a sense that, by doing one's duty, happiness will follow, and that is something that could only be possible in a world ordered by God.*
- **Freedom** – *because, unless you experience yourself as free, you will have no sense of being able to make a moral choice.*
- **Immortality** – *because you know that you might not see the results of all that you do in this life, and therefore presuppose that there is some future in which the present imbalance of actions and rewards will be rectified.*

Kant does not mean that you have to believe in these three things in order to respond to an 'ought' but that, once you do acknowledge the unconditional nature of that 'ought', it implies that you believe in them.

Not everyone would accept this, for it is based on the idea that there is a rational structure to our thought that underlies our instinctive reactions. This may not be so. We may feel an obligation for the worst of motives, or from unconscious needs.

This highlights a major problem with Kant's ethics. It is designed for a world where people act out of good will and moral duty. In the real world people are far more complex, seldom completely rational in their moral and personal choices, and sometimes act out of plain hatred or ill will. Is it wise, in such a world, to remain a moral innocent?

The creative response

There is a further point to note here – one to which we will return in the next chapter. For the natural law and utilitarian approaches, we look out at the world and analyse either its structure (if you are looking for purpose) or the likely results of action (if you are a utilitarian). But when a person makes a moral choice, he or she is not merely responding to an external situation but creating something new – taking an active step to change the world, not merely to respond to the way it is.

This active side of moral choice shapes both external circumstances and the personality of the person who acts. Character is shown and developed through such choices. Our moral choices change our world.

Insight

We do not find a 'categorical imperative' out there; it is not a piece of data in the world. To a person who says it does not exist, there is no objective proof to offer. It is not part of the world, but a feature of the way in which a person responds to the world.

Morality is therefore about creative response, about interpreting the world in such a way that we give it value. Things have value for us, and we are sometimes required to express those values, or choose between conflicting values, but those values do not inhere in external objects, but in the relationship that we have with them.

But values and commitments are not decided on rational grounds alone. Individuals and groups develop their own criteria for value and therefore for moral judgement. What one group regards as morally acceptable, even praiseworthy, another condemns. This is a feature of the 'moral relativism' debate, but it can be applied to each moral theory, including Kant's. If people cannot agree on what is 'good', then they are never going to agree on the means of evaluating actions as right or wrong. This stark fact was brought home to the world with terrible force in September 2001.

Elsewhere in the world, however, the attack was celebrated by Islamic militants as a triumph. To some young Muslims, Osama bin Laden was seen as a hero and those who carried it out were seen as martyrs, rather than terrorists.

Here, in its starkest form, is the dilemma for ethics. A universally accepted ethic is only possible if all agree on the values and principles on which it can be based. Both natural law and utilitarianism tried to find that basis, but both have presuppositions that may be challenged. The categorical imperative of Kant (particularly in its first form) assumes that an action is morally right if the person performing it can will, at that time, that it should become a universal law. But that too requires the acceptance of a set of values that are deemed to be 'good'.

What an American citizen and a member of al-Qa'ida would seek to make a universal law are two utterly different things. Each sees the rightness of his or her own cause; each feels the force of the categorical imperative, that there is an unconditional moral demand.

Insight

One aspect that does not come under question is Kant's second formulation of the categorical imperative: that people should never be used only as means, but always also as ends. Terrorism of any sort uses people as a means to an ideological end.

Kant seeks an ethics based on the pure practical reason. It should therefore provide universal guidance, acceptable to all reasonable people. In practice, that simply is not the case. These matters are not based on reason alone, but on deeply held convictions.

Determined and yet free?

Before leaving Kant, let us refer back to the issue with which we were concerned in Chapter 2. Kant argued that our minds impose space, time and causality on the phenomena that they encounter. From an external point of view, everything is conditioned. When I observe someone else making a choice, my mind naturally seeks out the causes that led to that particular choice. In the world of phenomena, there can be no freedom. But Kant held that all we know about are the phenomena that come through our senses. We know things as they appear to us, not things as they are in themselves. (Things-in-themselves Kant calls **noumena**, our perception of them **phenomena**.)

On this basis, Kant is able to say that we are *at one and the same time* phenomenally conditioned (perceived from the outside, I have no freedom), and noumenally free (I experience my freedom to act – something that I know, but nobody else can observe). There are therefore two ways of understanding the moral act:

▶ *from the standpoint of one who observes the choices that are made, with their consequences and the implications they have for an understanding of humankind*
▶ *from the standpoint of the person who is actually confronted with a choice and who, in a moment of creative action, actually responds on the basis of his or her values and convictions.*

This distinction is of crucial importance for ethics. When the logical positivists argued that the meaning of a statement was its method of verification, they dismissed ethics as meaningless, because it could not be verified by experience, in other words, by *phenomena*. And yet – as we saw in the reaction against that position – people continue to find moral statements meaningful. This highlights the division of perspective between a person who observes and analyses the phenomenon of human activity, and what it is to experience a moral 'ought'. As we are in ourselves, we can act morally, and no amount of analysis and observation is going to be able to remove either the experience of freedom and choice, or its moral significance.

THINGS TO REMEMBER

From this chapter, remember that ...

▶ *conscience implies freedom and knowledge of the 'good'*

▶ *conscience has a personal authority independent of rational argument*

▶ *conscience may be innate or acquired*

▶ *a hypothetical imperative takes the form 'if ... then ...'*

▶ *Kant's first form of the categorical imperative is that you should be prepared for the maxim of your action to become a universal law*

▶ *his second form is that people should always be treated as ends in themselves, never as means*

▶ *his third form is that you should act as though legislating for a kingdom of people who are treated as autonomous moral agents ('ends')*

▶ *a moral choice is creative and informed by values, not simply reactive*

▶ *there may not be a rational way of deciding between conflicting values*

▶ *people may be perceived as determined, and yet experience themselves as free.*

7

Personal development and virtue

In this chapter you will learn:

- *about Hume on benevolence*
- *about Nietzsche's challenge*
- *to explore the moral and existential implications of personal development.*

Before the sixteenth century, moral thinking in the West was dominated by the influence of Aristotle and mediated through Christian theologians, of whom Aquinas was the most influential. It was heavily dependent on the authority of religion and of the Church. With the Reformation and the intellectual upheavals that followed, that authoritarian structure was replaced by the desire to find a rational basis for action. From the seventeenth and eighteenth centuries we find the development of two lines of approach to personal ethics. One is utilitarianism; the other is represented particularly by Kant and the categorical imperative.

Both were dependent, in one way or another, on the values of the older 'natural law' view of the universe. Utilitarianism falls back on values – as it seeks to say what constitutes happiness, or the good of the greatest number. Kant, on the other hand, having come to the conclusion that you could not prove God, freedom or immortality by examining the phenomena of the world, decided that he should reinstate them as *postulates* or *presuppositions* of the practical reason.

Insight

Both utilitarianism and Kant require the prior acceptance of values and qualities, without which we would have no reason to want to achieve the greatest good for the greatest number, or recognize a sense of absolute moral obligation.

But what if we set this tradition aside and explore values that are not found 'out there' in a general understanding of the world, but are ones we create for ourselves as we act and make choices? Can we create values as an artist creates an abstract picture, rather than discover them, as a photographer might record a beautiful but external scene? Can we, as individuals, stop *asking* what is right, and start *deciding* what will be right?

This will be an important question as we look at moral choice from the standpoint of the human individual and his or her personal development. But first of all, it is important to recognize that such development takes place in a social context. So how does personal development relate to the way in which we treat other people?

Altruism?

Can human beings act genuinely for the benefit of others?

Thomas Hobbes, in *Leviathan* (1651), argued that, if people voluntarily give up their rights for the benefit of others, they do so in order to achieve something good for themselves. Indeed, he claimed that every voluntary act had as its aim some good to be obtained for the person performing it. On this basis, although the benefit done to oneself may be less tangible than the benefit offered to the other person (e.g. feeling good for having been charitable), nevertheless in some way, even if we appear to be helping others, we are actually acting in a way that benefits ourselves.

By contrast, Hume's *Enquiry Concerning the Principles of Morals* (1751) takes the view that people do actually experience 'sympathy' – that is, they respond when they see the suffering or the joy of others. He makes this experience basic to his ethics, in that if there were no sympathy there would be no development of altruistic qualities.

This does not mean that people respond to the sufferings of others in a generous way all the time, rather that everyone can experience some degree of sympathy. A psychopath, for example, is someone who has no sense of right or wrong, and who is not going to be persuaded by reason, but who has urges (to kill, for example) that are totally devoid of any sense of sympathy for his or her victim. In other words, for the psychopath, other people are 'things', not fellow human beings who have feelings and to whom one might want to relate in a personal way. In this case, the exception illustrates the general rule – that people are capable of responding to the sufferings of others.

Hume also holds that people can exhibit qualities that give happiness to themselves as well as being useful to others. These 'virtues' include justice, faithfulness and politeness, which are not directly related to self-development or happiness, but to the interests of others. In fact, Hume regards *benevolence* as the highest quality of which human nature is capable.

Insight

Such virtues are qualities that a person can develop. In this sense, altruism is a sign of personal development. But this is very different from personal development that is pursued for selfish reasons, or at the expense of other people.

In section 9 of the *Enquiry* ... Hume seems to step back from saying that sympathy is always its own justification. He points out that, even if someone appears to lose out personally because of some action for the benefit of others, he or she will feel inner peace of mind and satisfaction – which lead to personal happiness.

So, in assessing personal development as a feature of morality we need to reflect on three possibilities:

▶ *That people are basically selfish, and if they are honest they will admit it.*

▶ *That people think they are unselfish and considerate to others but, in fact, they are really just satisfying their own deeper needs.*

▶ *That people can genuinely feel and respond to the situations of others, and can show honest altruism.*

There is one other important feature of Hume's idea of 'sympathy' to keep in mind. When we looked at Aristotle in Chapter 4, we saw that he attempted to get some objective criterion for moral statements. His idea of what was right stemmed from reason, and an intellectual conception about the purpose of human existence. Hume, by contrast, sees reason as taking a secondary role to the emotions. It is the latter that provide us with the values we need for directing our action; reason is their handmaid, selecting options and possibilities to enable them to be expressed in practical action.

If a person is to develop, that development takes place within a social context. In other words, personal development implies personal worth in terms of relationships. It would be difficult to develop personally in total isolation from others, and if a person could achieve a high degree of personal growth in isolation (for example, through some form of religious asceticism), it would still depend on the religious and social ideas that set up the conditions for that growth in the first place. This social context was emphasized by F.H. Bradley in an essay called 'My station and its duties' (in *Ethical Studies*, 1876). Bradley argued that self-realization was the basis of ethics, and he followed the philosopher Hegel in pointing out that people need both self-expression and recognition if they are to enjoy the good life. That recognition can come through family relationships, through local society or through the state, because (according to Hegel) these are the basic spheres of influence.

Central to Bradley (and Hegel) is the idea that self-realization (achieving one's full potential as a unique human being) takes place in society, not in isolation. If freedom is needed to allow for the personal development and autonomy of an individual, we need to remember that it comes with a price, and that one person's freedom may well curtail that of another.

Nietzsche

The thinker who most radically challenged traditional moral thinking and placed human development at the centre of a value creating system of thought was Friedrich Nietzsche.

It is often valuable to consider a thinker's work against the background of his or her personal circumstances – although with many philosophers this is discouraged by the way that they present ideas in a cogent fashion, inviting logical comment only. Nietzsche is different. His writing is vivid, and his ideas are sometimes presented as images. It may be worth reflecting therefore that he was born in 1844, the son of a Lutheran pastor and of the daughter of a country vicar, and that as a young man he was a lover of solitude, enthusiastically religious, and also highly talented.

Insight

Nietzsche composed a motet at the age of 10, and by 14 had written some 50 poems and had decided that he wanted to be a writer. His abilities are literary as well and his complex character and brilliance shows through his unconventional style of writing – often stringing together short aphorisms, each of which, on reflection, have profound implications.

We shall approach Nietzsche's work through four key features.

'GOD IS DEAD'

The first of these is the idea that **God is dead**. This is not a casual comment from one who has not taken religious seriously; it is a conclusion about the state of things as Nietzsche saw them in the 1880s. In *The Joyous Science* he has the image of a madman who comes into the town with the message that 'God is dead': not that God had never existed, but that people had killed him. The character asks if his hearers do not sense that it is growing darker, that they need lamps, even at noon. He tries to explain that people have cut the world loose, and that (without God) it is wandering without fixed values and without direction.

This is perhaps the starkest recognition of what had taken place, almost since the Reformation – the replacement of an authoritarian and metaphysical structure of thought, believed to have been given by God, by human reason. His point was that, whatever they may claim to believe, people in fact create values based on themselves, not on God. They are the centre and measure of life.

It is presented, not as something good or bad, but as an observation – something that he is amazed others have not realized.

Insight
Without God, humankind is forced to take responsibility and establish its own values. That immediately sets an agenda for ethics which continues the trend started by Kant – that values are not to be found 'out there' but established by the human will. Hence, of course, we also have the responsibility for establishing what is 'good', and therefore of finding a morality that fits our new 'godless' perspective.

'SUPERMAN'

The next feature is the **superman** (a rather poor translation of *Übermensch*, which means something that goes over or beyond man).

In *Thus Spoke Zarathustra*, the sage Zarathustra comes down his mountain. He opens his teaching by saying:

> *I teach you the Superman. Man is something that should be*
> *overcome. What have you done to overcome him?*
> *All creatures hitherto have created something beyond*
> *themselves: and do you want to be the ebb of this great tide, and*
> *return to the animals rather than overcoming man?*

(translated by Hollingdale, Penguin, p. 41)

Here the context is evolution. As the ape is to humans, so humans will be to the superman. He then takes an important step: 'The Superman is the meaning of the earth. Let your will say: The Superman *shall* be the meaning of the earth!' In other words, from this moment on humanity is to choose its values and its direction by an act of will. We humans are to be the creators of value. Nietzsche is critical of those who sought some heavenly goal, accusing them of being poisoners, weakening humankind. Instead, the true goal is to be found in the future – the *Übermensch*. It is an affirmation of life, and of the human will that shapes and determines that life. In other words, you are free to define your world!

'THE WILL TO POWER'

The third feature is the **will to power** – which is the force behind Nietzsche's moral thinking. It does not mean a crude attempt to get power, but the affirmation of life, and the will to develop and move forward. It is the will to power that, for Nietzsche, is the source of all values and therefore the source of morality.

Nietzsche's thought is highly individualistic. Wanting to be equal with others and showing humility – key features of democracy and Christianity, as he sees them – are signs of decadence and weakness. They sap the will to power and desire for personal development. For this reason, Nietzsche opposed both democracy and Christianity. According to Nietzsche, exploitation is one of the basic features of life, and self-development is fundamental. Therefore we should be free to adopt whatever means we need in order to secure that power. In *Beyond Good and Evil*, he sees the world as divided into masters and slaves, and he holds that the morality that suits the one will not suit the other. Masters are free to do what their own creative development requires. Nietzsche rejects both democracy and Christianity because they are associated with slave values, not with master values, and cause the decay of the state because they are based on the false assumption that all are equal. He also attacks Christianity because it allows people to deny themselves on Earth for the sake of God and a heavenly reward.

Insight

Nietzsche's background is in nineteenth-century Protestantism: not everyone taking a religious position today would view Christian values in quite the way he did. Nevertheless it is true that some ethical views emphasize humility and co-operation, while others stress personal development and the competitive spirit. Nietzsche's is one of the latter.

'THE ETERNAL RECURRENCE'

Finally, there is the **eternal recurrence**. This is a difficult and complex idea. Perhaps it may be approached by contrasting it with the ideas of Aristotle or traditional Christian views. To Aristotle, everything has an end or a purpose. It achieves its goal once it fulfils that end. In the traditional Christian scheme, the world looks to something outside itself to justify its existence – God. But for Nietzsche, God is dead. There is no way that this present life can be simply tolerated because it leads to or points to something beyond itself. Nietzsche therefore held that one should be prepared to accept life as it is; to affirm it and work with it.

His graphic way of presenting this is to pose the challenge of accepting that everything that happens will be repeated over and over again. Can you look at such an endlessly repeating life and still affirm it? Can you enjoy it just as it is, without asking for some external compensation or explanation? Nietzsche presents a challenge – a necessary challenge in any world that has consciously or unconsciously discarded religious belief and the old metaphysics that went with it. **The challenge of 'the eternal recurrence' is to accept life as it is.**

Nietzsche's writings *are* a challenge, and these notes hardly touch the surface of what he has to say on the topic of morality. They are included here because Nietzsche looks at morality in a way that is very different from the older 'natural law' and 'utilitarian' arguments – in place of a fixed purpose or happiness, the key to Nietzsche's morality is a commitment to the future of humankind.

A point for reflection

Through the 'will to power', one should 'give style' to one's character and the greatest enjoyment is 'to live dangerously!' In *Beyond Good and Evil*, Nietzsche said of morality: 'Every morality is a rationalization of fear, a set of safety instructions on how to live at peace with the most dangerous aspects of one's self.'

▶ What might a modern psychologist make of this?
▶ How is it possible to be afraid of aspects of oneself, or to regard oneself as dangerous?
▶ What might be the ethical implication of admitting that, consciously or unconsciously, we have a 'will to power' and that it is the source of our values?

Virtue ethics

Rather than starting with questions about whether a particular action is right or wrong, it is equally possible to approach ethics by asking what it means to be a 'good' person. In other words, we ask what virtues or qualities a person should possess if they are to live the good life.

This **virtue ethics** approach goes back to Aristotle, who was concerned to understand what constituted the good life. Virtues are those qualities that can enable someone to live well and fulfil themselves as a human being. There are various lists of virtues, but the **cardinal virtues** listed by the Ancient Greeks were temperance, justice, courage and prudence.

If these qualities enable a person to express and live out his or her true – or essential – nature, then there will be parallels between virtue ethics and the natural law approach that we examined in Chapter 4. Natural law understood morality in terms of conforming to one's essential nature; the virtues summarize the personal qualities that enable that to happen.

With the rise of utilitarianism and Kantian ethics, alongside the older Natural Law approach, the virtues had not featured much in ethical debates until the 1950s, when virtue ethics was examined again, particularly associated with the work of Phillipa Foot and Elizabeth Anscombe. Although the basic argument – seeing virtues as dispositions to act in a particular way, and as a means of self-fulfilment – was not new, what was new was that it shifted moral debate away from general rules and principles of behaviour and towards more general questions about value and meaning in life, and the qualities that were worth developing and encouraging.

In particular this appealed to feminist thinkers, who had seen the rationalism of other ethical theories as being influenced by particularly male ways of approaching life, based on rights and duties, whereas they sought a more 'feminine' approach that included a recognition of the value of relationships and intimacy.

It also had the advantage of being a naturalistic ethic, in that it moved away from the idea of simply obeying rules, to an appreciation of how one might express one's fundamental nature and thus fulfil one's potential as a human being.

There are important questions raised by virtue ethics:

▶ *Do we have a fixed* **essence?** *Are there, for example, particular feminine qualities that all women should seek to express, and which constitute feminine virtues? Or is our nature dependent on our surroundings and upbringing?*

▶ *If our actions express our essential nature, and if our nature has been shaped by factors over which we have no control (e.g. the culture into which we have been born; traumatic experiences in childhood) are we* **responsible** *for our actions?*

▶ *How do we relate the expression of an individual's virtues to the needs of society?*

▶ *If there are different ways of expressing the same virtue (e.g. out of love, one person might seek euthanasia, another seek to prolong life), how should you choose between them? At that point, is it necessary to fall back on one of the other ethical theories?*

Example

Consider the difference between murder, committed in the course of a robbery, and killing a loved one who is seriously ill, in order to prevent further suffering. The latter – euthanasia – is treated differently, because the intention of the person doing the killing is quite different. In the first example the vice displayed is greed, in the second, the virtue displayed is compassion, and that makes a fundamental difference to the moral significance of the act itself.

Notice here that moral praise of blame focuses on the virtues or vices of the people concerned, not on the absolute legality or results of their actions.

Existentialism

Existentialism is the term used for a school of philosophy, developed during the nineteenth and twentieth centuries, concerning human existence and its meaning. The basic idea of existentialism is that our life is shaped by the choices that we make. We are all in a process of becoming, of changing and developing as we respond to our circumstances. We are free to choose what we shall become, but that freedom can be seen as terrifying in its implications.

Although existential questions had been raised earlier, Søren Kierkegaard (1813–55) is regarded as the originator of existentialism. He emphasized the inwardness, the subjective importance of choice. It was less a matter of *what* one chose to do, as of *how* one chose it – not in a superficial way, but with earnest integrity.

Another thinker who set the agenda for existentialism is Martin Heidegger (1889–1976), although he did not regard himself as an existentialist. He pointed out that we are 'thrown' into the particular circumstances of our life, and we respond to them. While it is relatively easy to wear particular masks to fit the roles that we perform (as a son or daughter, a student, a worker, and so on), to hide behind a mask is to opt out of our real task, which is to live in an authentic way – being ourselves, in all our uniqueness, not what others expect of us because of our social or family role. Thrown into life, Heidegger considered that we are also all too aware of death. We are finite, and it is therefore a challenge to find meaning in our lives – meaning that is not negated by death.

For reflection

In response to the sense of gloom in Germany that followed the defeat in the First World War, Heidegger looked for some figure that could give people self-respect, direction and hope for the future. He saw just such a figure in Hitler. Like Nietzsche, who saw

(Contd)

the Übermensch as the direction of the future, in the absence of God-given value and direction, so Heidegger saw self-respect in following a leader who could promise a positive and self-affirming future. This has made him a most controversial figure, but two things need to be kept in mind:

▶ With hindsight, his commitment to the Nazi cause in the 1930s was a great mistake, but it would be wrong to identify Heidegger's views with later Nazi atrocities.
▶ Clearly, elements in Heidegger's thought influenced his political views, but that should not detract from the value of his work as a whole.

Clearly, there is much in Heidegger's thinking that relates to ethics – quite apart from his controversial support for the Nazi movement, and his later examination of issues concerning mechanization and the environment. Notice the key feature here is *authenticity*. Heidegger does not tell you what you should choose to do – but he does argue that, whatever you choose, you should do it with integrity, as an expression of your authentic self, not simply to conform to the expectations that society might impose on you.

A similar emphasis is found with the key figure of the existentialist movement, Jean-Paul Sartre (1905–80). The key phrase that encapsulates his existentialism is 'Existence precedes essence.' In other words, I do not have an essential nature which is then expressed through what I do. Rather, my life and its choices shape who I am; I am the creation of my life, the result of the choices I make.

Insight

This led some (particularly the novelist Albert Camus) to argue that life is fundamentally absurd, in that there is no basic rational justification for what motivates us and no God to guarantee or explain what life is about. The only meaning to be found in life is the meaning that we choose to give it.

As with Heidegger's masks, Sartre emphasizes the difference between authentic and inauthentic human existence. Human consciousness is a matter of *être-pour-soi*, being for itself, as opposed to the world of objects, *être-en-soi*. The danger for human authenticity is the temptation to opt out of the responsibility of human development – to see oneself and others as objects, rather than as individuals able to take and shape their world.

Existentialism is a huge and fascinating area of study, and there is no opportunity to examine it in any depth here. However, we should be aware that the significance for ethics is that it makes personal development – learning what it means to live an authentic existence – the fundamental value. There is one huge problem with this, of course. If there is no fundamental rationality – if there is no fixed essence that natural law or virtue ethics can take as an objective starting point – then how do you decide whether the self that you choose to shape is good or bad? Integrity and authenticity may be fine, but if that authentic self is one that exploits others without hesitation and without shame, one might claim that, integrated or not, there is something fundamentally wrong. If there is no rational basis or essence for human existence, then we are free to make whatever we like of ourselves – and doing that authentically seems to be the only guideline that existentialism is able to offer.

Humankind, Marx and Freud

If we are to use the personal development of individuals as a criterion for morality – in the sense that what is 'right' is what enables individuals to develop to their full potential – then we need to look at the broader context of human life and motivation. What are the circumstances that influence moral choice? What motivates such choice?

Clearly, if you accept that humankind has a fixed and knowable 'essence' then, following the 'natural law' approach, it is relatively easy to set about evaluating what human development means – it is whatever enables people to express their true essence or nature. However, if you accept that human nature is something to be developed, rather than something given, then there will be other factors to consider. One of these – but quite beyond the scope of the present book – is to look at the biological and evolutionary aspects of humankind. It could be argued, for example, that certain traits in behaviour give the species a biological advantage, and will therefore be promoted by the process of natural selection. Hence you could argue that there is a biological basis for ethics – in effect, that the 'good' is what enables your species to develop.

However, that raises another problem. On what basis can we argue that the 'good' is what benefits the human species rather than any other? Is there a criterion that stands over and above the competing claims of different species in this world of competition for limited food and space? If not, then, if we opt for saying that human development is what counts, we need to recognize that our ethical system is based on a preference rather than a logically defensible argument. After all, the world was developing for millennia before the appearance of humankind; why should we assume that, having arrived, humankind will be a permanent feature of global evolution? Nietzsche spoke of creating a higher form of man. Why not accept that there may be other species now in existence that will one day take over the dominant position held now by humankind?

But quite apart from such global, environmental and biological issues, there are two other factors to be taken into account when we consider the personal development of individuals as a moral criterion: the Marxist and Freudian perceptions of humankind. Both Marx and Freud (along with those who followed and developed their work) have had an enormous influence on modern ethics, and both of them look to self-realization of the individual as a criterion in evaluating their theories.

MARX

Marx saw the proletariat suffering from the way in which the wage labourer was separated off from the product of his labours.

In factory conditions, the worker could no longer get pride or personal satisfaction from his or her work, but was simply a function in a process from which someone else made a profit. This Marx called **alienation**.

Whatever the practical consequences of Marx's thought – and, indeed, the huge moral issues that arise when we contemplate the application of this thought now – we can at least acknowledge this fundamental problem of alienation. Being recognized and valued for what one creates is an important element in maintaining self-worth. To be alienated in the workplace is to be cut off from an important feature of life, namely the acknowledgement of one's role in creating goods and services, in other words, of participating creatively in the social sphere.

When it comes to applied ethics, the area that might be influenced by this is business and work ethics. How should employees be treated? What is the status of wage labour? We saw that the second form of Kant's categorical imperative was the fundamental statement that everyone should be treated as an 'end', never only as a 'means'. Clearly, a fundamental problem with all forms of work that alienate the worker is that the worker becomes de-humanized (theoretically replaceable by a machine), a mere mechanical function.

Those who follow Kant's second form of the categorical imperative would argue that workers should be regarded as autonomous human beings and therefore ends in themselves, not simply means to a corporate productive end.

Insight

As well as this aspect alienation and personal development, the other major feature of Marx's philosophy that impinges on ethics is his idea of class conflict, where an individual acts (and justifies that action) as a representative of his or her class.

FREUD

In his analysis of the self, Freud introduced a threefold division: the id, the ego and the super-ego. Of these, the super-ego was the 'conscience', the source of moral commands, taken in as rules during childhood and now (for those who are psychologically unhealthy) unconsciously inhibiting the free expression of the rational self, the ego. For health, according to most psychological theories, the ego needs to be in control. Health is the freedom to understand one's needs and wants, to see how one might develop to achieve them, and then to take steps in that direction, free from neurotic guilt.

That approach – and it is, of course, not limited to Freud – takes the personal development and fulfilment of individuals as its fundamental aim. Whatever inhibits that development is 'bad', whatever enables it is 'good'. Might it be good or morally right to be inhibited, or to bring up children in a way that makes it more likely that they will grow up inhibited? Clearly not. Conscience, the super-ego, and all the structure of moral claims and principles that the super-ego looks to for support, are therefore subject to self-development as their criterion.

There is far more that both Marx and Freud could contribute to our study of ethics, but for now it is important only to recognize that they both emphasize this central feature of personal development. They also follow Nietzsche in seeing the moral self as creating something positive, and not just responding to circumstances. Marx sought to change the world rather than simply to understand it, and his thinking did shape the course of the twentieth century, while psychotherapy of all sorts seeks to set clients free from all that inhibits the natural flowering of their personality.

THINGS TO REMEMBER

From this chapter, remember that ...

▶ *We may create, rather than discover, a basis for ethics*

▶ *Hobbes argued that people are basically selfish*

▶ *Hume argued that everyone has a basic sense of altruism*

▶ *Nietzsche argued that the 'superman' should give a sense of direction for humankind*

▶ *Nietzsche contrasted slave and master morality*

▶ *Nietzsche argued that one should affirm life exactly as it is*

▶ *virtue ethics explores the qualities that make for human flourishing*

▶ *existentialism argues for personal authenticity rather than accepting social roles*

▶ *Marx saw impersonal working conditions as leading to alienation*

▶ *Freud saw personal development as inhibited by neuroses.*

8

Law and order

In this chapter you will learn:
- *to explore the political and social aspects of morality*
- *about some key thinkers on the topic of law and order*
- *to examine the issues of punishment, self-defence and civil disobedience.*

Society and moral choice

Some people might want to argue that there is no such thing as 'society': there are just collections of individuals. You cannot ask 'society' what it thinks; you can only ask particular people. Yet people who live together tend to develop sets of principles, expressed sometimes through laws, to make their common life easier. This means that an individual can take these agreed principles or laws into account when faced with a moral dilemma. They can be thought of as constituting conventional morality, expressing the agreed views of a society, and varying from one society to another.

In the fifth century BCE, the Greek Sophist Protagoras argued that moral rules were conventions created by society, rather than absolute truths. He believed that they were necessary in order for society to function, but that they could be challenged and changed. However, both Plato and Aristotle wanted to go beyond this idea of conventional morality, to show a link between virtue and happiness in order to find a more objective basis for moral rules – showing them to be in accord with nature. We have already seen the way in which Aristotle's views on this formed the basis of the natural law argument.

In Plato's *Republic* there is a debate about the function of rules within society. As we saw in Chapter 2 (when considering freedom), Thrasymachus argues that conventional justice promotes the interests of the rulers, and that the only reasonable basis for ethics is self-interest. Glaucon, in reply, points out that, if everyone acts from selfish motives, all will end up suffering in some way, exploited by others. The conventional rules, imposed by society, are therefore a way of protecting everyone from the basic selfish desires of everyone else.

Phone tap evidence?

Should evidence gained by the police or intelligence agencies by covert means – such as secretly tapping a phone – be allowed to be used as evidence in a court of law? Covert surveillance is an intrusion into the private lives of individuals, and most would argue that it should not happen routinely. But what if society is threatened by terrorism or organized crime? Should that not justify setting aside the right to privacy?

Here there needs to be a balance between the rights of the individual to be free from intrusive investigation, and the need to secure convictions. Since the latter is intended to make society safer, the individual might benefit either way. Most social legislation requires a balance of benefit and harm. A moral case can be made for either side of the argument.

Plato wants to take the debate further, and presents the idea that all elements in society (like parts of a human body) need to work together for the general health of the whole. He takes the view that justice offers the happiest life, because it is the expression of health. Injustice is a sickness that is liable to cause suffering in all parts of society. Controlled by reason, Plato considered that happiness lay in achieving a harmony within one's life, and thus also within society.

Of course, not everyone is willing or able to think rationally about the moral and social implications of every action. Plato considered – in *Republic*, Book 11 – that society should therefore be ruled by philosophers (because they are able to look at the needs of society as a whole in an unbiased way), and that ordinary people should be required to obey the laws that they devise.

Insight

But are philosophers really as objective and rational as that? Is it realistic to assume that they do not have presuppositions and values of their own to impose? And if they have no personal commitments and values, would they be able to understand and legislate?

Both Plato and Aristotle could be said to base their ethics on reason, but one should beware of assuming that they were therefore free from the prejudices of their day. For example, Aristotle (in *Politics*, Book 1, Chapter 5) is quite prepared to say that the proper function of slaves is to obey their masters, and that women should naturally obey men. These are huge social presuppositions that slip into the rational argument, illustrating the way all philosophy (and therefore all ethics) takes place within a particular society and reflects its values.

We cannot have value-free ethics, for in a value-free situation most ethical debate would be meaningless. It could be argued that ethics is based on experience and reason, but these alone do not provide the stimulus for the questioning of morality. Computers can handle experience quite effectively, and are also efficient at the application of logic. A computer cannot be moral or immoral, however, because it lacks an inherent set of values with which to assess its choices.

This brief look at early debates on social ethics illustrates three points:

> ▶ *Society imposes laws, and encourages moral principles, in order to maintain social cohesion and minimize the damage that would be done by the exercise of unbridled individual desires.*
> ▶ *Any moral or legal system will therefore be the result of a negotiation between the needs of society as a whole and the freedom of the individual.*
> ▶ *Rational arguments about the needs of individuals or of society spring from (but may well hide) value judgements and presuppositions.*

When we look at moral issues concerned with law and order, and the punishments that society imposes on those who break laws, we need to keep in mind three questions:

> ▶ *Does society need this particular law for its own well-being?*
> ▶ *Has this law achieved a suitable balance between any conflicting needs of the individual and society?*
> ▶ *On what values is it based, and are these values widely accepted within society?*

In whose interest?

In Plato's *Republic*, Thrasymachus argues that justice is the interest of the stronger. A ruler controls his or her subjects simply because he or she has the authority, backed up by power, to impose chosen laws. Justice therefore depends on the form of government; an absolute monarchy will be different from a democracy in the way that its laws are framed and applied.

In modern times, Thrasymachus' views have been reinforced by the Marxist critique of society, in which society progresses by way of conflict between classes. For Marx, the ideal is a classless society in which such struggles are overcome, and in which no one group is able to impose its will on others. His assumption is that, in such a society, the free development of each individual depends on, and enhances, the development of all.

But how, in a society of many different people and interests, are you to find a common basis for social ethics? Each person and each group will have particular goals and aspirations. Plato, in *Theaetetus*, ascribed to the Sophist Protagoras the idea that the wind feels cool to one person but warm to another – and in the same way values depend on the society within which they are encountered. If there is no general set of values, independent of the kind of society in which they are found, how do we assess or criticize any existing legal or social situation?

We therefore need to ask two basic questions:

1 *Does this imply that there can be no objective standards in law and social morals?*
2 *Is any political system as 'good' as any other? If not, by what criterion can you decide which is better?*

Beneath these there still lurks the more general problem of how to balance the needs and aspirations of the individual with those of society as a whole.

Example

Clearly, terrorism is a threat to individuals who may become caught up in an act of violence, as well as to society as a whole. The protection of society therefore requires some loss of individual liberty, in order that the threat of terrorism may be contained. Hence the need for a balance between freedom of the individual, freedom of information, and the imposition of laws to enable measures to be taken against terrorists. Like Protagoras, however, what feels like a major infringement of civil liberties to one person may be of almost no concern to another.

Is equality possible?

David Hume argued that it was impossible to achieve a justice based on what people deserve, simply because people never agree about what each deserves. But he also felt that it was not practically possible to seek a justice of equality. He sought to protect the property of each person, even though people were unequal in what they owned. He does not say that it would be *wrong* for people to have equal shares, but that it is impractical to expect that such equality could be enforced. The reason he gives is that people are by nature unequal in their abilities, and some will prosper more than others.

Whereas an individual act of redistribution might be beneficial (e.g. stealing something that a rich person will not miss to benefit someone who is poor), the application of that principle to the whole of society would not be practicable, and would have harmful consequences. In this, Hume uses a 'rule utilitarian' argument (see Chapter 5). In the example given above, the point to consider is not 'Will I actually benefit someone by breaking the law of theft in this particular case?' but 'What will be the result of everyone breaking the law of theft in this way?'

A social contract

Laws are created artificially. They are devised by legislators (with or without the consent of the people) and imposed on society. The way in which laws are applied, and the punishments that are deemed to be appropriate for those who break them, may be established and refined as particular cases are brought to court.

Some social rules do not have the force of law, but may become established over a period of time by custom. But these too are artificial, and may vary from one society to another.

Some philosophers have therefore put forward ethical theories based on a social contract (an agreement made between people to abide by certain rules) which limit what they are able to do, in order to benefit society as a whole and to allow everyone a measure of freedom and security.

HOBBES (1588–1679)

Thomas Hobbes argued for a contract to be made between people and their ruler. In such a contract, the ruler should agree to protect the natural rights of the people, to act as an arbiter in disputes, and to establish just laws. In return, all who live in the area of the ruler's jurisdiction agree to accept the authority of that ruler and of such governments and laws as are established. Hobbes thought that, if the ruler did not have absolute power, there was a danger of social disintegration. He therefore placed the ruler above the law.

For Hobbes, someone taking a minority view, or refusing to agree to any social contract, could not 'opt out' of this arrangement. Simply by living in the geographical area covered by that political regime, a person became bound to accept the contract.

Insight

Hobbes wrote against the background of the chaos of Civil War in seventeenth-century England. He considered the natural state of man, deprived of the benefits of law, as 'nasty, brutish and short' devoid of the benefits of trade and social cooperation.

LOCKE (1632–1704)

Locke took a different view. In *The Second Treatise on Civil Government* he argued that people are required to surrender some of their individual rights to the community, but that nobody (not even the ruler) should be above the law. Authority should reside in the institutions of state, as chosen by the majority of the people. Individuals are given rights – free speech, freedom to worship, freedom to hold property – and it is the duty of government to uphold these rights. Unlike Hobbes, Locke was anti-monarchist and opposed the idea of any one person being given absolute power. He wanted to ensure that bad rulers could be removed and replaced.

Insight

Locke is hugely important for the development of political philosophy. The general principles of individual rights, coupled with democratically supported responsible government, are basic to modern democratic systems.

ROUSSEAU (1712–78)

Ideas put forward by Locke are found also in the works of Rousseau. Social contract forms the basis of individual liberty, and in a democracy people and rulers have the same interests – they work together for mutual benefit. Rousseau was therefore against the divine right of kings, and his ideas influenced the French Revolution, although he did not live to see it.

He argued that primitive people have two basic emotions: self-preservation and repugnance at the sufferings of others (sympathy). These appear to form quite a reasonable basis for co-operative living. He felt that civilization, and the rules that go with it, tend to corrupt people (e.g. by imposing ideas of private property, thereby creating inequality and consequent resentment), which destroys the simplicity and co-operative possibilities of the primitive state. He argued that, under a social contract imposed by 'the general will', people would agree to give up some of their natural liberty in order to establish 'civil liberty'. In this way, an individual subsumes his or her will to that of the community as a whole.

Mugging for gadgets

People increasingly walk the streets listening to MP3 players or talking into mobile phones, and every wireless hot-spot and café is packed with people trying not to spill coffee over their laptops.

(Contd)

The latest technology is there to be seen – and its ownership conveys status. But this inevitably increases the desire to own them, and hence provides increased opportunities for street crime.

Rousseau would, no doubt, claim this as endorsing his view that the proximity of desirable goods only encourages resentment, which leads to temptation and theft – another example of the corrupting influence of society.

THOMAS PAINE (1737–1809)

Paine developed a similar view of the social contract. He argued that an individual should be given liberty, and allowed to do anything (including the right to pursue his or her own happiness) as long as no harm is done to others in the process.

Paine's views lie behind the American Declaration of Independence, which allows to each person life, liberty and the pursuit of happiness as a fundamental right.

J.S. MILL (1806–73)

Mill highlights another feature of the social contract. In *On Liberty*, he is concerned that, under a social contract, individuals and minority groups might suffer by being made to conform to the wishes of the majority. His answer to this is that a majority should interfere with a minority, only if that minority is doing something that is directly harmful to the interests of the majority.

Therefore, free speech should be allowed, even if the person speaking is thought to be clearly wrong or misguided. He considered that this was less dangerous than allowing an authority to decide what could or could not be said, which would result in loss of liberty for all.

Jailed for Holocaust denial

Denying that the Holocaust took place is illegal in some countries. In Austria in February 2006, the historian David Irving was sentenced to three years in jail for having denied, in speeches he made 16 years earlier, the murder of 6 million Jews and the existence of the gas chambers. This was in spite of the fact that he expressed regret for some of the statements that he had made earlier, and accepted that there had been gas chambers in Auschwitz. The state prosecutor called Irving a 'dangerous falsifier of history'.

There is a mixture of ethical issues here. One is the responsibility of a historian (or any non-fiction writer) to give the best available interpretation of the facts. Another is the utilitarian assessment of the damage caused if deliberately false information, or unsound interpretation, is given credibility by being published. (In this case, there was the danger of neo-Nazis using such ideas to justify their political views.)

But, at the same time, there is the issue of free speech. In democratic countries it is generally considered better to allow free speech than to forbid it. There are exceptions, however. Any speech that is likely to incite racial hatred or soliciting to murder is illegal (as was made clear in the case against the radical Muslim cleric Abu Hamza in the UK in January 2006). Here a utilitarian assessment is that the harm caused by such speech outweighs the right of an individual to express his or her views.

There is a further issue: is it right that some things are protected in this way, but not others? However horrific the historical events surrounding the Holocaust, they (like all historical events) are subject to interpretation, and no subsequent account of an event is guaranteed to be 100 per cent accurate.

JOHN RAWLS (1921–2002)

A modern version of the social contract theory is found in the work of Rawls. In an article entitled 'Justice as Fairness' (1957) and in his major book *A Theory of Justice* (1972) Rawls introduced the idea of 'fairness' into social morality.

He imagines a situation in which a number of people gather to decide the rules under which they are to live. But (by some curious form of amnesia) they forget who they are. They do not know their age, their colour, their wealth, their social position. They decide what they want from society, therefore, without any reference to any special interest group that they might otherwise represent.

He presents two principles on which justice, so framed, would be based:

1 *Each person has an equal right to the maximum amount of liberty compatible with allowing liberty for all.*
2 *Inequalities are to be allowed only if there is reason to think that such inequalities will benefit the least well-off in society.*

He introduced what he called 'the principle of priority', by which liberties come first and social equality second. You should not therefore surrender a liberty even if, by doing so, you could argue that the least well-off in society would benefit.

Rawls thought that people would choose to help the poorest in society because – not knowing whether they themselves were poor or rich when they met to decide their rules – they would play safe, in case they found that they were in that poorest category.

A situation

The public provision of health care would seem to be based on a social contract: people pay money in taxes with which the government provides a service. Since nobody knows the extent to which they might need medical help, it is perfectly reasonable that all contribute on the basis that it will be equally available for all who need it.

But life is never that easy ...

At the time of the first edition of this book, in the early 1990s, there was a debate about whether doctors should be allowed to refuse to operate on those who, by continuing to smoke, were making the outcome and recovery from an operation more problematic. The argument in favour of offering smokers surgery on the same basis as for non-smokers is that it is wrong to deny treatment to any group of people, even if they have an added (and voluntary) risk factor. Other people are treated for self-inflicted injuries – hospitals do not require that sportsmen give up their sport before they treat their injuries. Why should smokers be refused treatment on that basis?

The same argument could be made in terms of the increase of instances of cirrhosis of the liver as a result of binge drinking, or those who, by their diet and lifestyle, contribute to problems of obesity and diabetes. Should only the healthy be entitled to full treatment? Should treatment be conditional on lifestyle changes?

▶ Do you start with the rights of the individual to equality of treatment, irrespective of his or her lifestyle?
▶ Or do you take a utilitarian approach, looking at how the limited resources of the health service can be used most effectively to bring benefit to the greatest number?
▶ Over eating, over drinking and smoking are not illegal. Would it be different if they were? What responsibility does society have towards those who have a lifestyle that takes them outside the law, e.g. by drug taking?

(Contd)

- ► Do those who go against advice, or act unlawfully, effectively opt out of the social contract? If so, can they make demands on resources provided for society as a whole?
- ► Is there a basic responsibility to provide care for human individuals, no matter who they are and what they may have done? If so, how is that responsibility defined? Does it have limits?

In these social contract arguments there is a balance between the rights of an individual and the needs of society – and for the democratic and liberal approaches to social morality it is the individual who takes priority, by being given rights and by being allowed a say in the process of government. Any utilitarian assessment of a situation (e.g. about the allocation of health service resources) is therefore tempered by the sense that there are rights to which every individual has a just claim.

Insight

One problem with Rawls' position is that it does not take into account the genuine values and priorities that individuals have. In real life, these determine how one chooses to act – we can never stand back from our circumstances or forget who we are.

Crime and punishment

There are, in general, five reasons why society may impose a punishment on those who break the law.

1 *To protect society from those who have committed crimes, in order to stop them repeating their offences.*
2 *To deter others from breaking the law.*
3 *To reform the criminal.*

4   *As retribution for the wrong that has been done (i.e. it is felt
    that the person deserves punishment for what he or she has
    done).*
5   *To vindicate the law (i.e. unless punishments can be imposed,
    people will stop having respect for the law, and the result will
    be anarchy).*

Of these, 1, 2, 3 and 5 can be justified on utilitarian grounds. They
see punishment as a means of minimizing suffering and protecting
society. The punishment imposed on one person allows many
others to live unmolested.

Reason 4 tends to be defended on the basis of what might be
called 'natural justice'. In a natural state, people might be expected
to take revenge if they are wronged. Unlimited revenge leads to
anarchy. Therefore society limits what is appropriate by way
of punishment.

Just as Kant pointed to a sense of 'ought' that does not depend
on results, so there is a sense that justice requires punishment,
irrespective of whether or not anything positive by way of reform
or restitution can be achieved by it.

Example

In November 2009, John Demjanjuk, aged 89, who had been living
in Ohio, appeared in court in Germany, charged with being an
accessory in the murder of 27,900 Jews in a Nazi death camp. This
followed a 30-year campaign to prosecute him. He protested his
innocence and his lawyers argued that he was too ill to face trial.

Clearly, putting an old person on trial for a crime committed more
than 60 years earlier cannot be justified in terms of protection of the
public, reform or even realistic deterrence. The sole moral basis for
this would be that natural justice requires that some crimes deserve
punishment, irrespective of the time delay or circumstances.

Various crimes require various forms of punishment – depending on their severity, on the danger posed to society by the person committing the crime, and on the practical implication of the punishment – in terms of whether or not it can reform the criminal, and whether it is necessary to deter others, or to vindicate the law. In terms of the moral issues involved, one form of punishment deserves some special attention: capital punishment.

Capital punishment

As with other life and death issues, there are three main lines of approach.

1 *One is to affirm that there is an absolute right to life, and that nothing can justify taking the life of another human being (this also underlies opposition to abortion and euthanasia).*
2 *Another is to take a utilitarian approach – balancing the loss of life against the cost to society of keeping a person in prison for life, or the potential suffering that could result if that person is released from prison and offends again.*
3 *There is also the need to deter others from committing murder or other serious crimes.*

The first of these is based on an absolute moral conviction – either of the 'natural law' or the 'categorical imperative' variety – and is thus not swayed by the nature of the crime or the needs of society. If human life is paramount, then other forms of punishment and protection of society are necessary.

The second and third points are made more difficult by the great variety of serious crimes. Many murders are committed in the course of arguments between close relatives, others take place in the course of robbery or drug dealing, still others are politically motivated, as where a terrorist plants a bomb or carries out a shooting. It is difficult to balance the effect of a custodial sentence or capital punishment on any of these – a political murderer may well be prepared to face capital punishment, thereby achieving martyrdom. On the other hand, a domestic murder may lead to profound remorse, and it is highly unlikely that the person involved would offend again.

Generally, where capital punishment is legal, there are a number of special conditions that apply. In Texas, for example, not every act of murder carries the death penalty. It applies to murder of a public safety officer or fire-fighter, murder while carrying out a serious crime, murder for financial gain, murder of a prison guard or during an escape, multiple murders and murder of anyone under six years of age.

In considering the utilitarian and deterrence arguments, two things need to be kept in mind. The first is that, from the operation of capital punishment in the USA, it may eventually cost up to six times as much to execute a prisoner as to keep him in prison for life. The reason for this is that execution takes place only after a lengthy series of appeals, which may last many years and are very expensive. For example, Excell White was executed in Texas on 30 March 1999 after spending 24 years on death row. The second point is that, although it is reasonable to assume that the existence of capital punishment should be a deterrent, there is no firm evidence that it actually works as such. Countries with capital punishment do not automatically report a lower incidence of murder.

A further moral point for consideration is whether or not a prisoner should be allowed to choose to be executed, if it is genuinely his or her wish, rather than be kept alive in prison for life. In this case, the utilitarian or deterrence arguments are less relevant – the issue becomes that of the 'right to die', and therefore of the autonomy of the individual.

Insight

The death penalty is final and cannot be reversed! Legal systems are fallible, and in some cases convicted murderers have had their convictions overturned after many years. Any question of the justice of capital punishment must therefore be linked with questions about the reliability of convictions.

In self-defence?

The law does not consider whether something is morally right, but whether or not it is legal. Nevertheless, in looking at evidence in court, a judge and jury have to decide both what actually happened and whether the person accused intended to commit the crime for which he or she is accused. In this, the intention to do something illegal is crucial. This is particularly well illustrated in cases of murder. If the accused killed deliberately, then it is murder. If the killing was done while the person was deranged, or provoked to a point at which he or she lost control, then a charge of manslaughter is considered. If the killing is done in genuine self-defence, then the killing is not a crime. The courts must therefore ascertain a person's intention, as well as his or her actions.

A situation

In December 1997, a 30-year-old woman was given a life sentence for the murder of her apparently loving partner, having stabbed him in the course of an argument.

After serving a year of her sentence, and having also suffered from being separated from her 10-year-old son, she secretly admitted to the one person she felt she could trust, a psychiatric nurse, that she had suffered sexual, physical and mental abuse at the hands of her husband. She had felt too ashamed to reveal it at her trial but was eventually persuaded to reveal the details to her lawyers. As a result her murder conviction was quashed, and she pleaded guilty to manslaughter on grounds of diminished responsibility. Having already served a year in prison, she was sentenced to three years' probation.

This case raises an interesting issue: if she had killed her husband in self-defence while he was attacking her, it would not have been a crime. Her case was subsequently considered to be one of 'diminished responsibility' because she was aware of what she was doing, and not (apparently) in immediate danger, but had been provoked to such an extent that she was not wholly responsible for her action.

In this case, therefore, the husband takes partial responsibility for the situation that led to his being killed – in that he had provoked his wife to the point at which she stabbed him. But if that argument is extended to the situation before the stabbing, one might argue that the wife (morally, but not legally) should take some responsibility for allowing the situation to develop in which her husband became increasingly violent. Is allowing such a situation to continue the reason why she felt 'ashamed' and was unwilling to speak of it in court, even though her silence meant that she was found guilty of murder?

Insight

Legally, blame and punishment are related to an action, and this is generally also the case with ethics. But in the case of domestic or marital issues it may be unrealistic to single out actions rather than consider the dynamics of the underlying relationship.

A further example

Two men from a Norfolk village (referred to in newspaper reports as 'village vigilantes') lay in wait for a local teenager, whom they suspected of stealing. They forced him into a van, tied his hands and threatened him with violence. They freed him, unharmed, 20 minutes later.

They were sentenced to five years in jail for kidnapping. On appeal, their sentences were cut to six months, much to the satisfaction of a large number of villagers who had campaigned on their behalf.

The argument against the vigilantes was that you cannot uphold the law by breaking it – which they did by kidnapping the youth.

(Contd)

That argument is independent of the issue of whether the youth was actually guilty of any offences.

Notice that, as with the previous example, the intention was all important. To commit murder you have to intend to kill. Here, however, the intention is overruled by the action. It is not enough to say that the men 'intended' simply to warn the youth about what would happen if he stole things because they actually carried out (and pleaded guilty to) the crime of kidnapping.

This case raises an important issue of social morality. There are things that one person can do but another cannot. A surgeon can cut a person open with a knife; his or her social function makes that quite reasonable. However, if I were to walk into a hospital wearing a white coat and brandishing a scalpel, I would not be morally justified in going to work in the operating theatre.

On this basis, it is quite lawful for a policeman to arrest a suspect, to bind his hands in handcuffs, and to take him to a police station. There the suspect may be spoken to very sternly, threatened with legal action if he is apprehended committing a crime and then (following a formal caution, if he has been caught actually committing a minor offence) released.

The problem with the vigilantes is that they were taking on a role for which society has agreed that only certain people are to perform. Of course, if the two vigilantes had caught the youth in the act of committing a crime and had forcibly taken him to a police station (provided that no unreasonable force was used), they would have been carrying out a citizen's arrest, which is legal.

Civil disobedience

Do you have an absolute duty to obey the law of the land? Are there occasions when it would be right to break the law?

You could argue, for example, that if a law goes against fundamental human rights, the law is wrong and should be opposed. Remember that laws are artificial things, devised and imposed. Even though, according to the theory of social contract, they may have been established by the agreement of a majority of people, that does not mean that they are absolute – they are not created by logical necessity, and do not apply to all people at all times.

Those who contemplate civil disobedience might want to take the following into consideration:

▶ *Is the law the product of a democratic process? If there are no democratic controls on the law then you could argue (on utilitarian grounds) that it is right to oppose the law for the benefit of the greater number of people. This would be the case if there was a law that was imposed on people, but benefited only the ruler or small elite rather than the people as a whole. On the other hand, if the law is established within a democracy you cannot argue that opposing it will be in the interests of a majority, unless you can show that the majority were duped by the rulers or legislators. 'We didn't realize, when we elected this government, that this would be the result' would launch an argument of this sort.*

▶ *Is there any other way in which you can pursue the cause that you are supporting? For example, could the law be changed? If so, by whom? Can you influence those who could do so?*

▶ *Is there a categorical imperative – a sense of moral obligation that is absolute, and that opposes the law in question? In this case, you may feel justified in challenging or breaking the law. Although, of course, you will need to be prepared to take the consequences in terms of any punishments that society may impose on you.*

Examples

There are many famous examples of civil disobedience bringing about change: Gandhi's opposition to British rule in India; the

(Contd)

struggle for civil rights in the United States and against apartheid in South Africa. There are mass protests which go ahead in spite of government restrictions – as, in 2009, against the government in Burma, or in protest against the presidential election in Iran.

In each case, the protest was not merely that a minority view had prevailed over the wishes of a majority, but that there was a fundamental moral situation to be addressed that took precedence over obeying laws which, even if established through democratic means, were seen as fundamentally wrong, or as representing the interests of a government that had lost (or never had) legitimacy.

REVOLUTIONARY CHANGE

Although there *are* acts of civil disobedience from time to time, it is more usual for laws to change through the normal legislative procedures of the democratic process that framed them. Changes like this come because of practical or scientific advances (e.g. the time limit on termination of pregnancy was lowered in the UK in 1990 because scientific advances were allowing the survival of foetuses at an earlier stage), or because the attitudes of society change (e.g. the legalizing of homosexual acts in private between consenting adults).

▶ *If laws can be changed peacefully then – on the basis of utilitarianism or social contract – it would be right to avoid any violence or revolution.*

▶ *If the law cannot be changed peacefully, then (on a utilitarian basis) an assessment should be made about whether the cost of that revolutionary change, in terms of suffering or loss of life, is worth the benefits to be gained by it.*

▶ *Violence could be justified on a utilitarian basis if it were to be shown that it is simply a defence against an already existing violence. For example, it might be argued that a repressive regime imposed such financial hardship on its people that it amounts to 'economic violence'. In this case, some might argue that it could legitimately be opposed by using physical violence.*

Changes in society come about for a variety of reasons; some political, some economic, some because of a gradual change in attitudes and values. It is sometimes difficult to assess exactly how much change has been brought about by exactly which political actions.

A violent demonstration against a law could take place at a time of growing sense of general dissatisfaction with it and recognition on the part of a democratic government that it will not be re-elected if it does not change the law. Are those who took part in the violent demonstration therefore entitled to claim that their violence was justified because their chosen end has actually come about? Might the change not have happened anyway?

WHO TAKES RESPONSIBILITY?

When people are involved in civil disobedience or in the violent overthrow of a government, they tend to become bolder as they act together in a group. In the course of a demonstration, for example, there might be a great deal of damage done, looting of shops, etc. The general atmosphere of violence and change appears to sanction the sort of actions that individuals might not contemplate in more peaceful times. Does this loss of social restraint justify individual acts of violence against people or property?

Insight

This is part of a larger question of whether we ever act as fully autonomous individuals, or always in a social context and under social pressure. Are we, or is the situation, group, social class or nation to blame? We might need to assess the consequences of refusing to conform to the expectations of the group to which we belong.

If Nietzsche were a civil servant ...

Civil servants generally operate along carefully controlled and monitored lines.

First of all they gather data. They produce reports, setting out statistical evidence. To do this they gather together advisers, experts in particular fields. They are required to be well informed. Based on that information, they set about implementing the will of their political masters. In doing this they are governed by two things – the laws of the land, and the goals that politicians have set. What they do may be monitored through the checking process within the civil service, and through select committees, which can require them to explain their actions.

A good civil servant is meant to have no political views. His or her task is simply to act on the guidelines given, within the constraints of budgets, national and international law. The criterion on which a civil servant is often judged is not whether the decisions implemented were right or wrong – that is something for politicians to sort out – but whether he or she was effective in putting them into practice.

Civil servants, like chess players, work creatively within carefully controlled and defined structures. They are answerable only for decisions made within a very specific brief. Ultimately, they have no 'I' that operates in choosing what to do. They use personal judgement, of course (which is why they cannot be replaced by computers), but their judgements are based on values that are given to them, not generated by them. That does not mean that civil servants are without power, but their power lies in their ability to manipulate rules and values to achieve their chosen result.

Contrast the civil servant with the campaigner. He or she is someone who takes up an issue, decides on a particular point of view, and argues it with moral conviction. Campaigners lobby politicians. They present one side of an argument, the side about which they feel strongly. They tend to be visionary, to think long term, to be idealist in their aspirations. They are frustrated by bureaucracy and restrictive legislation. They wish to change laws by changing the values and priorities on which those laws are based.

Between the civil servant and the campaigner lies the politician. Some might be presented as genuine transmitters of the values and aspirations of those they represent, seeking to frame laws that will benefit their constituents. Others seem to be followers of Machiavelli, seeking their own power, and ruthless in maintaining their establishment. In either case, in order to survive, a politician has to take a line that is half-way between the campaigner and the civil servant. He or she has to explore situations and values, and use them as the basis of legislation.

Insight

Imagine a television sitcom involving a civil servant, a politician and a campaigner – in a caricature, their styles of speech, dress and lifestyle would be quite different from one another.

Alongside the political and civil establishment is the judiciary. Judges, magistrates and lawyers seek to implement law, but they do so with a degree of flexibility that allows the particular situation to influence the application of the general rule. Moral questions are sometimes raised when it is considered that a particular legal decision strays too far from the general rule (e.g. when a man found guilty of rape is given a very light sentence, or someone is fined heavily for dropping litter). The judge is required to be an expert in law, a balanced assessor of what is appropriate in terms of punishment, and also a subtle inquisitor of human nature and of the way in which values and laws impinge on each individual.

These characters are introduced here (albeit in the form of caricature) to illustrate different positions that may be taken in terms of the ethics of law and society. All are needed in society. Without the campaigner, there is no direct application of values to practical issues. Without the politician there is no way of

Yet the central challenge of Nietzsche remains: in the absence of God (who might have guaranteed and fixed a set of values), by what criterion – other than the development of that which is 'beyond' each individual in terms of personal development – can one judge what is right? Is society there fundamentally as the environment in which each individual can grow to his or her full potential? Or is the individual simply one part of a social pattern, defined and valued within it?

Both perspectives – the personal and the social – are needed. Neither makes sense without the other. But in moral debate there is a constant process of balancing the two: too far one way and the result is anarchy and chaos; too far the other and there is authoritarian rule and loss of personal freedom.

In an ideal ethical system (and an ideal world within which to operate it) every social contract would allow the personal development of each individual. Equally, personal development would enhance the relationships of which society is made up. If (like Rawls) we could see the world from a completely selfless point of view, then the ideal system might be devised. Unfortunately, no such global amnesia exists, and self-interest remains a powerful feature in human choice.

THINGS TO REMEMBER

From this chapter, remember that ...

▶ *Plato argues for all sections of society to work together*

▶ *it will always be practically difficult to redistribute wealth fairly*

▶ *Hobbes thought that a social contract would protect against the chaos of anarchy*

▶ *Locke placed the law above the ruler and emphasized the rights of individuals*

▶ *Rousseau thought people were naturally innocent but corrupted by society*

▶ *Mill argues for personal freedom, except when it harms other people*

▶ *Rawls argues for justice and fairness, initiated by an act of social amnesia*

▶ *there are five reasons for punishment*

▶ *capital punishment is irreversible and difficult to justify on a utilitarian basis*

▶ *civil disobedience is easier to justify if there is no democratic input into the legal process.*

9

Religion and moral values

In this chapter you will learn:

* *how religion is related to ethics*
* *about the ethical norms of the major world religions*
* *to explore the issue of religious freedom.*

The moral choices people make, and the values they express through them, depend (consciously or unconsciously) on their understanding of the nature of the world and the place of humanity within it. But these are also things with which religions are concerned. Each religion:

▶ *presents a particular view of the world*
▶ *promotes a set of values by which its followers should live*
▶ *gives specific advice on how to live – in terms of either rules to be followed or attitudes to be taken.*

Religious rules or values may be based on:

▶ *the authority of a religious leader or holy book*
▶ *the cumulative experience of that religious community*
▶ *rational thought, or an understanding of what is 'natural'.*

Religious values may influence society in general, not just practising members of that religion. For example, many of the ethical arguments that we have examined so far are based on ideas and values that have been promoted by the Christian religion. This does not mean that every ethical thinker is Christian, but that everyone who lives within Western culture is liable to be influenced by Christian ideas, simply because they have come to pervade so much habitual thinking. The same would be true for someone living in a predominantly Jewish, Muslim, Hindu, Sikh or Buddhist society. The assumptions people make about the nature and value of life often reflect their religious background, or a deliberate reaction against it.

How are religion and morality related?

There are three possibilities:

1 **Autonomy** – *morality may be autonomous if it is based on reason alone, without any reference to religious ideas. If its values are the same as a particular religion, that is seen as purely coincidental.*
2 **Heteronomy** – *morality may be said to be heteronomous (i.e. rules coming from outside itself) if it depends directly on religious belief or on a set of values given by religion.*
3 **Theonomy** – *morality is theonomous (i.e. comes from God) if both it and religion are thought to come from a common source of inspiration and knowledge, a source that religion may refer to as 'God'.*

SOME ARGUMENTS IN FAVOUR OF AUTONOMY

▶ *Responsible moral choice depends on freedom and the ability to choose rationally. But some religions speak of rewards and punishments offered after death – in terms of heaven or hell, or rebirth into higher or lower forms of life. Are you behaving morally if you obey religious rules for fear of punishment?*
▶ *Different religions (or even different sects within a single religion) may take different approaches to moral issues. In order to choose between conflicting religious views, a person*

has to use his or her reason as the ultimate deciding factor – which is autonomy!

▶ If I subscribe to one of the theistic religions (i.e. I believe in God), then I will believe that God already knows what I will choose to do before I do it. If he is all-powerful, he should be able to prevent me from doing what is wrong. If he does not do so, he is responsible for the consequences of my action, aiding and abetting me through divine negligence! In which case, I lose my moral responsibility.

Insight

The standard view of atheists is that human beings are quite able to create their own normative values and opt to live by them. What is more, they tend to gather together in groups of like-minded people, who therefore give each other added reason for keeping to those norms.

SOME ARGUMENTS IN FAVOUR OF HETERONOMY

▶ People cannot escape from the influence of religious values and attitudes. They have an unconscious effect, even for those who reject religion. Better, then, to acknowledge that influence than try to deny it.

▶ As soon as you try to define moral terms (such as 'goodness' or 'justice') you are using language that has been shaped by the prevailing religions. Natural law, for example, may have come originally from Aristotle, but today it is understood largely through the use made of it by Aquinas and the Catholic Church. Religion has largely supplied the language of ethical debate.

▶ It is one thing to understand what is right, quite another to have the courage or conviction to put it into effect. It can be argued that religion is the source of such courage and conviction, and that it provides a community within which values and moral attitudes can be shared and reinforced.

▶ Philosophers often assume that everyone is reasonable. Religions, by contrast, are well aware of human selfishness and unreasonableness. Religion is likely to offer a more *realistic view of human nature than philosophy, and therefore be better able to guide moral choice.*

Religion or politics?

Sometimes headlines can suggest that an issue is religious when it might equally be regarded as political. Take this one, from the *Independent*, 24 February 2006:

Five days of violence by Nigerian Christians and Muslims kill 150

On the face of it, this is a clash between religious groups, sparked by Muslim protests against the publication of cartoons of the Prophet Muhammad. Mosques and churches were burned; dead bodies were left in the streets. But beneath this is the fact that the Muslims are mostly from the Hausa, and the Christians from the Yoruba and Ibgo ethnic groups. Hence the clash is as much ethnic as religious. Neither Christianity nor Islam, considered as religions, would condone such violence, but that does not prevent the religious differences becoming an opportunity for other resentments to be sparked into life.

SOME ARGUMENTS IN FAVOUR OF THEONOMY

▶ *Intuitionism was right in saying that there are certain things that are known, but cannot be described. We have an intuitive sense of the meaning of the word 'good'. This intuition lies behind both religion and morality.*

▶ *It can be argued that religion and morality have a common source in 'mystical' experience – moments of intuitive awareness of a sense of meaning, purpose or wholeness in life, of well-being and acceptance. This is a basic feature of religious experience, and gives the impetus to act in a purposeful and moral way.*

▶ *Metaphysics (the rational exploration of meaning and purpose in the world) can be seen as a basis for morality (as in Greek thought, in the 'natural law' tradition, and as explored today by, for example, Iris Murdoch in* **Metaphysics as a Guide to Morals***) and as fundamental to religion.*

THE EUTHYPHRO DILEMMA

Named after one of Plato's dialogues, the Euthyphro Dilemma poses the question of the relationship between autonomous morality and religion is a most succinct way. It asks: Is something right because the gods command it? Or do the gods command it because it is right?

If you take the first option, you have to ask yourself whether it would be right to obey any divine command, however much it went against your personal sense of right and wrong. Take the example of Abraham, in the Old Testament, who was commanded by God to sacrifice his only son. Reprieved at the last minute, Abraham is praised for being prepared to kill his son at God's command. There have been many atrocities (judging by autonomous morality) carried out in the name of religion. If it is believed that God did indeed command them, does that make them right?

If you take the second option, you acknowledge a sense of right and wrong that is independent of God – and hence the priority and autonomous nature of morality. In effect, you assess the morality of God's commands against your own reason.

Insight

It is a sad feature of religious extremism that normal human restraint and morality can be set aside in the name of God. A terrorist, claiming to act according to God's will, kills innocent people. How – unless you accept the priority of autonomous morality and human reason – can you prove that he or she is wrong to do so?

The basis for religious ethics

There is no scope within this book to look in any systematic way
at the actual lifestyle, attitudes or values of each religion; these
can be found in books on the individual religions within the Teach
Yourself World Faiths series. Our task here is to examine not so
much what they hold to be of moral value, as why they value it,
and how they therefore justify their moral principles.

JUDAISM

Jewish morality is based on the Torah, which means 'teaching' or
'law'. It is found in the first five books of the Hebrew Bible, and
includes many rules for ethical and social matters. The most famous
of these rules are the Ten Commandments (Exodus 20:1–17), and
the Torah was famously summed up by Rabbi Hillel in the first
century BCE in one of the various forms of the 'golden rule':
'What is hateful to you do not do to another.'

The body of the Torah developed over the centuries, as each law
was applied to new situations. Eventually (by about 600 CE) a
complex encyclopaedia of rules and traditions, the Talmud was
completed. It contains the Mishna, a collection of oral traditions
believed to have been originally given to Moses by God, along with
the written Torah, and further commentaries on the Mishna, called
the Gemara.

Jews are required to follow these in the correct way; this is called
the *halakah*, or 'path'. Different groups within Judaism vary in
the strictness with which they put these rules into effect. Some
take them literally in every detail, others follow rather more
general principles, adapting where necessary to some perceived
requirements of modern life.

In terms of morality, the Jewish approach is one of rules. Reason
and conscience have their part to play, but mainly in terms of
interpretation and application. It is important to emphasize,

however, that the rules are not regarded as arbitrary. They are seen as having the authority of God, given to humankind for its benefit. The many layers of tradition that surround the original Torah represent the cumulative experience of generations. There is a real sense that, in keeping the rules of his or her religion, a follower of the Jewish faith is not simply adopting a particular style of life, but entering into a community and a tradition.

With any monotheistic religion, the issue of free will is relevant, because if an omnipotent God can overrule human decisions, moral responsibility is taken away. It is clear that, for Judaism, this is not the case. Moses Maimonides (1135–1204) said about free will:

> *Free will is granted to every human being. Should he so wish, he has the power to incline himself to the good way and to be just; should he so wish, he has the power to incline himself to the evil way and to be wicked ...*

(as quoted in *Making Moral Decisions*, ed. Jean Holm with John Bowker, Pinter, 1994, p. 133)

Insight

There is a particular issue concerning the building of Israeli Jewish settlements on former Palestinian land. The claim that God gave the land to the Jews is made on the basis of a literal interpretation of scripture. The question is whether such a view (the historical validity of which is in any case a matter of debate) should be able to overrule secular moral principles about the rights of individuals and the ownership of property.

CHRISTIANITY

Because it developed out of Judaism (Jesus was a Jew, and his first followers formed a sect within Judaism rather than a separate religion), Christianity accepts the moral basis of the Ten Commandments and the Jewish Torah as part of its own scriptures.

Christianity interprets the rules of the Torah in the light of the life and teaching of Jesus Christ. In the New Testament, a significant feature of this is that Jesus was prepared to set aside the detailed requirements of the Law, but insisted that in doing so he was not setting the Law aside, but rather fulfilling and completing it. This has allowed Christian morality a measure of interpretative flexibility.

Early in the history of the Christian Church, it was agreed that its members should not be required to keep all the rules of the Torah (the crucial issue being the distinctively Jewish practice of circumcision), thus allowing Gentiles to accept an equal place with Jews in the new religion. Nevertheless, Christians and Jews hold a common core of moral tradition.

Christianity emphasizes faith in God and in Jesus Christ, rather than obedience to religious rules as the basis of its way of life. It is therefore less rule-based than Judaism, even where it shares the same values.

Forgiveness

A key feature of Christian spirituality is the ability to forgive those who wrong you. When Anthony Walker was murdered in July 2005, his mother said of those convicted of the racist killing 'At the point of death, Jesus said: "I forgive them for they know not what they do." I have got to forgive them.' The following March, the Reverend Julia Nicholson resigned from her post as vicar of a parish because she could not bring herself to forgive the person who killed her daughter Jenny in the London bombings of July 2005. Her bishop appeared on television and praised her integrity and courage in making that decision.

It is argued that the courage to forgive sets the action – however terrible – in the broader context of recognition of what Christians describe as the universal human phenomenon of 'sin' – a falling short of what humans are designed to be.

Sources of authority for Christian morality vary from one Christian denomination to another, but they include:

▶ *the authority of the Church (believed to be inspired by the Holy Spirit), including the Pope, the Bishop of Rome*
▶ *the authority of the Scriptures*
▶ *human reason (used in applying a 'natural law' basis for morality)*
▶ *conscience*
▶ *the direct inspiration of the Holy Spirit.*

The fact that there are a number of different sources of authority is significant. Thus, at the time of the Reformation, the authority of the Church was challenged on the basis of the authority of the Scriptures. Reason and conscience are significant in re-examining the relevance of particular teachings to changing cultural and social circumstances.

Insight

Should human reason and conscience take priority, or does that lie with scripture and tradition? That will determine where, for example, a Christian is likely to stand in relation to, say, homosexuality.

ISLAM

The word 'Islam' means 'submission'. Muslims believe that most things in the world submit naturally to God, the source of life. Humans are the exception, for people can either choose to submit to God, living in a natural way, or refuse to do so. Fundamental to Muslim ethics is the idea that everything should submit in a natural way to the life of the universe. Indeed, Muslims believe that every child is born a Muslim, and only later may adopt another religion or decide to have no religion at all.

Muslims believe that Allah (the Arabic term for God, the source of life) revealed his will for humankind through various prophets (including Jesus, and figures from the Jewish scriptures), but that his final revelation was given through the prophet Muhammad.

Muslims have two written sources of authority:

▶ **The Qur'an** – *this is believed by Muslims to be the revelation of the will of God, given to Muhammad in a series of visionary experiences. It is traditionally thought that Muhammad was illiterate, but that he was told to recite what he heard. The Qur'an is the written record of that recitation.*
▶ **The Hadith** – *this is a collection of the sayings and deeds of the Prophet Muhammad.*

These form the basis of *Shariah*. This term, which means 'path', describes a natural law, created by God, which determines everything in the universe, from the movement of planets to the details of how people should act. It seeks to give expression to the fundamental Muslim belief in the unity of God (Allah), and forms not only an ethical system and legal framework, but effectively a whole way of life.

As they apply the Shariah to present-day situations, Muslims use the principle of analogy – linking a present issue to a decision found in the Hadith or Qur'an. Where there is doubt about what is right, a gathering of Muslim scholars (called the *ulama*) is called together to reach a decision on a point of law. Muslims believe that their community can never agree together on something that is wrong and therefore decisions by the ulama are authoritative.

One particular feature of Muslim moral thinking is the requirement that Muslims should defend of the faith of Islam and of the community of Muslims. The term used for this is *jihad*, and it takes two forms. The greater jihad is the internal struggle that every Muslim is required to undertake to overcome his or her personal faults. The lesser jihad, however, is the requirement to defend both the faith and the worldwide community of Muslims against external threats.

Example

The term *jihad* has become known in recent years through its use by those Muslim groups who claim that Islam is under attack from secular (particularly Western) forces, whether that threat is seen in military, political, economic or social terms.

It is used by al-Qa'ida to justify its terrorist campaign – seeing Western society and its economic and military might as a threat to Islam that requires to be countered. It is found in terms of confrontation between radical Islamic groups and what they perceive as symbols of Western culture and economics – as, for example, in the targeting of young Western tourists in the Bali bombings in 2004.

It is also found in the clash between secular freedom of expression and any perceived insult to the Prophet Muhammad. This was the case when Salman Rushdie published *The Satanic Verses* in 1989, and most recently in the worldwide protests by Muslims against the publication of cartoons of the Prophet in a Danish newspaper, and their subsequent reproduction elsewhere.

But we should note two things:

▶ The vast majority of Muslims, while accepting the need for both the lesser and greater jihad, would not endorse the activities of extremist 'jihadist' groups.
▶ For Islam, submission to Allah and the defence of Islam and the Prophet are paramount, whereas in secular society, emphasis is placed on the rights of the individual and freedom of expression. This clash of values is fundamental, and it is difficult to see how a compromise can be achieved.

Notice how this view contrasts with the libertarian approach of J.S. Mill. For Mill, everyone should be free to express his or her own opinions, even if they are obviously misguided. For him, freedom of the individual takes precedence over the dissemination of right

(Contd)

views. The autonomy of the individual within a democratic society is the basis of utilitarianism, and is the unquestioned assumption behind much discussion of right and wrong in a secular Western context. For a Muslim, this can never be the case; defending the truth of Islam takes absolute priority.

Insight

Extreme caution is needed in any discussion of Islam and terrorism. The principle of Jihad may be invoked in situations where the *principal* motive is political, rather than religious, and where actions are carried out which are not approved of by the vast majority of the Muslim community.

HINDUISM

Hinduism is the name used for a variety of religious traditions that originated in the Indian sub-continent. People do not generally call themselves 'Hindu', but say that they are devotees of Krishna, Shiva or one of the other gods.

Because of this, it is difficult to set out ethical guidelines that will apply in detail to all who might be called Hindu. There are scriptures that are used by a large number of them – the *Ramayana* or the *Bhagavad Gita*, for example – but there is no set way of interpreting them, and some Hindus do not read scriptures, but depend on oral traditions for understanding their religion.

Nevertheless, there are certain features that apply widely, and concepts that may be used in understanding the personal and social values of Hindu society.

Dharma

This is the term used for 'right conduct' or 'duty', and it is this that determines what is morally right. Your particular Dharma depends on who you are, and what stage of life you have reached.

Caste

Hindu society is divided up into caste groups, within each of which there are various sub-groups. The main groups are:

- **Brahmin** – *the priestly caste, generally the most highly educated, and traditionally much involved with education and religion.*
- **Kshatriya** – *traditionally the warrior caste, these tend to be involved in military and administrative posts and in the law.*
- **Vaishya** – *the 'merchant' caste, often involved with business and agriculture.*
- **Shudra** – *this is the caste for manual workers.*

Today, there is flexibility between the castes: some Kshatriyas, for example, hold university teaching posts. What is important to recognize is that those who are born into one of the three upper castes may be expected to have a sense of their duty and social position.

Below the four castes come those who are outside the caste system, who tend to take the most menial of work. There are situations in which the caste system allows people to remain in poverty, or favours those of higher birth, even if they do not necessarily have the ability to match. However, the caste system is not meant to promote inequality, but difference. People are to be given respect, whatever their place in society.

The Ashramas

The Ashramas are the four stages in life. Each of them has certain duties, and each implies certain moral choices:

1. **Student** – *at this stage a person is expected to work hard, to show respect to parents and teachers and to develop self-discipline. Students are expected to abstain from sex, alcohol, tobacco and drugs.*
2. **Householder** – *during the middle years of life a person is expected to be involved with marriage, family and career. The social rules for this stage are the most lenient.*

3 **Retired** – *traditionally, from the time of the arrival of a grandchild, it is expected that both husband and wife may start to stand back from family and business concerns. At this point they can choose to hand over control of a family business, for example, to the next generation.*

4 **Ascetic** – *a few Hindus, in the last years of their life, choose to divest themselves of all possessions and devote themselves to the practice of their religion. Most remain in the retired stage, however, and continue to live with their families.*

Hinduism recognizes that different people have different abilities and are able to take on different responsibilities.

Insight

Hinduism does not pretend that society is uniform, or that an equal distribution of goods, or equal rights, will in itself produce happiness or justice. It attempts to work with collaborative difference.

BUDDHISM

Unlike most other religious traditions, Buddhism is not actually based on a belief in God but offers a practical set of guidelines for spiritual development.

A Buddhist may say that his or her aim in life is to overcome the suffering caused by greed, hatred and illusion while developing in a way that leads to peace, joy and insight. Buddhists believe that all ethically significant actions (*karma*) have their consequences. What you do today will affect the sort of person you become tomorrow – not in the sense that there is any externally imposed law to that effect, but just because actions have their natural consequences. Those who are foolish remained trapped in a cycle of craving and unsatisfactoriness.

Buddhists are encouraged to cultivate qualities of compassion, gentleness and serenity, and to overcome the 'poisons' of hatred, greed and ignorance.

Buddhist moral guidelines are summed up in the five basic precepts, undertaken by all committed Buddhists.

1 **Not to destroy life.** *This means avoiding killing other humans, and also (for many Buddhists) keeping to a vegetarian diet, so as to minimize the suffering of other species. It also implies that Buddhists should avoid a negative attitude towards life – denigrating people or situations – but should cultivate an attitude of* **metta** *(loving kindness).*

2 **Not to take what is not given.** *This requires avoidance of dishonesty and grasping for material goods in a way that may be honest, but implies craving. Buddhists should cultivate an attitude of generosity.*

3 **Not to indulge in harmful sexual activity.** *There is the general principle that sexuality should not be used in such a way as to harm people. Although many Buddhist attitudes are shaped by the cultures within which it has developed, in general, Buddhism takes a liberal and positive attitude to sex – although those who aspire to follow the spiritual path seriously may find that they are able to find personal fulfilment without sexual activity. This precept is sometimes taken in a broader sense of not harmfully over-indulging any of the senses.*

4 **Not to speak falsely.** *This is a general rule against lying, but also against anything that deliberately gives a false impression.*

5 **Not to take those things that cloud the mind.** *In order to increase their awareness, it is important that Buddhists should stay alert and be sensitive to their own and other people's feelings and responses. This cannot happen if the mind is dulled by alcohol or drugs, and so it is recommended to avoid them. Unlike in Islam, however, there is no absolute prohibition.*

Insight

The Buddhist precepts are not presented as rules to be obeyed but aids to spiritual training. To use Kant's term, they are 'hypothetical imperatives' – if you want to meditate well, you should abstain from alcohol.

As well as these principles, Buddhists are required to cultivate four mental states, known as the Brahma Viharas, which may be translated as 'the resting places of the divine spirit':

- **love** – *towards all creatures, and including oneself*
- **pity** – *compassion for all who suffer*
- **joy** – *an unselfish sharing in the happiness of others*
- **serenity** – *freeing oneself from anxieties of success or failure, and being equal minded in dealing with other people.*

Buddhists do not refer to actions as 'good' or 'bad', 'right' or 'wrong', but as 'skilful' or 'unskilful'. This implies that an action is assessed by the intention of the person who does it rather than by any external absolutes. As action is skilful if it is the result of insight and loving kindness, it is unskilful if it is the result of ignorance, greed or hatred. That unskilfulness is shown both in the action itself and in the results that come from it.

Like Christianity, Buddhism is a religion that has been very free to adapt itself as it has moved from one culture to another. The oldest forms of Buddhism, as found now in the Theravada traditions of Thailand and Sri Lanka, for example, are very different from those found in Tibet or Japan. The basic teachings of the Buddha are a common factor, but it is considered wise to use 'skilful means' to adapt and apply teachings to the particular society and situation in which people find themselves.

Although it does have its cultural traditions and ceremonies, and many Buddhists place great importance of the lineage of their teachings (the list of teachers who have handed down traditions from one generation to the next), Buddhism is essentially a process of self-examination, within broadly defined parameters. Hence it produces general moral principles and virtues, but does not generally offer narrowly defined moral rules. The main exception to this is the voluntary acceptance of numerous rules and traditions by those who choose to spend part of their life as a monk or nun.

But even then, monastic discipline is not an end in itself, but a means to create an environment in which people can practise the Buddhist dharma.

SIKHISM

Sikhs believe that, without the inspiration that comes from devotion to God, people live in illusion, and are dominated by the five evil impulses: lust, anger, greed, attachment to worldly things and pride. Sikhs are therefore required to cultivate their opposites: self-control, forgiveness, contentment, love of God and humility.

In practical terms, the guidelines for the Sikh way of life are set out in a book called the *Rehat Maryada: A Guide to the Sikh Way of Life*, a translation of a Punjabi work of 1945, produced by a group of Sikh scholars and regarded as authoritative for giving a summary of the Sikh way of life and the teachings of the ten Gurus on which the Sikh faith is based.

The Sikh community is concerned to emphasize equality. Every Gurdwara (a place of Sikh worship) has a kitchen and a place where worshippers can sit and eat together. This is a way of demonstrating the unity and equality of Sikhs.

Sikhs who belong to the Khalsa (those who have committed themselves in a ceremony to follow the Sikh way of life – the word itself means 'pure') are required to carry a sword (*kirpan*), to be used in self-defence. It should be used only when all peaceful means of resolving a dispute have failed, and only to re-establish justice where there has been a wrong (for example, to defend the Sikh community), or in a direct act of self-defence.

The Sikh religion came into existence against a background of opposition between Hindus and Muslims, and countered this by emphasizing the unity of all people before God. This not only colours Sikh worship, and the sharing of food at the Gurdwara, but is a key feature of Sikh attitudes towards moral issues – seeking a justice that goes beyond any religious or political divisions.

formulating laws for the common good based on those values. Without the civil servant, there is no application of laws to specific situations. Without the judge there is no application of law to individual situations in a way that allows justice to operate on an individual level.

Some thinkers might easily be typecast as one or other of these characters. Machiavelli, for example, would clearly do better as a politician than as a judge or campaigner! He might also do well as a civil servant – but he would have to be very skilled in achieving his goals without appearing to break too many of the rules under which he would be required to operate.

But what about Nietzsche? Is it possible to act as a civil servant if one's ultimate criterion of right and wrong is defined in terms of the ability of individuals to overcome themselves and develop something higher? Is it possible to promote personal evolution at the same time as maintaining social cohesion?

Nietzsche was a shrewd observer of the loss of faith in the nineteenth century, and he was not afraid to explore the consequences that this might have for morality and for human values in general. His 'will to power', like Hobbes' or Bentham's view that everyone seeks his or her own good, is an observation of what actually appears to take place as people make choices.

It is grossly unfair to see Nietzsche only from the perspective of those who later took some of his ideas (particularly that of the *Übermensch* or 'Superman') as the basis for racist elitism. His only elite are those who press forward, responding to the challenge to go beyond themselves.

Insight

The Nazi party in Germany, seeking to promote the idea of a superior Aryan race, exhibited a ruthless disregard of human life in the extermination of Jews, of gypsies, of the mentally ill. Nietzsche, by contrast, was against any form of racial or sectarian elitism.

Religious values and society

The moral choices that a person makes, and the attitude of a society as a whole to accepted moral norms, will depend to some extent on the vitality of the ethical life of that society. Some societies are clearly defined by a single religious and cultural matrix, but in today's world they are becoming the exception rather than the rule. It is more normal these days to encounter societies in which there is a mixture of religious and ethnic groups. What is more, it might have been assumed at one time that the ethical views of a particular religion would be the same wherever it was practised. This again is now in question. Members of a single religion, bound together by a shared religious tradition, are nevertheless divided by the lifestyle and expectations of the societies within which they live.

Hence there is real scope for problems of commitment and the acknowledgement of ethical norms. Someone who belongs to a religion, but lives in a largely secular society, is likely to respond to that situation in one of two ways:

▶ *By making a clear distinction between the lifestyle and ethics of his or her religious community and that of the rest of society. The temptation then is to define by difference, and to emphasize those things in which the religion differs from the accepted secular norm.*
▶ *By compromising on, or re-interpreting, religious rules in a way that brings them into line with the prevailing lifestyle. Once that happens, members of the same religion, living in different societies, start to disagree about their religious ethics.*

Making a responsible moral choice involves weighing up all the factors that influence your self-understanding. Are you basically a member of a religion, who just happens to be living in this secular society? Or a secular person and an atheist, who happens to live in a society dominated by religion? Or are you a member of this society, who happens to find the teachings of a particular religion helpful? How you weigh up such conflicts (or potential conflicts) in interest and commitment, will determine the way in which you balance secular and religious moral arguments.

'Protests as ferry firm ends Sabbath shutdown'

In an article in the *Guardian* (Friday 15 May 2009), Severin Carrell described the way in which people on the Hebridean island of Lewis were responding to the news that the ferry company was to start sailings on a Sunday. Lewis, a Calvinist Protestant island, had for centuries observed the Sabbath, with many people refusing to work, use a car or even watch television on a Sunday. Now it faced the prospect of an ending of 'the island's isolation from the modern world'. But does that make the 'modern world' right and Lewis's Calvinists wrong? Should morality and lifestyle be decided by majority vote? And how might a young person on Lewis balance commitment to the religious tradition into which they were born, against the world revealed by the media and the attractions of modern secular life?

Sometimes the moral principles of a faith community coincide with those of secular society, but the authority behind those principles and the way in which moral rules are justified may still be quite different.

Example

The deliberate killing of another human being is against the law in almost all societies, except in particular circumstances (e.g. when war is declared, or where a person is legally sentenced to death). A Buddhist living in that society would also wish to refrain from killing;

(Contd)

not because of the secular law, but from a profound respect for all living things. The Buddhist may also go beyond the secular law, opposing those forms of killing which are permitted by society (e.g. the killing of animals for food). The secular and religious viewpoints may or may not coincide in practical terms, but what is essentially different is the justification given in each case. Social observation is therefore inadequate in assessing the strength of religious moral influence.

In the case of Judaism, Islam, Sikhism and Hinduism, the religion tends to promote its own culture, and is therefore less influenced by the secular or cultural contexts within which it finds itself. Traditions of prayer, or the observation of Ramadan in Islam, for example, will be the same wherever in the world Muslims find themselves.

Buddhists and Christians, however, have tended to adapt their presentation of their fundamental beliefs to take into account prevailing attitudes and philosophies of the societies within which they have found themselves. Consequently, there is great variety within these religions to moral issues. Where the religion is established as the historical norm within a culture (e.g. Christianity in Europe or the United States, Buddhism in Thailand) it is sometimes difficult to distinguish what is an expression of secular culture and what has religious roots. Minority religious groups tend to stand out against their cultural background, and their ethical position may be more sharply defined.

Example

At the Lambeth Conference in July 1998, bishops of the Anglican Church agreed to ignore polygamy in areas where this was accepted by society. African bishops had argued that it was wrong to force Christian converts who had several wives to become monogamous as a condition of church membership. Although the Church did not endorse polygamy, it recognized it as something it had to live with, and agreed not to make pronouncements against it.

IS INTENTION ENOUGH?

The American philosopher, Daniel Dennett, writing in *Philosophers Without Gods* reflects on the help given during a life-threatening illness. He contrasts the assumption of many religious people that what matters is a person's intention to do the right thing, not necessarily their success in it, with the ethical demands made by medicine to make sure that, within human limits, everything possible is done. He concludes by saying:

> *I applaud you for your loyalty to your own position – but remember: loyalty to tradition is not enough. You've got to keep asking yourself: What if I'm wrong? In the long run, I think religious people can be asked to live up to the same moral standards as secular people in science and medicine.*
>
> (*Philosophers Without Gods*, ed. Louise Anthony, 2007, p. 117)

Although many religious people also find themselves following the demands of, say, the medical profession, what Dennett reminds us is that, without religion, medicine and science make strict moral and intellectual demands on their practitioners. In secular morality, as much as religious, it is not simply a matter of obeying rules, but of using all that is within one's power to do what is right. Good intentions alone are not enough.

Insight

There are questions about quality of life, euthanasia, the limits of treatment and so on, that require careful thought about exactly what the medical practitioner should be committed to. Professional rules are not foundational; they depend on insights about the nature of human life.

Should religious freedom be restricted?

There are situations where religious beliefs lead to actions that go against the prevailing norms of the society within which they operate.

Examples

1   In Waco, Texas, in 1993, a branch of the Seventh-Day
    Adventist Church, led by David Koresh, was besieged in
    its headquarters by federal agents, following a shooting
    incident. The cult members were heavily armed, and there
    had been considerable exchange of fire in which four agents
    had been killed. At the end of the siege, there was a fire in
    which Koresh and many of his followers died.
2   Some people refuse to accept medical attention on religious
    grounds. For example, Jehovah's Witnesses may refuse to
    accept blood transfusions. Sometimes Christian Science
    practitioners may refuse conventional medical treatment for
    themselves or their children on religious grounds.

Should a religious cult be allowed to operate outside the laws of the
society within which its members live? Does society as a whole have
a right to legislate about religious beliefs?

Historically, those who have deviated from the norms of religious
belief have often been persecuted and killed. In contrast, there is
wide acceptance today of the idea that the free practice of one's
religion is a basic human right. To what extent is there a moral
obligation on society, or on individuals, to monitor or take action
to prevent the spread of beliefs that (on the basis of the ethics of
society as a whole) are harmful?

The dilemma here is whether it is right, in the name of one set of
moral values, to deprive any individual or group of the freedom to
live by a different set of moral values.

- *Does the value of allowing individuals or groups freedom to
  act according to their own moral or religious views outweigh
  any potential harm (from society's point of view) that such
  freedom might entail?*
- *Which is better for society overall: freedom, with the risk of
  minorities doing things that the majority regard as wrong, or
  an enforced moral code?*

Recent freedom ...

Although the freedom to practise any religion or none is generally accepted in modern secular societies, we need to remember that this is a fairly recent phenomenon. Until the middle of the nineteenth century, Christianity dominated the establishment in Britain, and many positions in society (or even access to education) were based on a religious requirement. During the wars of religion, people were tortured and killed for holding religious views other than those of the government of the day. Those accused of witchcraft could be burnt at the stake. As recently as 1842, George Holyoake, a campaigner for secular humanism, became the last person to be sent to prison for denying the existence of God.

THINGS TO REMEMBER

From this chapter, remember that ...

▶ *morality may be autonomous, or (if derived from religious, social or political values) heteronomous*

▶ *the Euthyphro Dilemma considers whether God's commands or human reason should take priority in morality*

▶ *Jewish moral principles are based on interpretations and applications of the Torah, guided by reason and conscience*

▶ *Christianity seeks to balance the authority of Church and scripture with reason, conscience and direct spiritual inspiration*

▶ *the highest form of jihad in Islam is the battle to overcome one's personal faults*

▶ *Hinduism sees moral and social obligations as linked to a person's caste and stage in life*

▶ *Buddhists seek to follow five basic guidelines for spiritual training, rather than externally imposed rules*

▶ *Sikhs seek equality, the development of personal moral qualities and the right of self defence*

▶ *a religious believer may need to balance religious and secular moral principles and values*

▶ *freedom to practise a religion may compromise established moral norms in society.*

10

Scepticism and relativism

In this chapter you will learn:

- *to cast a sceptical eye over morality*
- *to examine the claim that morality is always culturally conditioned*
- *to explore whether moral absolutes are appropriate for a varied world.*

In the context of ethics, **scepticism** is the view that there are no solid foundations for ethical theories or principles. It may take the form of a scientific argument for a determinist position – thereby suggesting that freedom of choice is an illusion, and therefore that moral responsibility is also illusory. It may equally take the form of a logical argument that questions each assumption and attempts to show that there is no foundation for morality that cannot be challenged. It may even be expressed in the assumption that, whatever they may claim, people are only motivated by their own self-interest.

Insight

There is, of course, a logical problem with being an absolute sceptic, namely that you can be sceptical about scepticism itself! Why should we not challenge the validity of challenging all moral norms?

We shall look at one exponent of a political philosophy that comes as near as one might choose to scepticism, namely that of

Machiavelli. Whether *The Prince* was taken to be serious advice for the aspiring ruler, or written with the wry smile of one who has long observed how people actually survive in the political jungle, need not greatly concern us. It does, however, offer a moral scepticism that verges on the cynical.

An equal threat to those who would espouse absolute moral principles is **relativism**. All ethical theories are relativist to some extent – in the sense that it is widely accepted that moral rules should be applied in a way that is sensitive to the particular situation and context. However, relativism can be pursued to the point of saying that all moral norms and principles originate within a social context. Hence they are not autonomous and cannot be applied universally. Society decides what is right or wrong, and may be free to change its mind.

Because relativism appears to be sensitive to the autonomy of the individual and the cultural context of human action, it tends to be more 'reasonable' and perhaps even more moral that scepticism. However, a thoroughgoing relativism makes moral debate very difficult, for debate depends on agreed principles and norms, and if these are culturally conditioned then they too can be challenged and dismissed.

Insight

Perhaps the question to ask in this chapter is whether the combined influence of scepticism and relativism invalidates the ethical arguments and theories that we have been considering so far, or whether they are simply a restraining influence on those who would define morality too narrowly.

Philosophers or politicians?

Kant was a professional philosopher, and by all accounts his life was regular and carefully ordered. There is an anecdote told of him that he took the same walk each day, and that his timing was so precise that housewives seeing him pass could set their watches by him! His thought is precise and logical, as we saw in the examination of his 'categorical imperative' (see Chapter 6).

▶ *He looked at experience and realized that we play a large part in the ordering of what we see – we impose space, time and causality on the jumble of sense impressions that bombard us.*

▶ *He looked at the experience of behaving in a moral way, responding to a sense that there is something that one 'ought' to do, and analysed that too – in terms of both its implications and its presuppositions.*

▶ *He presents us with three simple rules – that we should be prepared to universalize the principles on which we act, that we should treat people as ends in themselves and not merely as means to our own ends, and we should act as though taking responsibility for legislating for a kingdom of ends. All three are eminently sensible criteria by which to assess our moral choices.*

▶ *He does not offer practical advice for specific situations, but the most general of guidelines.*

Why then might one hesitate to accept Kant as the ultimate judge of acceptable action? Perhaps because in the actual world of crises and moral decisions, life is seldom as straightforward as it would seem from Kant's standpoint.

To get a realistic view of moral choices we need to balance what we feel 'ought' to happen by a study of what does actually happen. From Kant's perspective, much of what happens (especially, perhaps, in the world of politics) might be regarded as immoral. But is that fair? Should we not look carefully at the actual choices that people make if they are to rule? Should we not balance the innocent simplicity of the categorical imperative against the experience of one who sees the consequence of always acting innocently?

For a very different perspective we shall therefore turn to a politician – a fifteenth-century Italian from Florence, a diplomat and shrewd (if cynical) observer of the realities of political life. His maxims are rather different from those of Kant, and he treats morality with a good degree of scepticism!

MACHIAVELLI

Machiavelli was essentially a practical man. His book *The Prince* gives advice to one who would seek to rule a principality, and it is set against the political intrigues of fifteenth- and sixteenth-century Italy. It looks at the realities of political life, the need for stern action, the need to use power in a way that is effective, the need to act creatively and decisively, breaking all the conventional moral rules if necessary in order to deal in a pragmatic way with the demands of high office.

Machiavelli's views are suitable to balance against Kant's for three reasons:

▶ *Kant is concerned with the 'categorical imperative' – the 'ought' that does not depend on conditions. Machiavelli is concerned almost all the time with 'hypothetical imperatives', such as what you need to do in order to retain power. The implication of this is that, in most practical situations, it is the hypothetical rather than the categorical that constitutes the normal sphere of 'moral' (to Machiavelli) operations.*

▶ *Kant argues that you should always treat people as ends, not as means. Machiavelli recognizes that there are occasions when a ruler must act cruelly against one person or group of people in order to establish fear as a deterrent against lawlessness, for example.*

▶ *Kant thinks one should legislate for a kingdom of ends. Machiavelli knows that treating people as ends in themselves might well lead to anarchy and chaos.*

Insight

If the Golden Rule is that one should do unto others as you would wish them to do unto you, Machiavelli's rule would be that one should do unto others before they get a chance to do unto you!

Let us look at just a little of Machiavelli's advice. Here, for example, are his words to a ruler who has taken over a state, but it might equally apply to a managing director who has taken over an ailing company, or a politician inheriting a new ministry.

> *So it should be noted that when he seizes a state the new ruler ought to determine all the injuries that he will need to inflict. He should inflict them once for all, and not have to renew them every day, and in that way he will be able to set men's minds at rest, and win them over to him when he confers benefits. Whoever acts otherwise, either through timidity or bad advice, is always forced to have the knife ready in his hand and he can never depend on his subjects because they, suffering fresh and continuous violence, can never feel secure with regard to him. Violence should be inflicted once for all; people will then forget what it tastes like and so be less resentful. Benefits should be conferred gradually; and in that way they will taste better.*
>
> (*The Prince*, section VIII)

Like a surgeon, forced in some extreme circumstances to operate without anaesthetic, one is sometimes in a position where the inflicting of pain is inevitable and ultimately beneficial.

It might seem irrelevant to ask 'Am I prepared for everyone to operate without anaesthetics?' because clearly the actual decision is not based on a general theory but on the immediate and unique situation. The surgeon might say 'This is not how I would choose to act, but in the circumstances it is right for me to do so.' What Machiavelli is saying (and using a utilitarian argument to justify it) is that less harm will be done by decisive action, than by a compassionate but indecisive muddle.

And here the advice to a ruler might be adapted for a new teacher, taking over an unruly class:

> *So a prince should not worry if he incurs reproach for his cruelty so long as he keeps his subjects united and loyal. By making an example or two he will prove more compassionate than those who,*

being too compassionate, allow disorders which lead to murder and rapine. These nearly always harm the whole community, whereas executions ordered by a prince only affect individuals.

(*The Prince*, section XVIII)

He acknowledges the traditional virtues, but comments:

... taking everything into account, he (the prince) will find that some of the things that appear to be virtues will, if he practises them, ruin him, and some of the things that appear to be wicked will bring him security and prosperity.

(*The Prince*, section XV)

Now this is not to dismiss entirely the idea that a ruler should do good, merely that a ruler should be flexible enough to recognize that it is not always prudent.

... he should have a flexible disposition, varying as fortune and circumstances dictate. As I said above, he should not deviate from what is good, if that is possible, but he should know how to do evil, if that is necessary.

(*The Prince*, section XVIII)

For our purposes, there are four features of Machiavelli's advice that we may need to take into account:

▶ *In many situations, traditional virtues may be set aside, and actions judged on a utilitarian basis. Keeping order and minimizing pain take precedence over traditional moral principles.*
▶ *Actions depend on the duties and responsibilities of the position you hold in society. A prince might be justified, therefore, in doing something that would not be acceptable in one of his subjects. Once you have accepted the position of ruler, you are obliged to seek the benefit and integrity of the state – your morality in other respects being subsumed beneath that overall obligation. Morality is therefore related to social position.*

- *In practical terms, one needs to be flexible, adapting moral principles to suit particular situations.*
- *What we do should depend on our awareness of the likely actions and attitudes of those around us. If everyone else were good, there would be no problem – but they are not, and so we remain naively innocent at our own peril.*

Example

During 2009 and 2010, there was discussion about whether the international forces fighting in Afghanistan should negotiate with the Taliban, and whether it was right to continue to support the government in Kabul, given that it did not seem able to eliminate corruption and that the president had been voted into office by an election in which there had been considerable fraud.

On the one hand, there was a feeling that one should not compromise when it comes to dealing with corrupt regimes or with those who are willing to shelter terrorists.

On the other, there was a sense that a pragmatic way forward would have to include compromise, the acceptance that any government is better than none, and that eventually there would need to be some form of negotiated settlement with the Taliban, so the sooner lines of communication are established the better.

To what extent does this view of political reality negate the Kantian attempt to settle moral issues on the basis of pure practical reason?

There is, of course, an answer to Machiavelli, but it is not an easy one. One could say: 'I will do what I know to be right, no matter what the consequences, to myself, my family and friends, my country. I will not compromise my integrity, however much pain that might cause.' That is a valid moral position to take, for someone who holds his or her principles very dear. Martyrs take such a stand.

It is also possible to take this position for other reasons: out of fear of being in the wrong; out of pride or stubbornness; out of the conviction that future glory awaits those who stand by their principles (in heaven, in a new incarnation, or in the perspective of history). T.S. Eliot put onto the lips of the soon-to-be-martyred Thomas à Beckett in his play *Murder in the Cathedral*, when Thomas is tempted to accept martyrdom for the sake of future glory, that the foulest treason is to do the right thing for the wrong reason.

Let Machiavelli stand for those who are sceptical about the application of moral principles. This is not a total scepticism about moral values – which implies that there are no values other than those that individuals choose to impose on life – it is just scepticism about the application of general rules to individual situations.

In almost all moral systems there is scope for individual flexibility. In extreme circumstances you are morally justified in doing things that would be wrong in the general run of events. Machiavelli takes this seriously, but in political life almost all events are extreme and unique, all demand that normal rules be set aside. Just how flexible can people be before they are 'unprincipled'?

Insight

Ask yourself: is Machiavelli really unprincipled, or just a realist, applying moral guidelines as best he can in the world where political survival is what counts?

Situation ethics

The natural law approach to ethics formulates rules and then applies them to individual situations. But is it right to apply rules in this way? Is not every situation unique? Does the practical scepticism of Machiavelli not suggest that we need to be far more flexible in our approach?

In the 1960s, largely as a reaction against what he saw as a paternalistic and imposed morality of traditional Christianity, Joseph Fletcher developed **situation ethics**.

He argued against the deductive method of ethics (in which you start with a rule or principle, and then apply it to various particular cases), and suggested that the individual situation should be paramount. He believed that there should be **a single moral principle – that you should do whatever is the most loving thing**. Ethical rules were of secondary importance; they might guide a person, but should not dictate right and wrong.

The requirement to do the most loving thing is not a rule or law – it does not say *what* you should do in any particular situation – it merely gives a motive and attitude that can inform moral choice. Of course, a person may act foolishly out of love, with disastrous consequences, but nevertheless, from a strictly situationist ethical perspective, it is still morally right. Each situation is taken and judged by what love requires, and if that means breaking some conventional moral rule, it is right to do so.

Other writers from the same period took a position half way between this radical 'situationist' approach and the conventional application of rules. Paul Tillich (in *Morality and Beyond*, 1963) pointed out that if there were no rules, everyone would have to work out what he or she should do on every individual occasion. This, he argued, was too much to expect. There should be rules to help people decide what love might require of them in any given situation.

For reflection

The principle of love may be fine as an ideal, but will it work in the real world? What would be the result if some people accept it and others do not? Are those accepting it not going to be at a disadvantage? And if they are, might they accept that disadvantage as part of the price they pay for following the value they hold most dear? How might Machiavelli have responded to that principle?

Situation ethics, in putting individual circumstances before fixed moral rules, nevertheless accepted one absolute principle: love. But what if there is no absolute principle that can be applied to all situations? This leads us to the general issue of relativism.

Relativism and moral absolutes

Any **absolutist** approach to ethics is going to argue that it is possible to find a basic feature of the world, human nature, biology or pure reason on which a system of ethics can be built. Once that foundation is established, moral principles and the right or wrong of particular actions can follow by logical deduction and practical application.

That is not to imply that absolutist ethics is inflexible; all moral systems need to take some account of particular circumstances, intentions and so on. However, every absolutist ethic is based on something other than itself, some reality or shared value, by which it is justified. Looking at the ethical theories we have considered so far:

- ▶ *natural law ethics is based on a rational interpretation of purpose within a rationally comprehensible universe.*
- ▶ *Virtue ethics is based on an understanding of the essence of what it is to be a mature human being, and the virtues that spring from that.*
- ▶ *Utilitarianism is based on the assumption that a rational person (whether from altruism or enlightened self-interest) will want a democratic sharing out of benefits.*
- ▶ *Kant based his ethics on the pure practical reason and the logical application of his categorical imperative.*
- ▶ *Even where personal development, whether with a fixed idea of the self or an evolutionary one, is used as a basis for ethics, it is based on an ideal of what a person can become and understands morality in the light of that.*

This does not imply that any of these are 'absolutist' in any narrow sense, but it does show that they all depend on some prior commitment or understanding, by which right and wrong can be judged.

Relativism also starts with a couple of basic assumptions, but they are very different from any of those listed above. It assumes:

▶ *that the only absolute rule is that there are no absolute rules*
▶ *that nobody should impose his or her morality on anyone else.*

Insight

Relativism has come to the fore in moral debate because we live in a multi-faith and multi-cultural world, and are therefore far more aware of cultural diversity than was the case in earlier centuries. Relativism is, in part, an attempt to respect all cultural, ethnic and religious views equally.

Early in this book (see Chapter 2) we made the distinction between descriptive and normative ethics. The former simply described what people do in particular situations, without attempting to label that behaviour either right or wrong. The latter – which then became the subject matter of all that followed, was concerned with defining and understanding moral norms. Descriptive ethics is relativist. In other words, if you say 'people in such and such a tribe practise cannibalism' you are not making a judgement about whether cannibalism is right or wrong, you are simply noting that it is socially acceptable in that tribe.

What a relativist approach to ethics is doing is extending descriptive ethics into the territory that was previously held by normative ethics. In other words, it argues that all issues of right and wrong should be seen as culturally, socially and temporally conditioned. We should not take moral norms or rules from one society and impose them on another; nor should we assume that the rules that applied in one era can be continued into another.

In looking at moral language, we saw that **emotivism** (arguing that moral language is merely expressing one's approval or otherwise) and **prescriptivism** (recommending a course of action) were logical ways of understanding what ethics is about, once you accept the logical positivism argument that moral language cannot be justified with reference to facts (see Chapter 2).

Relativism follows exactly the same logic. Because there are no facts that can decide between competing sets of moral rules or values, no one set can be any better or worse than any other.

Those who argue for any of the traditional ethical systems tend to regard relativism as a dangerous medicine; taken in small quantities it is useful (in warning against too rigid an application of ethical maxims), but overdoses can be fatal – in the sense that they tend to preclude the rational discussion of genuine differences of opinion.

THINGS TO REMEMBER

From this chapter, remember that ...

▶ *scepticism sees no solid foundation for ethical judgements*

▶ *scepticism and relativism challenge the validity of ethical theories*

▶ *the ideals of Kantian ethics may be challenged by circumstances*

▶ *Machiavelli looks at what is needed for a ruler to maintain power*

▶ *Machiavelli puts pragmatism ahead of principle*

▶ *one may need to compromise principles in order to establish negotiations*

▶ *situation ethics accepts only the law of love*

▶ *relativism sees values as culturally determined*

▶ *relativism opposes moral and cultural imperialism*

▶ *relativism is seen as threatening the validity of moral norms.*

11

....

Applied ethics

In this chapter you will learn:
- *to apply ethical theories to a range of issues*
- *about the variety of moral issues today*
- *to understand how different arguments reflect different standpoints.*

It may seem strange, at the end of a book that has already introduced examples of the way ethical thinking is applied to real-life situations, to have a separate chapter on 'applied ethics' – surely *all* ethics is 'applied'?

The reason for this is partly historical. Before the twentieth century, there is no doubt that ethical thinkers sought to apply their reasoning to practical situations. Bentham, for example, was concerned with prison reform and J.S. Mill campaigned for women to be given the vote. In the early twentieth century, however, in response to the logical positivist claim that moral statements were 'meaningless' because they could not be verified empirically, it became increasingly common for the philosophical discussion of ethics to be limited to the exploration of what moral statements might mean and how they might be justified – in other words, 'meta-ethics'. It did not presume to enter the real world and say what *should* happen. Philosophers were not expected to make pronouncements about what was right or wrong.

The last four decades of the twentieth century, however, saw a dramatic shift in emphasis, so that the range of ethical topics under consideration in the twenty-first century, both in an academic context and among the general public, is far greater than half a century earlier. The anti-war movements in the 1960s and 1970s, the coming of the contraceptive pill, the sexual revolution, feminism, environmental issues, global warming, terrorism and financial crises have all thrust ethics to the fore. In the professions (particularly medicine and nursing) there has been a range of very immediate ethical dilemmas, and pressure to define professional responsibilities in this area.

There has also been an increase in litigation. If people feel that they have been unfairly treated, they will sue; companies and individual professionals have needed to define their responsibilities and be prepared to defend themselves when challenged. There has also been an increase in interest in business ethics, again fuelled by the grievances felt when companies fail to deliver what they promise, or where corporate failure affects the lives of employees, who claim that they should have appropriate consideration.

Equally, with the coming of the Internet and global television coverage, people have far more access to information and – through interactive media – are able to make their views known or participate in campaigns against what they see as injustice. But the media not only reveal moral issues, they also become the subject of debate. It has become far easier for people to review and compare the performance of different media – comparing what is said in a newspaper with what appears on news websites or television stations from other parts of the world. Censorship, political manipulation and the balance of news coverage all have ethical implications.

Clearly, applied ethics covers a vast range of subjects, and any one of these tends to spill over into others. Take issues about *race*. These may include questions of legal and social equality, and the rights of ethnic minorities. Discussion of these can work both on the individual level, and also in terms of 'institutionalized racism' in organizations such as the police or the armed forces. Issues of race, like those of gender, tend to be rather different from other ethical issues, because they contribute an additional layer of complexity to an ethical analysis of a situation. For example, whether or not a police force investigates a crime adequately may be a matter of ethical debate (depending on the reasons for a failure of adequacy), but where it is suggested that there are racial or gender issues, these are superimposed over questions of existing rights and responsibilities. Ethical issues are seldom only about race or gender, they are about fundamental questions of human rights as well. Consequently, there is something slightly artificial about compartmentalizing moral issues – examine one and it has implications for many others.

Insight

Pick up any newspaper and you will see that moral issues are never far from the surface of public concern, as was illustrated in one-day news summary in the 'Only got ten minutes?' section at the beginning of this book. To keep pace with applied ethics, once you have a grasp of key arguments, the best thing to do is to scan the papers or the Internet for new issues and arguments that are constantly being raised.

In this chapter we shall take a brief look at some of the ethical issues in a range of key areas of human life, without attempting to give all the background details. Quite apart from the practical limitations of space, it is important to recognize that none of these issues is settled once and for all, and the ethical debates and arguments may well change with changing circumstances.

Insight

The key thing is to keep in your mind what sort of ethical argument is being used for each issue. Is it utilitarian? Or based on natural law? Or on a Kantian sense of moral obligation? Or the result of an agreed contract? What sense of fairness or justice is being argued for? If you recognize the type of argument being used, you are better able to question it and assess whether it is valid.

The natural environment

We have to recognize that the human species, both by its numbers and its technology, has a massive impact on the environment. Yet, until recently, almost all moral thinking focused on human happiness of benefit; directly so in the case of utilitarianism, indirectly in the natural law arguments or the categorical imperative. The tendency has been to seek human flourishing first of all, and to consider other species or other elements in the natural environment only insofar as they impact on humans.

A stone cannot feel pain, or express a preference; therefore, it has traditionally been ignored in moral debates. From a utilitarian point of view, the environment (and other species living within it) has too often only been seen as a moral issue when its destruction threatens to harm humankind.

Insight

The notable exception has been Peter Singer, who has argued for the interests of all sentient beings to be taken into account, on the grounds that they can experience pain and can therefore either suffer or benefit as the result of human action. We shall examine this in the section on animal rights (page 195).

This approach tends to be short sighted, however, since we are not able to assess the full impact of, for example, climate change on the human species, quite apart from the question of any moral responsibility towards other species or the natural environment for its own sake.

Example

If rainforests are destroyed, we may be concerned because:

▶ climate change will affect us all

(Contd)

> ▶ many medicines are discovered through analysis of rare plant
>   species, many of which are still to be found in the rainforests.
>
> In both cases, this reflects a narrowly utilitarian argument. It does
> not imply any responsibility towards the rainforest in itself, nor to
> the other species who live in it.

A second approach is implied by what has already been said
about the 'natural law' argument. Whether backed by religious
convictions or not, there may be a sense that everything –
humans, other species, the planet itself – has its place within an
overall scheme of things, a 'final cause' that is its natural destiny.
This approach is based on metaphysics, in that it goes beyond
descriptions of the physical environment to consider issues of value,
meaning and the fundamental structures of reality. It may conclude
that the world and its many species should be valued, quite apart
from any specific or demonstrable benefit to humankind.

For reflection

The human population is about 6.8 billion (as at December 2009,
a 300 million increase since the previous edition of this book in
2006, and more than double what it was in 1960) and is set to
rise to more than 9 billion by 2050. The planet cannot sustain
such growth in a species that has such a significant impact on the
environment. Whatever is done by way of ethically responsible
lifestyle changes in order to reduce the 'human environmental
footprint' (in other words, the impact of each person on the
planet) it remains true that the only way to reduce a person's
footprint to zero is for him or her not to be born! We immediately
move on to issues of contraception, population control, social
provision, education and so on – all of which impact on the birth
rate. And once you do that, moral arguments from a 'natural law'
perspective (opposing contraception, for example) start to come
into play, to be balanced against a utilitarian assessment of future
suffering due to an unsustainable population.

Whether arguing from a utilitarian or natural law basis, it is clear that lifestyle options have a direct impact on the environment. Those concerned to preserve the ecosystems on which life depends, need to make a case for changes in our attitudes to those things that most people take for granted as part of an affluent lifestyle.

Action on climate change

The climate change summit held in Copenhagen in December 2009 failed to achieve any legally binding agreements to lower carbon emissions, to the frustration of most of those involved. While accepting the scientific evidence for the impact of global warming on the future of the planet, and recognizing that something needs to be done to restrain the rise in temperatures, all that the summit achieved was a general statement of intent.

There were many complex political and economic issues standing in the way of an agreement, but in terms of ethics, the problem lay in conflicting utilitarian calculations. On the one hand, there is the long-term benefit to the planet of binding agreements to ensure the reduction of the human contribution to climate change. On the other, is the need for political leaders to calculate the benefits sought by their people in a world where nations compete against one another. In the end, national self-interest (and thus the satisfaction of the preferences of a majority of people in each country) seemed to take precedence over the preference of the global community.

When Rawls argued for justice as fairness (see page 135) he required those who came to decide on the principles of justice to forget who they were. The problem is, in the real world, those who come together to take decisions that affect the whole globe simply cannot forget where they come from or whom they represent.

Ethical discussions about genetically modified (GM) crops tend to start with a utilitarian assessment. On the one hand, GM foods may carry long-term health risks of which we are not yet aware, but on the other, the modified crops will have been specifically adapted to resist diseases, or give better yields, which are clearly beneficial. Into this assessment are thrown issues like the risk of GM crops cross-fertilizing with other species, with unknown results, against the fact that the selective breeding of plants and animals is seen as a normal and acceptable part of farming.

The problem for any such utilitarian assessment is that the potential benefits, in terms of the resistance of GM crops to disease, for example, are relatively easy to show, while the potential dangers of eating GM products are as yet unknown. The balance is therefore not so much between known advantages and disadvantages of the product, but between positive claims for the new crops and unknown risks.

But none of this answers the anxiety of those who feel that genetic modifications are 'unnatural', simply because, while breeding is carried out within the same or very closely related species – you can cross-pollinate two types of flower, or interbreed similar kinds of dog – you cannot find a natural way to cross a cabbage with a fish! On the other hand, you can introduce modified genetic material from a fish into plant DNA. And it is that 'unnatural' mixing of genetic material from very different species that is the main concern from the 'natural law' perspective – a perspective based on the idea that each individual species (and each individual within them) has a naturally designed essence, waiting to be fulfilled. To mess with such essences is to challenge the fundamental design of the natural order.

Insight

If the debate is between someone who follows natural law ethics and a utilitarian, no amount of additional evidence for the benefits of GM crops is ever going to be able to settle the matter. The clash will remain between morality based on respect for the design of the natural order, and that based on potential benefits.

Interestingly, another key feature of the GM debate is an economic one. Since companies make money by selling what people want to buy, GM produce on the one hand and organic produce on the other may flourish or decline depending on the market perception at the time.

For reflection

▶ Is market economics a sufficient basis for deciding whether manipulating food is right or wrong? It is morally right to sell something simply because people are prepared to pay for it?
▶ Should government increase the tax on those products (e.g. cigarettes) that it wants to discourage people from buying?

Economic questions such as these tend to mask the fundamental moral question about whether it is right to manipulate genetic material to create new products. That remains a matter of considering the relationship between humankind and the rest of nature, and whether nature is primarily there to be exploited to meet human need.

Animal rights

So far, everything we have been considering has been concerned with the way in which human beings treat one another, but humankind is just one of many species on this planet, so we need to ask if the sort of moral considerations that have been applied to the treatment of other human beings should be extended to include other species.

This does not imply that animals should behave morally – without reason, morality makes no sense. A cat, offered the prospect of killing a mouse, acts instinctively, but (as we shall consider in a moment) humans can choose how they will behave towards other species.

But do we as a species have any moral obligations towards other species? Do animals have rights – and, if so, how are those rights assessed? Let us look at the way in which some ethical arguments might be applied to animals.

Insight

In practical terms, we may want to ask:

▶ *Is it right to keep wild animals caged in zoos?*
▶ *Is the concept of making an animal into a 'pet' one that damages its original nature?*
▶ *Should we breed favourite species on grounds of aesthetic appeal?*

FAIRNESS

Ethical theories that are based on the idea of a social contract drawn up between people are concerned with the fairness within a relationship. Each party accepts responsibilities and in return receives rights. Can this sort of theory be applied to other species?

A pet is accepted into a human social setting for the benefit of the humans. For example, looking after a pet hamster may be a way of encouraging children to take responsibility generally, as well as giving them pleasure. A dog or cat may be good company, especially for people living on their own. A family pet may be thought to offer something positive to the life and atmosphere of a family home. A relationship develops between the pet animal and the humans, through expressions of affection and shared enjoyments (like dog and owner taking walks together).

In what way does the animal benefit from this arrangement? By being given food and shelter, veterinary care and all else needed, to enable it to live out its natural lifespan in a measure of comfort seldom offered in its natural habitat?

Where animals are treated cruelly, once accepted into the human environment, then it is clear that the humans have not acted fairly in terms of the implied contract between themselves and the animal.

Insight

In other words, if you accept a pet, you have a moral responsibility to care for it in a way that is appropriate to its needs. That is only fair, according to the implied contract you have with it. You may be prosecuted for inhumane treatment on that basis.

NATURAL LAW

It might be argued that humans have no right to be entering into such implied contracts with animals. The Islamic view of life, for example, is that animals should not be kept as pets or put into zoos. It regards this as basically unnatural, and therefore as violating the natural life and instincts of the animal. In this case, the argument being used is one of 'natural law'; that animals have their natural place within the scheme of things, and are not to be treated as pets. Respect for the animal demands that it should be treated as an animal, not as a quasi-human, manicured, clipped and paraded!

On the other hand, animals in the wild feed on one another. Humans are omnivorous, and therefore have a choice – they can either eat animals or remain vegetarian. A natural law argument might well accept that there is a place for the eating of meat, and therefore also for the farming of animals. But if the eating of meat in order to sustain life is justified under natural law, what about the conditions in which the farming of animals takes place? Most species do not have any choice about their feeding habits; they simply catch what they can. The human species, on the other hand, controls the production of animals for food. Does such control imply moral responsibility?

> ## Example
>
> A cat will play with, kill and eat a mouse. The sight of this might be extremely distasteful, but it is a cat's nature to do so. However much the cat may have been domesticated, it is still a natural hunter with killer instincts. On the other hand, if I decide to take a pet mouse out of its cage, set it free in a room and then chase after it, biting it from time to time before killing and eating it, I would be considered to be acting in a way that is unnatural, and the morality of having such a supper would be questioned. My feeding habits might feature in a tabloid newspaper, and I might find myself under pressure to accept psychotherapy. I would certainly be banned from keeping pet mice.
>
> ▶ What distinguishes me from the cat in this respect?
> ▶ Does my rationality and ability to choose other sources of food mean that I have a moral responsibility towards the mouse?
>
> If I were starving, would I be morally justified in eating the mouse?

The treatment of animals is connected with questions about diet and standards of living. If fresh meat is enjoyed occasionally, and a roast chicken is regarded as a delicacy, it becomes more possible to breed chickens in humane circumstances – fewer are needed and people will pay more for what is considered a delicacy. On the other hand, if people expect to eat meat every day, the demand goes up and artificial methods are found to maximize the efficiency of meat production. A change in eating habits and expectations therefore implies a change in attitude to animals, even aside from the issue of vegetarianism.

Insight
How do you assess the fairness of an implied contract in which a member of one species is born, reared and fattened,

and then killed to feed members of another species? All the gains would seem to be on one side. The animal used for food is not considered as an individual member of a species, but simply as a source of protein.

Natural law sees everything – and therefore every species – as having a place within the overall scheme of things within the universe. Hence animals are regarded as having significance, but not the same significance as human beings, since they have a very different essence. Where a metaphysics is evolutionary, or emphasizes the interrelationship between all life forms – e.g. within Buddhism – the welfare of one species is bound up with the welfare of others, and the treatment of animals is therefore most definitely a moral concern.

EXPERIMENTS ON ANIMALS

Animal rights activists target laboratories that conduct experiments on animals – and tend to do so irrespective of the purpose of the research being undertaken. In other words, they oppose the use of animals in this way, whether the aim is to find a cure for a serious human disease or whether it is to test cosmetics. In this, they are rejecting a utilitarian approach.

Using a utilitarian argument, the gains to be anticipated must outweigh the pain inflicted. Thus, if it is possible to use an animal in a test that might result in a cure for a serious disease, then many people would judge that a morally acceptable thing to do. Of course, it would need to be shown that as little suffering as possible was inflicted on the animals concerned. On the other hand, the testing of cosmetics on animals does not yield life-saving benefits. Cosmetics are not essential to life. The use of cosmetics that have been tested on animals is therefore optional, a matter of personal moral choice. One teenager, campaigning for the use of cruelty-free cosmetics, used the slogan 'Make up your mind before you make up your face' to highlight the nature of the choice involved.

Therefore, using a combination of a natural respect for the life of animals and a utilitarian approach to the expected gains from experimentation, the main moral questions about animal experimentation may be set out as:

▶ *Is it necessary to use animals in these tests, or is there some other way to obtain the same information?*
▶ *Are the tests carried out in such a way as to minimize the pain caused?*
▶ *Are the anticipated results of the tests of sufficient importance to justify the suffering involved?*

'Scientist backs animal testing for cosmetics'

A front page article in the *Guardian*, 4 March 2006, described a controversial statement, made in an interview with the newspaper, by Professor Aziz of Oxford, who had previously explained why he needed to use monkeys in his research into Parkinson's Disease. He suggested that it was not wrong to use animal testing in the production of cosmetics, if it could be shown to reduce suffering. Other scientists disagreed with this view, and made a clear distinction between animal testing for research into disease and testing for cosmetics.

The argument on both sides is broadly utilitarian. If the potential benefit to human health outweighs the consideration shown to the animals, then animal testing is acceptable. That might be the case for serious illnesses, but not for cosmetics.

THE RIGHTS AND NEEDS OF ANIMALS

The Australian philosopher Peter Singer is particularly well known for his work on the ethics of our treatment of animals – although he is influential across the whole area of applied ethics. His approach is utilitarian, in other words he wants to consider the happiness or benefit of all concerned. Unlike earlier utilitarians, however, he sees no reason why the argument should be limited to humans. Just because animals cannot express their preferences, it does not follow that the benefit or harm caused to them should not be taken into account in a utilitarian assessment. In his view, any creature that is capable of feeling pain deserves to have its needs taken into consideration.

Insight

Singer argues that, just as we now recognize that sexism and racism are wrong, so we should avoid 'speciesism' – giving privileged or exclusive consideration to the needs or preferences of the human species to the exclusion of all others.

In general, the argument of the animal rights movement – and others who want to consider the welfare of animals without considering themselves to be part of a campaign or movement – is that other species should be considered as worthy of consideration in themselves, and not used as the property of human beings. Hence, for example, some would argue that just as liberty and protection from the threat of cruel treatment is regarded as basic to the rights of a human being, so they should be extended to animals.

Just as, in any preference utilitarian argument, we need to look at the particular situation and needs of the people involved, so we may need to consider what rights are appropriate for each particular species. Part of that may be a consideration of those things that animals seek in order to live and reproduce. An example (given by James Rachels in *Can Ethics Provide Answers?*) is that of a bird building a nest. Clearly, if we watch a bird build a nest and then take that nest away, or deliberately destroy it, we are depriving that bird of something that it needs, and it will have to start building all over again. Similarly, if another bird takes over a nest that is already built, we might tend to see that as unjust. Hence, by looking at the needs of a bird, we might conclude that the right to gain benefit from a nest that it has built would seem to be a fairly clear right. And that amounts to giving property rights to the bird, since the bird has invested effort in taking twigs (nominally the property of nobody and everybody) and investing energy and skill in constructing a property out of them.

Insight

This extends to the bird the argument of John Locke that a person has the right to 'property', which is the product of mixing his or her labour with the things that nature provides.

This is further reflected in the fact that it is illegal to steal and sell rare birds eggs. A species of bird is deemed to have the right to reproduce itself, and that right is taken away if its eggs are stolen.

In this way, one can build up a case for some basic rights, appropriate to the essential needs of each species, the upholding of which will allow that species to survive and have the opportunity to flourish.

Unfortunately for those concerned about animal welfare, there are some today who might still follow the line taken by the eighteenth-century philosopher Immanuel Kant, who said:

> **But so far as animals are concerned, we have no direct duties. Animals are not self-conscious, and they are merely as means to an end. That end is man.**
>
> (from *Lectures on Ethics*, quoted by Rachels in *Can Ethics Provide Answers?*, p. 100)

Insight

That is a classic example of what Singer calls 'speciesism', but it is in line with Kant's moral theory – namely that he wants to consider human beings as autonomous and rational ends in themselves. We have already seen the difficulty of applying Kant's principles in a world where people do not behave rationally. That applies equally to a world in which sentient and sensitive beings happen to belong to other species and are therefore unable to have a rational discussion with us!

International issues

The moral choices people make, and the laws by which they live, generally reflect the overall self-understanding and values of their society. Even when people use a widely accepted and logical argument to justify their ethics (e.g. natural law or utilitarianism) the application of that argument to their particular situation will still reflect on the underlying values they hold. You may seek the greatest happiness for the greatest number, but what counts as happiness of benefit in your eyes will reflect your own situation and society. The more closely defined your group, the clearer can be its moral rules, because people in the group are assumed to have a common outlook on life.

The problem with international ethics is that there is no single global ideology, religion or political system. An international ethic needs to be based, therefore, on those things that can be shown to be good and right for all people in all places and at all times – and that is difficult to establish.

Example

In medieval Christendom, it was considered right to torture heretics in the attempt to get them to turn from their 'erroneous' beliefs back to orthodox Christianity.

From a modern perspective, based on respect for the freedom and integrity of the individual, such torture seems barbaric and utterly wrong. But the torturer would have believed that the immortal soul of the heretic was at stake: if he or she died holding heretical beliefs, the result would be an eternity in hell-fire. A brief period of pain now, even if it led directly to death, would have been seen as a merciful alternative.

A medieval inquisitor, transported through time to a modern society where it is acceptable to hold any or no religious beliefs, would think
(Contd)

Over recent decades, there has been an explosion of information from all parts of the globe. If there is famine, war, or natural disaster, we see it live on our televisions, and have come to expect some international effort in response – 'something must be done'. The problem with such international efforts is the degree to which they are hampered by any prevailing political or social ideologies in the countries concerned. Thus, what may be seen as an international peacekeeping force from one perspective, might be felt to be an unwelcome invasion of foreign troops from another.

Example

From the perspective of the Taliban in Afghanistan, British, American and other forces are effectively invaders, there to support a government that the Taliban do not accept. They see themselves as fighting to establish and maintain a strictly Islamic state. From the perspective of the international community, those same forces are there to stabilize and support a democratic government (however flawed) and to protect the rest of the world from Islamic terrorists who would use Afghanistan and Pakistan as a place to train and hide.

It is difficult to see how there could be a negotiation between these two perspectives, since they come from very different sets of values.

The problem with international issues is that no single moral framework, or line of approach, is likely to be acceptable to all.

Insight

As we saw in the introduction to this book, ethics requires both facts and values. Without the latter, there is no reason why one should accept any moral obligation. The first problem with considering any moral issues in the international arena is to establish a set of basic values to which all can commit themselves.

THE INTERNATIONAL COMMUNITY

There are two ways of approaching the ethical guidelines for international relationships: one considers basic human rights, the other is utilitarian.

The first approach is to start with the basic human rights that should be allowed to every human being, irrespective of the political, social or religious community in which he or she lives.

Examples of this are the United Nations (UN) Universal Declaration on Human Rights, and also the Geneva Convention, which deals with the conduct of war and the treatment of prisoners. Such an approach also recognizes the integrity and national sovereignty of individual countries. For this reason, the UN will operate within a country only if it is invited to do so by those whom it recognizes as the legal government.

A utilitarian approach, however, seeks to take into account the preferences of the maximum number of people. But utilitarianism comes up against two major problems when applied to these global issues:

1 *A person may have conflicting loyalties. I may think of myself as a citizen of a particular region, or of a wider grouping of nations, but I may first of all think of myself as coming from a particular county, or even village. In times of civil war, local loyalties conflict with national ones.*

Examples

During the wars in Bosnia and Kosovo, people of different ethnic groups who had previously lived together peacefully as part of a
(Contd)

village community were suddenly thrust apart, and regarded one another as enemies, each supporting a national rather than a local identity.

▶ Does being a Serb, Croat or Kosovar Albanian count for more than being a member of a particular village?
▶ Is it right to take action against former neighbours who are from a different ethnic, religious or national group, just because the majority of members of your own group demand that you do so?

Another dramatic example of this is Iraq, where the Sunni, Shi'a and Kurds see themselves as distinct, but yet also form a single nation. The fundamental question to ask of an individual looking at the political future, is whether it is possible to think of oneself first and foremost as Iraqi, or whether the first loyalty is to a specific community.

The same problem exists in Nigeria, where the north of the country is mainly Muslim and the south Christian. During the worldwide reaction among the Muslim community to cartoons of the Prophet Muhammad in early 2006, there were clashes and loss of life between Muslims and Christians in Nigeria – thus what starts as one moral issue unlocks the deeper issues of a country divided along religious lines.

Thus it is very difficult to find a consensus as to what most people would prefer, or what could actually be expected to bring the greatest happiness to the greatest number of people.

2 *Without any international standards with regard to what people consider the necessities of life, it is difficult to know how best to share out the world's resources. What might be regarded as living on the poverty line in Northern Europe, might seem like luxury for someone from the more impoverished nations of Africa, for example.*

Nevertheless, most issues of international aid, or warfare, imply a combination of both ethical processes. There is talk of human rights and responsibilities, but there is also a utilitarian attempt to deal fairly and allow each nation or group to express and live by its own preferences.

However, the whole dilemma of the ethics of international relations is that there are few means of enforcing the decisions taken. There is a gap between what may be perceived as right, and what is possible. Whether it is in the field of national sovereignty or of destruction of the environment: argument, economic and political pressure, and exclusion from international bodies, are the only available means of persuasion (and some nations consider that their own internal perceptions and aspirations take priority over those of the international community).

International pressure is brought to bear, however, by the threat to withhold the normal process of international trade in the form of sanctions, or the cutting of international political or financial ties. The problem is that such pressure works in the long term, whereas the issue it is meant to address is immediate.

For reflection

Machiavelli recommended that, if a ruler had to administer punishment, he should do it quickly and efficiently. This would produce least resentment. But sanctions – as a means of enforcing international agreements – produce their results only slowly, and maximize resentment. They affect all those who live in a country, not just its rulers, and may produce a sense of national solidarity. On the other hand, sanctions do not generally involve loss of life.

There seems to be no way in which an international moral code could be translated into enforceable laws without loss of the principle of national sovereignty. The nearest that the UN would appear to come to such a situation is, for example, in the terms imposed on Iraq after the first Gulf War. These include 'no fly' zones over areas of the north and south of the country, seeking to give some protection for the Kurds and the Marsh Arabs respectively. But even so, without military on the ground, it is impossible to prevent persecution of minority groups within a state.

But here there is another dilemma. If you maintain national sovereignty, how do you deal fairly with those groups of people who do not form a nation? An example of this is the Kurds, who are found in Iraq, Iran and Turkey.

For reflection

▶ Is it better for a nation to keep its borders open to receive those who are fleeing persecution in other parts of the world, or to close them in order to preserve the standard of living of its own citizens?
▶ In a democracy, should people be balloted on whether or not to allow citizens from other countries entry permits?
▶ If its own citizens enjoy a far higher standard of living than that of the refugees, are they morally required to take a small cut in their own standards in order that their government can offer a considerably improved standard of living to the refugees?

POVERTY AND INTERNATIONAL AID

In his book *Practical Ethics*, Peter Singer argued that if deliberately allowing people to die is no different (in moral terms) from actually killing them, then we are all guilty of murder, because we allow a situation to continue in which millions of people starve to death. On the other hand, he recognized that cutting one's standard of living to the bare minimum, in order to do all that might be possible to help others to life, would require 'moral heroism' far greater than simply refraining from killing.

A point for reflection

Imagine a situation where people from various developed and developing countries are sitting in a single room, each in the exact situation that would apply in his or her home territory. In one corner people would be naked and starving, in another they would be well clothed and fed.

In such a situation, it would not be too difficult to imagine sharing both food and clothes. Indeed, it would be very difficult not to do so, because the emotional impact of the proximity of poverty and starvation would be intense.

But the single room situation is an unrealistic abstraction. In practice, it is easy to refrain from sharing necessities because:

▶ *No one individual is to blame.*
▶ *Social pressures and expectations are connected with a particular standard of living: to give all that up and accept shared poverty would require great determination. It could also affect others, who might not share your personal commitment to such poverty.*
▶ *Although they can be seen on television, for much of the time the starving are out of sight. Although there is intellectual awareness of their plight, there is no immediate emotional pressure to respond to, in the way that there might be if they were visible and present.*
▶ *When confronted with a particular emotional challenge, a person can take practical steps. For example, many people respond emotionally to appeals on the television: some make a practical response by donating money; a few take on a longer-term commitment, as when Bob Geldof was moved by reports of the starving in Ethiopia in 1984 to found Band Aid, and the Live Aid concerts, in order to raise money and awareness to benefit those who were starving.*

► It is possible to justify inaction by arguing that much poverty is not caused by simple lack of food, but by the political situation. Most areas of starvation are also those hit by military conflict. In the absence of such conflict, it is easier for people to move and get food, or for external agencies to give aid effectively. It is also possible to plan long-term agricultural development if there is peace.

Aid is therefore a complex issue: it cannot be reduced to the single room situation. Some major ethical issues connected with it are:

► How, on a utilitarian basis, do you determine what is an appropriate level of wealth or poverty? (One person aspires to a level of material support that another might fear, thinking it the most abject poverty.)

► How do you give aid, while maintaining the personal integrity and independence of the people who receive that aid? (This is based on the moral principle that sees human autonomy and independence as of primary importance.)

► Does the presence of a factor over which I can have no control (e.g. a civil war in a developing country) be justification for taking no action to alleviate a condition which, in theory, I can control (e.g. by giving a donation to an aid agency to help famine relief, even though that agency realizes that the underlying cause of the famine requires a political solution)?

It depends on what you produce!

The poppy fields of Afghanistan produce a large percentage of the world's opium, and it is the main source of heroin in both Europe and America. Drugs do harm and the money made from drugs funds the Taliban, therefore it would seem to be morally right to destroy the poppy fields. However, doing that will cut off the livelihood of many poor farmers, for whom the poppy is their only crop. Hence there is a dilemma – unless you want to create further suffering, you need to make it possible for alternative crops to sustain the local economy. However, that cannot be done until the opium poppy and the drug trade based on it is removed. But that cannot happen until ... and so on.

International aid charities also face moral dilemmas. They cannot operate without the consent of the governments in power, but that may itself require something of a moral compromise, and runs the danger that their work will be identified with that of the government.

There is also the issue of whether it is right for aid workers to be sent into situations where their own lives are put in danger. Some may volunteer to take on work that is dangerous, but those charities employing them have a duty of care for the welfare of their workers.

Insight

On the international scene, aid is never a simple moral issue. Governments may be highly suspicious that aid is in fact a cover for political influence – and who can blame them, since there has been a long history of colonial powers claiming to bring civilisation to parts of the world that they have subsequently plundered.

Fair trade

If those who live in the developing world are to be allowed to help themselves, they need to receive a fair price for the goods they produce or the food they grow. Apart from ensuring a long-term solution to the problem of poverty, this promotion of fair trade overcomes the stereotype of the charity as being an organization for doling out money to those it deems worthy to receive it. Fairtrade labels now appear on clothing, food, jewellery, flowers and cosmetics. By choosing to buy Fairtrade products, the customer at least knows that he or she is not exploiting those who have produced them.

In an ideal world, trade would be fair and aid would be given without political strings attached. In the real world, there are so many overlapping interests that the moral issues are seldom simple.

> **Insight**
>
> In his book *The Life You Can Save*, Peter Singer makes a clear utilitarian argument for taking radical action to alleviate world poverty. He takes a very challenging position, that most people have more than they need and that, if suffering can be prevented without thereby sacrificing anything morally significant, then it is right to do so.

War and peace

War is the most destructive of all human activities – not just in terms of the loss of life and the damage done to the infrastructure of a country, but in the broader sense that war takes away the basic security that enables civilization to continue, for civilization depends on security and peace. Ethical issues arise whenever peace is threatened by an act of aggression, and, in general, actions are deemed 'just' or 'right' if they aim to re-establish peace and justice. But if a just peace can only be secured by the use or threat of violence, does that make it right?

It is not surprising then that there is an ongoing debate about the ethics of war, and this section will try to outline just a few of the key issues. The debate centres on a number of questions:

▶ *When, if at all, is it right to go to war?*
▶ *Who has the right to declare war? A single nation? The UN?*
▶ *How should wars be fought, if they cannot be avoided?*
▶ *Is any one form of weapon inherently morally better than another?*
▶ *Is the use (or even the possession) of weapons of mass destruction ever justified ethically?*
▶ *How do you distinguish terrorism from warfare?*

▶ *Is it possible to guard against terrorism and warfare without eroding either civil liberties or the right of nations to self-determination?*

And behind these questions are others relating to the relationship between individuals, minority groups and nations, where these give rise to conflicting loyalties. There is also the question of religion, and how that relates to the divisions between or within nations.

THE 'JUST WAR' THEORY

The starting point here is whether, and in what circumstances, a war can be considered just. There are two categories of issues here:

▶ *Those concerned with the right to go to war (jus ad bellum).*
▶ *Those concerned with the way in which a war should be fought (jus in bello).*

The principles for this were set out by Thomas Aquinas in the thirteenth century, but with later developments. A just war approach would argue that:

1 *It may be just to go to war if:*

▶ *It is done by proper authority (e.g. by a nation, not by an individual. Can a terrorist group be a 'proper authority'? And what of 'state-sponsored' terrorism – if the group has the backing of one or more sovereign states, would that make the act a valid act of war?)*
▶ *There is a good reason to go to war (e.g. in self-defence. But does that give a nation the right to a pre-emptive strike against another, for example on the basis of intelligence that suggests the other is in possession of weapons of mass destruction?)*
▶ *The intention of going to war is to establish peace and justice (in other words, war should not become an end in itself, but only a means of restoring justice).*

2 *The conduct of war is considered right only if:*

▶ *It is waged against military personnel, not against civilians. (But is it ever possible to wage war without civilian casualties, either directly or indirectly? Can 'smart weapons', which claim to minimize 'collateral' damage, be seen as more acceptable morally? What about the economic harm and further suffering that civilians face even when the war is over?)*

▶ *The force used is proportional. (In other words, the harm likely to be caused by an action should not outweigh what that action sets out to gain. It is very difficult to judge this, but an example of its failure might be the huge loss of life in some of the battles of the First World War, for a negligible gain.)*

▶ *Minimum force is used in order to achieve one's end (which would preclude the use of all weapons of mass destruction, or excessive conventional force against a lightly defended target).*

Those who go against the accepted norms of warfare may be accused of crimes against humanity if, for example, they deliberately set out to kill civilians. Here the issue is intention; was that killing the accidental consequence of military action or its deliberate aim? In other words, if civilians are killed because a bomb fails to hit its intended military target, does this have the same moral force as the deliberate disregard for civilian life? In weighing up such things, we need to ask if sufficient care was taken by those planning the attack, and so on.

Suicide of war criminal

Milan Babic, a former Croatian Serb leader, was found dead in his cell in the detention unit in The Hague in March 2006; he had apparently hanged himself. He had admitted war crimes from the early 1990s. During his trial in 2004, he admitted that he had taken part in 'the worst kind of persecution of people simply because they were Croats and not Serbs' and added:

'Even when I learnt what had happened, I kept silent. Even worse, I continued in my office, and I became personally responsible for the inhumane treatment of innocent people.

> *These crimes and my participation therein can never be justified. I'm speechless when I have to express the depth of my remorse for what I have done and the effect that my sins have had on the others.'*
>
> Perhaps the most terrible point of moral choice was when he remained silent, and thus became drawn into accepting responsibility for what was going on. Responsibility here is quite different from that of a military commander who, within established conventions, makes decisions as a result of which many are killed. Here it is action outside the conventions of the 'just war'.

In terms of the ethical principles that underlie the conduct of war, there are two basic lines of argument. One is conformity to agreed statements about rights and responsibilities in the conduct of war. An example of this would be the Geneva Conventions about the treatment of those military personnel who are captured in war, prohibiting torture and so on. The other approach is to use a utilitarian assessment – whether it is the overall aim of a war, or the use of a particular weapon, there is a balance between what it is hoped to gain (e.g. ending the war sooner, restoring justice, saving the lives of other military or civilians) against the destruction and loss of life involved.

TERRORISM

In general, acts of terrorism are condemned on a 'just war' theory, even if those carrying them out claim that their cause is just, because:

▶ *They are not backed by legitimate authority. (But should a nation state constitute that authority, or the United Nations? Can a religion constitute valid authority?)*
▶ *They are generally (but not always) aimed at causing civilian casualties as a means of influencing public and political opinion.*

In a war situation, the invading nation has a responsibility to restore peace to the country it invades. Failure to take proper steps to manage the aftermath of war, detracts from any moral validity in conducting that war in the first place. With terrorism, this is simply not possible. The terrorist causes destruction as a political gesture, as an act of anger or defiance. He or she is not in a position to restore the situation to normality after the damage has been done. Hence the normal rules of war are set aside, and it cannot be argued, for example, that minimum force has been used to achieve an aim.

There is a fundamental problem with historical perspectives on this. Yesterday's terrorist may, in retrospect, be seen as a freedom fighter and become an ally. This is particularly significant where terrorism has been limited (or has attempted to limit itself) to attacks on military personnel or other representatives of the state, rather than on the civilian population. Hence, the terrorist of today may see his or her action as an expression of a struggle that will one day vindicate the acts of terror.

Insight

The standard counter to such an argument is that all other methods to restore justice should have been exhausted before resorting to violence, which is seldom the case. However, it is asking a great deal of people who are being oppressed that they should continue indefinitely to press for peaceful means of change.

But even if all other means of bringing about change have been tried and failed, it is still far from clear how you establish a utilitarian justification of violence in terms of its long-term results. The terrorist might claim that his or her action will, in the long run, contribute to an overall justice and will therefore be justified. Others will argue that the intended end result, however just in itself, cannot be used to justify acts that deliberately cause suffering to the innocent.

WEAPONRY

All weapons which by their nature and method of use are likely
to cause civilian casualties, are not a proportionate response to
a threat or do not represent minimum necessary force, may be
deemed wrong. In the extreme case, the use of weapons of mass
destruction (i.e. nuclear, chemical and biological weapons), which
by their nature cause widespread damage and loss of life, cannot
be justified. The only justification for holding such weapons
is deterrence. On the other hand, conventional weapons, used
inappropriately (e.g. the systematic bombing of cities) can have the
same devastating effect as weapons of mass destruction, and can
therefore be condemned on the same basis.

Smart weapons are designed to destroy their pre-selected targets
and minimize collateral damage. The sight of a cruise missile
flying along a street in Baghdad, before turning right to seek out
a particular basement of a government building, is awesome in
its use of technology for warfare. The aim is that, with smart
weapons, a country might be subdued with minimum loss of life.

Insight

Is a smart weapon inherently more moral than one that
kills in a less well targeted way, or that causes more civilian
casualties? Clearly, from a utilitarian standpoint it is, since it
aims to minimise suffering. But that does not imply that the
use of the weapon is right in itself – the situation may be one
in which it is wrong to use any weapon, smart of otherwise.

RELIGION AND WARFARE

Historically, many wars have been fought between nations or
groups that are from different religions, or different branches of
a single religion. Are such religious differences the cause of war, or
are they used as a proxy for deeper social and economic divisions?
Modern examples might include the conflicts and tensions in
the Middle East between Jews and Muslims, in Kashmir between
Muslims and Hindus, in Nigeria between Christians and Muslims,

in Iraq between Sunni and Shi'a Muslims and in Northern Ireland between the Catholic and Protestant communities. Looking further back in history, there were the Crusades and later the Wars of Religion in Europe, following the Reformation.

The just war arguments presented above came from a Western tradition that was largely influenced by Christianity. But Judaism and Islam also have clearly defined principles of self-defence, regulating when it is appropriate, or even necessary, to take up arms.

According to the Talmud, both Jews and non-Jews may kill a pursuer in order to save their own life. It is also permissible to kill an attacker who is threatening the life of another person. But it is obligatory for a Jew to attempt to stop, and if necessary to kill, a person who is trying to kill another Jew. These come from the scriptural principle of the right to self-defence. But it is wrong to kill a person after he or she has committed the act and is allowed only as a way of preventing them from doing so. So, according to Jewish principles here, killing should not be for the purpose of punishment only – it is only permitted in order to seek to prevent further harm.

When it comes to warfare itself, the principle again is one of self-defence. In general the interpretation of the Talmud does not permit warfare for the purpose of territorial expansion and aggression. Warfare should also be restrained. So, for example, in laying siege to a city, one should do so on three sides only, never completely, so that civilians and those who do not wish to fight should be given some means of escape. On the other hand, it is clear that, if Israel or a Jewish population is under threat, there is an obligation to go to war against the aggressor.

In Islam, there is the principle of *jihad*, which may be translated as 'struggle'. It takes two forms: the 'greater jihad' is the spiritual struggle of every Muslim to overcome personal faults, but the 'lesser jihad' is obligation to struggle against external threats to Islam or the community of Muslims.

Valid reasons for performing the lesser jihad are:

▶ *to defend the Ummah (the Community of the Islam) against*
  external threat (e.g. if a Muslim country, or the Muslim
  population within a country, is threatened, jihad against the
  aggressor becomes an obligation)
▶ *to fight on behalf of the oppressed against injustice (whether*
  or not the victims of that injustice are Muslim).

However, there are rules about how jihad should be put into
practice. It should be used only as a last resort, when peaceful
means fail to defend the community, it should be carried out with
compassion, causing minimum suffering to achieve its aim, and it
should seek to establish justice. A Muslim is therefore obliged to
protect both himself or herself and other people against injustice,
but not to initiate violence.

Insight

The key text for this in the *Qur'an* is Sura 2: 190–191. 'Fight
in the way of God against those who fight against you, but
begin not hostilities. Lo! God loves not the aggressor.'

Within both Hinduism and Sikhism there is a tradition of self-
defence, although within Hinduism there is an ancient principle of
ahimsa, refraining from taking life of any sort. This same principle
is found in Buddhism, and particularly in Jainism. Hence, for these
religions, the consequences (*karma*) of taking life are very serious,
and warfare is to be avoided by all means possible. Passive resistance
has been a key feature of the ahimsa approach to perceived injustice.

Gender issues

It may be argued that much traditional thinking has been biased
against women, since most ethical thinkers have been male, and
their values and arguments have been influenced by their gender.
Feminist thinkers are therefore quick to point out that many

views are not reached as a result of rational argument, but are the unquestioned norms of a particular society and culture, norms that frequently disregarded the views, needs and abilities of women.

Feminism arose out of this perceived gender injustice, and to appreciate ethics from a feminist point of view it is therefore useful to reflect on the historical relationship between the sexes and its influences on women's consciousness and moral concerns.

The feminist movement generally traces its origins to the eighteenth century. With the coming of the Industrial Revolution, more men took paid employment away from home, while the women remained at home to bring up the children and became dependent on male earnings. For the previous two centuries men had started to demand more religious freedom and civil rights, but had done so in a way that largely excluded women.

From that period, stimulated by Mary Wollstonecraft's *A Vindication of the Rights of Women* (1792), 'feminists' (to use the term in a broad sense of those concerned with women's rights and gender equality) campaigned for education, for equality in work and for a place in civil and political life. They argued against what they saw as domestic tyranny and unfair treatment, in a world in which the laws, the economic system and socially accepted ways of behaving were devised for the benefit of men.

Insight

By the second half of the twentieth century, the issues had broadened to include an overall critique of the language and culture that reflected male-dominated social structures, along with a new awareness of the value and significance of womanhood and of female sexuality.

One particular criticism of existing moral systems from a feminist perspective, was that they were based on arguments formulated by male philosophers, emphasizing the place of reason rather than intuition or emotional commitment, and therefore biased against women (the earlier view, held by Wollstonecraft and others, was that reason was 'gender neutral'). The 1950s saw the modern development of virtue ethics (see Chapter 7) as one way to get away from 'masculine' discussion of rights and duties, towards a consideration of the qualities that enable people to flourish.

Headteacher decapitated by Taliban

In January 2006, armed men dragged a secondary school headteacher into a courtyard and forced his family to watch as they cut off his head. This took place in Qalat, Afghanistan. And the reason? The school offered education to girls. In the previous months, threatening notices had been pinned to walls in the town, calling for an end to the education of girls. The previous month a teacher in another province had been pulled out of his classroom and shot. Many schools closed altogether, and only 8 per cent of the pupils in those that remained open were girls.

This followed a series of attacks on schools and colleges, of which 165 had been either burnt down or forced to close.

Clearly, there is a fundamental difference in the perception of the place of women in society, between the Taliban militants on the one hand and the Afghan government and the agencies that are attempting to assist it on the other. Those campaigning for the right of women to be treated equally, whatever society they live in, could argue that the very brutality of the attacks illustrates the problem of a male-dominated political and religious ideology.

Although Islamic society tends to treat women differently from men, it is essential to distance the actions of a radical minority from the generally-held views of Islam as a religion and way of life.

This is made more complicated because it is often difficult to determine where religion ends and politics begins: deeply held social and political attitudes (which are themselves not justified by religion) tend to become associated with the religion of those who hold them.

A key question for feminist ethics (as for virtue ethics) concerns essentialism: is there a particular, fixed 'essence' of womanhood? In other words, are there particular features of being a woman that influence her emotions, aspirations and sexuality, or are these things simply created by society and therefore able to be changed by common consent? The overall aim of much feminist thinking was to find structures that would enable women to fulfil themselves as women. Hence feminist ethics has, to some extent, taken the 'personal development' approach, along with an appreciation of distinctively feminine virtues.

Feminist views impinge on many areas of ethics, including business ethics (e.g. the 'glass ceiling' above which few women manage to rise; the inequality of opportunity in the workplace), environmental ethics and sexual ethics.

Insight

Of the ethical theories we have considered, notice that both Kantian ethics (with its emphasis on the autonomy of the individual and the right to be treated as an 'end' rather than a means) and utilitarianism are – at least in theory – gender neutral. That is not to say that all ethical thinkers have maintained such neutrality, but any bias comes from their social assumptions rather than their ethical theories.

DIVORCE

When divorce was introduced into English law in 1670, it was available to men (not women) by an Act of Parliament, and only on the grounds of adultery or life-threatening cruelty. Prior to that, divorce was granted only by the Church courts, and on the basis of non-consummation, impotence or insanity.

When divorce was rare, difficult and expensive, many women (and no doubt some men – although they were generally less socially and economically constrained) were trapped within marriages that did not allow their flourishing, but saw no realistic means of escape. Any gender equality was further hampered by the fact that legal and financial control of the household was in the hands of the husband.

The UK divorce rules, set down in the 1969 Divorce Reform Act, introduced the idea of a 'no fault' divorce, on the basis of mutual consent and two years' separation. The morally significant feature here is that divorce can take place where a marriage relationship has failed, not simply where one or other partner has committed an offence.

With the changing grounds for divorce and the huge increase in the numbers of people divorcing, there has come a very different view of the nature and expectation of marriage.

In the eyes of the Catholic church, for example, a marriage is for life and can be ended only if it can be shown never to have been a valid marriage in the first place. In other words, its validity is based on something deeper than the legal formality of marriage.

For others, the relationship is what counts, and the formalizing of that in terms of marriage is a secondary matter – and one that is determined entirely by social convention. From that perspective, if the relationship has broken down, then divorce is simply the legal acknowledgement of what has already happened. The acceptance of divorce on the grounds of 'the irretrievable breakdown of the marriage', rather than because of some particular 'fault' on the part of one or other of the partners, implies that it is the future (or lack of it) for this particular relationship that constitutes the basis for divorce.

When it comes to the practicalities of divorce – division of property, the proper care of any children of the marriage and provision for the welfare of all concerned – the criteria used shift towards the utilitarian; seeking to minimize pain, if not actually to promote happiness.

Sexual issues

It is a caricature of medieval society to say that the sexual act was often one expressing power and property rather than love, or even straightforward lust. Nevertheless, it is true that for many societies and for much of history the legitimate expression of sexuality has been controlled by social norms, including the stability of family life (requiring sex to be confined to marriage partners), the prohibition of homosexuality, and the use of marriage as a means of forging political, financial or social links between families or even nations. Clearly, in such situations the moral dilemmas are more to do with power and control, with treating other people as ends rather than means, and of the relative importance of society and the individual.

By contrast, the twenty-first century world is one that displays an amazing range of attitudes to sex. What is cheerfully accepted in one society is condemned by another, with a broad consensus condemning sexual exploitation, particularly of the young and vulnerable.

Sexual morality is a topic in which relativism and existentialism have considerable influence – for the quest for meaning in life generally involves understanding one's own sexuality, and when it comes to sex, proclivities and expectations vary enormously, and what seems natural and right to one person may disgust another.

The history and variety of human sexuality need not concern us here, except to point out that, in modern debates about sexuality, there are at least three different ethical approaches.

THE 'NATURAL LAW' APPROACH

This approach, exemplified by the views of the Catholic Church, tends to separate the sexual act itself from general issues of sexuality and sexual orientation, and to regard it as objectively either right or wrong, depending on whether or not it includes the possibility of fulfilling its natural function, the procreation of children. As we argued previously (see page 71), such an approach tends to regard masturbation, homosexuality, oral and anal sex as wrong, simply because they cannot lead to conception.

Sexual orientation, if it does not lead to specific sexual acts, is a different matter. Commenting (in July 1993) on discussions about whether the age of consent for homosexual sex should be lowered, the late Cardinal Hume is reported to have said that, while homosexual acts are 'objectively wrong', they (homosexuals) should not feel guilty about their sexual orientation. The Vatican speaks of homosexuality as a 'disorder', but that should not imply a sinful situation or even a sickness.

Notice an implication of this distinction. A homosexual relationship – in the sense of an emotional attachment between two people of the same sex – is not itself sinful. This means that, if you take personal development and fulfilment as a criterion of morality, then there is nothing wrong with homosexuality. The debate is between those of the 'natural law' view, who see specific acts of homosexual sex as wrong, and those who, examining mainly the relationship and its implications, judge it as they would a heterosexual one – the actual nature of the sexual acts being considered less important than the emotional commitment and affection that they express.

Insight

The difficulty with this natural law position is that it seeks to make a distinction between sexual orientation and its practical expression. You can feel it, but you should not show it. But is personal integrity possible in such circumstances?

UTILITARIANISM

When it comes to the problems of sexual relationship, the agony columns of magazines are full of utilitarian advice, which generally takes the form 'if you do X, the likely consequence will be Y'.

Hence, for example, contraception is recommended in order to avoid unwanted pregnancy, which in turn is presented as a situation likely to lead to unhappiness, either because it ends up with an abortion or through motherhood for someone not ready or able to take on that commitment.

On that basis, wearing condoms is advised, to avoid pregnancy and HIV infection. The fact that it frustrates the natural 'end' of sex in the conception of children is of less consequence. Indeed, for the person asking for advice about their situation, conceiving a child was most unlikely to have been their intended 'end'. Sex may have been all to do with lust, self-esteem, not wanting to be considered prudish, seeking to please or not wanting to be left out. Hence the issue of whether sex is 'right' or 'wrong' depends, for a utilitarian, on a whole range of 'preferences' for those involved.

A typical utilitarian view might be expressed as:

'It's not hurting anyone, and it's what we want, so why shouldn't we?'

Insight

And this follows John Stuart Mill's famous 'harm' principle in his discussion of liberty – see page 43 – avoiding harming others is central to any utilitarian argument.

Let us assume that this view is taken by a teenager, confronted by a parent who realizes that he or she is in a sexual relationship. The parent might argue:

1 *'It's wrong unless you're married.'*
2 *'It will lead to unhappiness because ...'*
3 *'Well, if you're going to have sex anyway, just make sure you use contraception.'*

The first of these is based on an absolute rule, which could be backed up either in terms of a religious or social tradition. Marriage is a contractual and social phenomenon, not a biological one, so it is no good trying to argue the case for sex being restricted to marriage by some form of natural law argument. It can be countered only by opposing the authority on which it is based.

The second is clearly utilitarian, and will probably become the fall-back argument if the first is challenged. The third is equally utilitarian, and illustrates the way in which a utilitarian argument can shift with changing circumstances. While there is a possibility that the young person may be dissuaded from having sex, the utilitarian argument sets out the possible hazards, but once it becomes clear that the option in favour of sex is inevitable, then the next best moral outcome is one that attempts to minimize harm to the people involved.

Insight

It is interesting to note that, although the arguments presented by the parent and the young person may sound very different – the one authoritarian and the other libertarian – they may actually be using very similar utilitarian methods of assessment.

So, for example, in advertising about contraception and the risks of HIV infection, the arguments in favour of taking a 'responsible' approach to sex are utilitarian. The same utilitarian approach surrounds issues of adultery and the break-up of marriages. Very often the crucial factor in the discussion is not the fact of the sexual desire of a married person for someone other than their marriage partner, but on the potential harm this might do to others, and particularly to children of the marriage.

And the utilitarian assessment spreads outwards from the adulterous relationship – to take both the particular people involved, and the more general point about the number of single parent families in society, their dependence on the state for welfare help and so on. In these arguments, the sexual act is not considered from a traditional 'rule-based' point of view, but from one that includes the emotional, social and economic consequences that result.

PERSONAL GROWTH

Increasingly, people claim that they embark on a sexual relationship as part of the quest for personal fulfilment. The ideal relationship is portrayed as one that enables both partners to grow as individuals through their contact with one another. Sex is seen in that context – as a pleasure in itself, but also as a way of becoming intimate with the partner, sharing in a way that has an effect on the relationship as a whole. Unlike those motivated by lust, this approach sees sex as a means to an end, not necessarily an end in itself. If the sex helps to cultivate a good, fulfilling relationship, then it is good.

This approach is increasingly used to justify the establishment or break-up of a relationship. The image of the bored and depressed housewife, whose life is stunted through a relationship that offers her no personal fulfilment, has been the starting point of books and films. Equally, the middle-aged man, sexually attracted to a younger woman, finds that he starts to take new interest in his appearance. By falling helplessly in love, he discards conventional values by which he has lived for years. He also discovers things about himself.

These vignettes are not in themselves the subject matter of ethical debate – although, fleshed out with details, they can become so – but they illustrate the fact that in many spheres of modern Western society, the criterion used for the assessment of sexuality and marriage is that of personal development, and of self-discovery, renewed energy and self-confidence through a fulfilling relationship.

There have been (and still are) societies in which a wife is regarded as the property of her husband. In Britain, until 1882, women had no control over their own property or money once they were married. What does this sort of control and power do to the physical side of sexual relationships? Power, independence, and women's control over their fertility have made sexuality a much more balanced thing, and have allowed personal development within a sexual relationship to be viewed as a realistic expectation.

RAPE

The sexual urge is probably the strongest of all human inclinations, and it is 'natural' – both in the sense that it fits in with what people would do in a natural state, unchecked by laws and social conventions, and because it is experienced as a natural response to a deep biological urge.

Although social customs and laws vary from one country to another, heterosexual intercourse is generally legal, provided that:

▶ *the partners are over the age of consent*
▶ *consent is freely given*
▶ *it does not cause public nuisance (e.g. it should be done in private).*

Rape is the term used for an act of sexual intercourse where consent is not given, or where a partner is below the age at which valid consent can be given (statutory rape). It is the violation of one person by another, as opposed to legal sexual intercourse, which is enjoyed (hopefully) by mutual agreement. But once we start to ask about what is natural, there are many issues to be considered.

▶ *According to natural law, every act of intercourse should be open to the possibility of conception, and should (on a strict interpretation) have that as its 'end'. Does this mean that the forcible act of intercourse imposed by a husband on a wife in order to conceive a child (assuming that the wife does not want to conceive) is therefore right?*
▶ *Is marital rape possible, or does marriage imply acceptance of sexual intercourse under all conditions? Is there a point at which it is 'natural' for one or other partner to refuse to have sex?*

► In the case of the rape of a stranger, it is assumed that the person committing the rape finds the victim sexually attractive. If the person raped actually dresses in a way that is sexually provocative, or behaves in a provocative manner, can he or she be considered to have contributed to that act of rape, by deliberately behaving in a way that invites sexual attention? Is it 'natural' to want to look sexy? If so, can one then argue that it is wrong for a person to respond to that implied sexual invitation?

Date rape

Two students attend a dance and both become drunk. They return at the end of the evening to the girl's room and sexual intercourse takes place. The following day, realizing what has happened, the girl claims that she has been raped.

In defence, her partner argues that they were both drunk at the time, and that the girl was a willing partner in the sexual act, and was not subject in any way to force.

► If there are no strict social rules (e.g. if it is believed that other students in a similar situation would willingly take part in sex), does acceptance of a situation (returning to her room) imply consent?
► Can rape be retrospectively applied to an unwise sexual act?
► How specific does consent have to be? Does it have to include verbal agreement, or can it be intuited?
► 'Date rape' is a feature of social ambiguity. Two people go out together, each expecting something different of the other. Is it reasonable to separate out the act of intercourse (which gives rise to the claim that rape has taken place) from the rest of the social situation?
► Does it make any moral sense, in the case of date rape, to ask about what is 'natural' as opposed to what is agreed by written, verbal or implied contract?

This issue of date rape highlights the difference between 'natural law', what is 'natural' and what is socially acceptable. It is an area where legislation seems most difficult to frame, simply because it is open to the personal interpretation of the parties involved.

Rape, of course, may take place in both heterosexual and homosexual contexts, and between people of similar or very different ages. The key moral question is that of the ability of a sexual partner to give consent. If the partner is too young, or is deliberately drugged or made drunk in order to render him or her unable to withhold consent (or even to be aware of what is happening), then that person has been violated as an individual, quite apart from the physical nature of the sexual act that takes place.

Here the key ethical thinker is Kant – who (in the second form of his categorical imperative) argued that people should always be treated as ends in themselves, never as means to our end. Rape is the deliberate use of another person as the means to own our sexual gratification.

Protection for rape victims?

In Libya, women and girls who have been raped are placed in centres for what may be described as 'social rehabilitation.' Accused of 'brainwashing' by a human rights report, the Libyan government responded by arguing that the report ignored Islamic values and the protection of women who might be in danger of 'honour' killings by their family.
   (Reported by Anne Penketh, *Independent*, 28 February 2006)

One issue to consider here is how you balance an international standard by which human rights might be judged against the expectations of a particular society or religion. When does protection become punishment?

It is curious to reflect that, in common parlance, 'immorality' is often identified with unconventional sexual behaviour. We have seen in this book that moral issues are found in all aspects of life, but sexuality still has an important part to play in a person's overall moral stance, because it is one area of life where physical and emotional needs come into direct conflict with externally imposed rules and social conventions, and decisions about right and wrong feel most immediate.

Some issues in medical ethics

Medical ethics is concerned with the moral principles that govern the work of doctors, nurses and other healthcare professionals. It is of crucial importance for the professions because it guides the framework within which they are able to practice. It also sets the minimum standards required in terms of their dealings with patients.

In general, the guiding principles are utilitarian – in other words, in any course of treatment, the intention must be to maximise the benefit offered to the patient. Where the possible outcome of treatment is uncertain, a patient should be told the potential risks as well as benefits, in order to be able to give their informed consent.

But behind that utilitarian assessment of results, there are other ethical theories that influence what is done. Kant's second form of the categorical imperative – that people should be treated as ends and not as means – is fundamental. After all, it is important that a patient receives what he or she needs, not what a doctor prefers to offer (i.e. the doctor should not use a patient simply as a means of trying out a medical procedure).

There is also a fundamental question of human flourishing and what constitutes a full human life – questions that spring from the natural law and virtue ethics approaches. These are particularly important in matters concerning the beginning and end of life, euthanasia and issues concerning the potential quality of life offered as a result of medical intervention.

Quite apart from these professional ethics, there are moral questions about the way in which research is carried out, and the appropriate use of limited resources within a health service.

In this section we shall look at just two issues – research and organ transplants – and will then, in the following section, move on to the issues of life and death.

RESEARCH

In 1964, the World Medical Association set out principles that were intended to guide doctors who were to be involved with medical research. Two of these principles are definitely utilitarian, as follows.

▶ *That the objectives of the research should be in proportion to the inherent risk to the subject (in other words, the probable results should justify what is being done).*
▶ *Before starting any clinical trial, the risks involved should be assessed in terms of the foreseeable benefits to the subject. In other words, the person taking part in the medical trial should be expected to benefit personally. It would not be acceptable to expect a person to accept a risk just for the sake of some future unspecified gain in medical knowledge, however important that might be held to be.*

Of course, if a healthy person is paid to test out a new drug, he or she will not expect to benefit medically, but the company running the clinical trial would still have a duty of care towards those on whom its product is tested.

During the Second World War, medical experiments were forcibly carried out, under the Nazi regime, on inmates of concentration camps. These were regarded as crimes, because there was no intention to offer the subjects any benefit – they were harmed simply for the sake of gaining medical knowledge.

There are general questions to be asked about the morally acceptable limits of medical and scientific procedures as well as basic research. If such procedures are to be evaluated in terms of potential benefits (i.e. on a utilitarian basis), it is likely to be difficult to specify exactly how much is to be gained, or from which particular experiment.

Insight

Research, by its very nature, deals with what is unknown. One may guess the results, but cannot guarantee them. It makes no more sense to limit medical research to those areas where results can be quantified, than to limit university research grants to those areas that directly benefit the economy! To do so is to shut off the possibility of work that will yield as yet unknown and unexpected future benefits.

In deciding the limits of research or the development of a procedure, a utilitarian assessment is the most likely way to evaluate whether something is morally right. You need to establish the benefits on offer, but in doing so there are a whole range of other questions. For example: would you want (e.g. through genetic engineering) to be able to choose the sex and physical characteristics of your yet unborn child? If so, would you like to live in a world where everyone's characteristics had been selected in that way?

If it were possible, would you be prepared to authorise a brain transplant for someone close to you? Either enabling life to continue with a familiar body but an entirely new set of memories, thoughts and mental characteristics; or maintaining a familiar person with a strange new body? In either case, who would that 'new' person be?

Would you authorize the development and use of a medical technique that could save lives, but would be so expensive that is would starve other medical services of funds?

One controversial area concerns the use of 'spare' embryos (collections of cells that could, in suitable circumstances, develop into a human being, produced over and above what are needed for a course of fertility treatment) for experimentation. The argument against such experimentation is based largely on when human life is considered to begin – and therefore on whether the use of these early embryos is the equivalent of killing human beings. The argument in favour is based on a utilitarian assessment of the potential benefit to be gained from such experimental work.

Insight

Few things in this life are unambiguous. With the best of intentions on the part of those conducting it, research or medical treatment may produce harmful results. The key moral question is to ensure that, when embarking on such work, all known risks are benefits are considered and made known to those involved.

ORGAN TRANSPLANTS

There are two ways in which utilitarian arguments are used in this issue. Let us consider the situation with kidney transplants. Many thousands of people suffer kidney failure in the UK each year, and at any one time a significant number of them are waiting for a kidney transplant. If doctors were allowed to take the kidneys from any healthy person who was killed in an accident, more patients would benefit. This might suggest that there should be an 'opt out' clause for the transplantation of organs, so that doctors could be free to operate on anyone who had died unless he or she carried some identification deliberately forbidding such an operation.

> **Insight**
> At the moment, permission for organ donation has to be obtained from next of kin, often in very difficult and distressing circumstances. Giving consent in such circumstances is itself a morally admirable act, taking thought for the potential benefit to a stranger while in the midst of your own grief.

Issues here include:

▶ *freedom of the individual (to allow or forbid transplantation of organs)*
▶ *whether or not a dead person has rights*
▶ *whether a relative of a recently deceased person is morally justified in refusing to allow transplantation of their organs, given the benefit that can be gained by doing so*
▶ *whether the scale of human medical need should be allowed to overrule other considerations – allowing automatic removal of suitable organs, including those of brain-dead but artificially sustained patients.*

A second moral issue regarding transplantation is quite different. It examines the cost of transplant operations, and compares it with the benefit to the health of people through routine screening and other less costly forms of treatment. A utilitarian might then ask if it is right to give one person a heart transplant, if the money for that operation could have been used to benefit a greater number of people with less dramatic illnesses. This is not the same as the choice between forms of treatment (e.g. between a kidney transplant or maintaining a person on dialysis), but whether the cost of either is justified, given the state of human health globally, following a strictly utilitarian moral line.

Sometimes transplantation involves a living donor; for example, with bone-marrow transplants, the donor is often a close relative. In the case of a relative, or a volunteer discovered as a result of the search for a compatible donor, there is little by way of a moral problem. A person is free to give something for the benefit of another. On the other hand, should you create a person in order for them to become a donor? This rare moral dilemma is a real one.

Example

It was reported in the *Independent* in April 1990 that a woman in the USA had decided to have a second child in order that the baby might provide bone marrow suitable for transplanting into her 17-year-old daughter, who suffered from leukaemia.

This step was taken because a nationwide search had failed to find any compatible donors.

Tests on the mother showed that the then unborn child was a girl, and that she had a 99 per cent chance of being a compatible donor.

▶ Is it right to bring a child into the world with the specific intention of using that life to save another, even that of a close relative?

A strictly utilitarian argument would say that it is, provided that the newly born child did not risk death as a result of giving life. Those whose ethics are closer to the 'natural law' approach might argue that it is a misuse of the process of giving birth to do so only for the secondary reason of saving someone else. On the other hand, you might want to argue that many children are conceived as a result of a failure of contraception – is that more moral than to conceive for a specific purpose? What of the person who conceives a child in order to have an heir to inherit a personal fortune? Is that any more or less manipulative than to conceive in order to use the child for a more immediate life-saving medical process?

In many medical debates, two different forms of ethical argument are set against one another: 'natural law' (or at least a general view of the nature and rights of an individual human being) against 'utilitarianism', representing the results that are anticipated.

Clearly, there is a general moral duty on doctors and other health service employees to treat the sick to the best of their ability. However, when it comes to allocating limited resources, it is a matter of assessing how benefit should be spread across the range of deserving cases. The basis of decisions then becomes a utilitarian one – as competing claims are weighted against each other.

With the increasing cost of new treatments and the growing expectations of patients, who hear about the latest medical developments through the media and think themselves entitled to receive them, there is almost no limit to what could be spent on a health service.

On the other hand, basic hygiene costs little but has a dramatic effect of the health of patients coming into hospital, for example. Basic sanitation has had an even more dramatic effect of the health of whole populations. Given limited resources, how should money best be spent? That is a moral issue far broader than that generally considered under the heading of medical ethics, but it is one that will almost certainly come into increasing prominence in the future.

Insight

Connected with this is the question of whether healthcare should be free at point of need for all, or should be based on insurance or other payments. Is it right to have a two-tier system with some receiving better treatment than others? Strong moral views have been expressed on this matter in the debates in the US, where medical insurance has now been extended to the millions of Americans who were not formally covered.

The beginning and end of life

If ethics is concerned with examining moral issues that relate to the rights and responsibilities of individuals and to the value of human life that are implied by them, it is understandable that all matters related to choosing when life should begin and when it should end, are going to be of particular importance. Ethics is most sharply focused when it is a matter of life or death, whether that is at the beginning or end of the human lifespan.

ARTIFICIAL METHODS OF CONCEPTION

Statistics vary, but around 10 per cent of heterosexual partnerships are naturally infertile. Of these, the woman is infertile in about 85 per cent of cases.

The possibilities for overcoming this are:

▶ *If it is not possible for the couple to conceive through copulation, the male partner's semen may be used for artificial insemination – called AIH (Artificial Insemination – Husband).*
▶ *If the male partner is infertile, the couple could use semen from a donor – called AID (Artificial Insemination – Donor).*
▶ *If the woman cannot produce a viable ovum, this can be supplied by a donor, fertilized using the partner's semen, and then implanted in the womb.*
▶ *Where neither ovum nor semen are viable, both can be donated, brought together and fertilized artificially, and then implanted in the womb. In this case the whole embryo has been donated, with no genetic link with either partner.*
▶ *If either or both sperm and ovum are viable, but the woman cannot go through pregnancy and childbirth, it is possible to arrange surrogacy (womb leasing). Sperm and ovum are brought together – either being donated – and artificially implanted in the womb of the surrogate mother.*

Some issues raised by this:

1 *The last three of these methods have been made possible by in-vitro fertilization (i.e. the natural process of fertilization takes place in an artificial environment, literally 'in glass'). Is the development of this medical technique moral?*
   ▷ *Clearly, this is an artificial way of reproducing what happens (or should happen) naturally – giving nature a helping hand, rather than opposing it. A case can be made for saying that this is therefore natural in itself (just as a wound will heal naturally but more efficiently in a sterile environment). From a utilitarian standpoint, of course, the conception of a child is itself justification for the procedure.*
   ▷ *However, you might argue that, in a world where there are quite enough unwanted children, it is immoral to develop expensive techniques to conceive more. Infertile couples should therefore be encouraged to adopt children instead.*
2 *Where either semen or ovum (or both) has been provided by a donor, should the resulting child ever be given information about that donor or donors?*
   ▷ *What is the basis of human individuality? Is it the genetic link with parents as providers of semen and ovum, or with parents as those who care for a child and bring it up? Is the donor really a parent? You might want to contemplate the difference between a child who is adopted, and who claims the right to find out details of his or her natural parents, and the child who is actually born from the womb of his or her 'mother', but who finds that genetically he or she is linked with one (or two) unknown donors.*
   ▷ *If the donor could be traced, should the child be able to inherit from that donor, or make any other claim? Alternatively, should a donor be able to make any claim on a child born as a result of that donation?*
3 *With surrogacy, this problem has an added complication because the 'natural' mother and the 'parents' are in touch*

with one another, and the situation is reversed – in that it is the donor (or donors) who find themselves bringing up 'their' child.

▷ In the UK, following the 1990 Human Fertilization and Embryology Bill, the 'mother' in such cases is defined as the woman who gives birth, and the 'father' is her husband, provided that he has agreed to the procedure (i.e. the person who donated the semen is not considered to be the legal father of the child, whether that person was an unknown donor or the person commissioning the surrogacy). This means that the couple who want to use a surrogate mother place themselves in the position of donors – once the child is fertilized, the legal 'mother' is the person in whose womb that embryo is lodged. The commissioning couple then have to adopt the child once it is born, although this adoption is not legally enforceable. It is possible for the surrogate mother to change her mind and refuse to hand over the child.

▷ The surrogate mother may be a close relative of the donor couple, or she may be previously unknown to them. She may give her services free, claim only her expenses or (illegally in the UK) receive payment.

▷ The British Medical Association (BMA) published a report on surrogacy in 1990, offering guidelines to doctors. The ethical basis of the recommendations was that all decisions should be made in the best interests of the child. It also advised that surrogacy should be considered only after the failure of all other methods of fertility treatment.

4 The conception of a child is a biological process, part of which may be carried out in an artificially constructed environment. But the birth is also a matter of personal relationships and the emotions associated with them. In a 'natural' context, these two features of human reproduction come together in an act of sex that leads to pregnancy and birth.

▷ The BMA guidelines mentioned above take the basis
of ethical decisions as the welfare of the child to be
conceived – this is a utilitarian argument, based on
expected results. A natural law argument would want to
consider the welfare of the child that is to be born, but
would do so in the context of whether or not the actual
process of conceiving that child was in accordance with
an understanding of what is the natural place of sex and
childbirth in human life. In doing this, it would separate
out the actual technical acts involved with the conception,
and assess each of these rationally.

▷ You might argue, on the basis of natural law, that,
because the sexual act is the natural way in which
fertilization takes place, the attempt to replicate that
process in a clinical environment detracts from the unique
and personal context of natural fertilization. If you take
this line of argument, you might need to accept that
many other medical techniques – from life-saving surgery
to the use of antibiotics – could also be challenged. The
whole basis of medicine is to change the natural course of
disease or to make good a disability. A natural law basis
for ethics could equally claim that this is the product of
human reason, and that the development of medicine is
therefore a natural human function, given the desire to
relieve suffering.

▷ A further ethical line to be considered here might be
the right of the individuals concerned to have certain
experiences in order to further their own personal
development. You might wish to ask at this point whether
'motherhood' or 'fatherhood' is a right that people can
claim on the grounds that they will not be fulfilled as a
person unless they experience it.

▷ In the UK, most treatments for infertility are undertaken
privately, and are quite expensive. Should infertility be
considered an illness, for which there should be free
treatment?

Is infertility a 'disease'?

Commenting on the issues of funding for the National Health Service, Lord Winston suggested that realism was needed about the costs or treatment and who should pay, arguing that patients must eventually be required to contribute to the cost of their treatment. But he also commented on the lack of funding for fertility treatment, arguing that childlessness should be considered a 'disease', and was not presently given the priority it deserved.

(As reported in the *Independent*, 6 January 2006)

▶ If childlessness is a disease, is there a 'norm' to which all people may expect to conform?
▶ Should having small breasts or large feet be considered a disease worthy of treatment?
▶ Should embryo selection be a suitable treatment for those who are 'diseased' by having too many children of one gender when they would have preferred to have a child of the other?

These may be extreme examples, but it does raise the ethical issue about what is normal and what is 'disease' and therefore deserving of treatment.

5   *In the course of in-vitro fertilization, several eggs may be fertilized successfully. If more than one of these is implanted successfully, the result is a multiple birth. There is therefore a limit to the number of fertilized embryos that can be used immediately. The remainder could be frozen to be used later, discarded, or used for research.*

▷   *The embryo has the potential to become a person – indeed, it already has the genetic information that will determine all the characteristics of that human being into which (given the right conditions) it will grow. Should it therefore be treated as a person? Is it right to discard a 'person', or to use him or her for research?*

> ▷ In the normal course of events, only about 60 per cent of embryos actually succeed in establishing themselves in the womb and growing into babies, and in the case of in-vitro fertilization the success rate is much lower. In depriving a 'spare' embryo of implantation, we are not depriving it of a certainty of development, but only of a possibility.
>
> ▷ If the embryo does not become a human being at the point at which it is fertilized (and therefore genetically defined), at what point does this humanization come about? This point is debated especially in the context of abortion, but it applies equally to all issues of fertility and the very early stages of life.

Choosing the sex of a baby

When conception takes place 'in vitro', embryos of both sexes may be produced, and since a selection is taken from these for implantation in the womb, it is possible to select either male or female embryos, or a mixture. It is therefore be possible to choose the sex of the child to be brought to birth.

There is a valid medical reason for selecting embryos by sex (e.g. to prevent the continuation of genetically transmitted diseases – muscular dystrophy, for example, affects only boys). But should it be done to fit the social requirements of the parents, perhaps as a result of cultural pressure to produce male offspring?

The fundamental issue here is whether, at the point at which a child is conceived, that child is to be an end in itself or a means to an end (to use the important distinction set out in Kant's second version of the categorical imperative).

Any child born for some already determined purpose – e.g. to be a male heir – is treated as a means to an end. Only if that child is free to develop equally as male or as female is it treated as an end in itself.

ABORTION

Of all the ethical issues people face today, abortion is probably the one that most clearly illustrates the contrasting bases on which moral judgements are made. The facts are not in doubt, the arguments have been presented time and again, and yet there is no consensus view.

The issue of abortion can be approached logically, pragmatically, or from the standpoint of the personal, physical and emotional needs of the woman who seeks the abortion. It can be seen as an intensely personal issue, or one that is a touchstone for the protection of human rights throughout society. Abortion may be seen on one side as a woman's right, and on the other as the first step towards compulsory euthanasia, selective breeding and wholesale denial of the uniqueness and rights of each human person.

Abortion has frequently been presented, from a feminist standpoint, as an issue of personal choice and freedom. As the growing foetus is essentially still physically part of her, should a pregnant woman not be free to make decisions as to its future? Both abortion and contraception are close to the original agenda of feminism, because childbearing was at the heart of the imposed domesticity of women. Taking charge of one's own fertility was seen as a major step in the direction of freedom and equality.

British law requires that the agreement of two doctors be given for a pregnancy to be terminated. Abortion can be legally permitted if the foetus is seriously defective, if the risk to the health of the mother from having the child is considered greater than the risk of the termination, and if the birth of the child would have a seriously damaging effect on the mother, taking into account the psychological and social situation of the mother and other members of the family.

Abortions can take place (according to British law) up to 24 weeks after conception. However, they can be performed after that if there is a risk that the mother will be permanently injured by continuing with the pregnancy, or if the child is seriously handicapped.

An anti-abortion argument

Both the ancient Greeks and Romans killed weak or deformed babies by exposing them to the elements. This was justified ethically by both Plato and Aristotle, on the grounds that death was to be preferred to a stunted life.

Christianity opposed this, on the grounds that each person had an eternal soul, and was made in the image of God. The decision about when a person should die was to be left to God alone. The crucial question: When does human life start? If the foetus has a 'soul' then it should be protected.

St Augustine thought that the foetus was 'animated' (received its soul) 60 or 80 days after conception. English law originally followed this principle, and distinguished between abortions before and after 'quickening' – the time when a mother might feel the movement of the child within her.

At the moment of conception, when the ovum is fertilized, a unique genetic code is fixed, which will determine the characteristics of the individual. Does this mean that a 'person' should be considered to exist – and therefore protected and given rights – from that moment?

A problem – twins

There are three stages at which the tiny bundle of cells that can become a human being may divide and produce two or more individuals:

- It can happen on about the fourth or fifth day after conception – this is at about the eighth cell division. In this case, each twin will go on to develop its own placenta.
- It can happen around the time when the bundle of cells becomes implanted in the womb. In this scase, the twins will have the same placenta, and may be identical.
- It may happen at about the twelfth or fourteenth day, by which time the resulting twins will have to share the same amniotic sac, and may be joined ('Siamese twins').

The genetic code is established at conception. But at any stage through until about the fourteenth day, one could not say whether that genetic code was going to result in a single or multiple birth. Is it therefore reasonable to say that there is a unique human person before the possibility of twins forming?

There are cases of cells dividing to form twins and then, during this early stage, coming together again to result in a single birth. If each is an individual with rights from the moment of conception, does this mean that the surviving foetus is guilty of murder? Of cannibalism, even, if it has absorbed another human individual into itself?

This situation highlights the problem of taking genetic identity as the unquestioned basis of human individuality.

The problem over the separation of twins does not preclude the idea that from the time of conception there should be respect for (or even human rights given to) an embryo, but it does raise questions about exactly when human identity is established.

In the UK (following the 1990 Human Fertilization and Embryology Act), the age limit for abortions was lowered to 24 weeks (except in exceptional circumstances, where the health of the mother is seriously threatened). In the USA, the Supreme Court decision of 1973 set the time limit for abortions at six months.

The general recognition here is that it is wrong to kill a foetus if it is capable of surviving independently. At this point, it receives the right of protection as a separate human being. The point made by the anti-abortionists is that such right of protection should be extended back to the earliest stages of conception.

It could be argued that many pregnancies are terminated naturally, which might make an abortion an 'elected miscarriage', and that therefore there is no reason why an individual foetus should be protected. But this argument is not logical. Human beings are being killed naturally all the time. If I stab someone through the heart, I cannot plead in my defence that many people suffer sudden cardiac arrest, and that I am simply electing that the person should die in that particular way. To induce a cardiac arrest is an action for which I would be morally responsible. To terminate the life of a foetus is also an action for which moral responsibility should be taken, irrespective of whether or not nature might have done the same thing.

Those who oppose abortion also point out that, once life is devalued at one particular point, then all life is under threat. They may present abortion as a touchstone for assessing issues like involuntary euthanasia, or even eugenics (selective breeding). Once the principle is established that it is legally and morally acceptable to destroy life in one particular case, then life in general is threatened.

The pro-freedom argument

This argument is not presented as pro-abortion, because very few people would actually choose to have an abortion. It is not regarded as a 'good' to be sought, but rather as the lesser of two evils. The argument is about who should decide whether an abortion is to be carried out.

Those who say that a woman should be free to decide whether or not to have an abortion generally do so on two grounds:

> ▶ *That the foetus is essentially part of a woman's body until it is capable of independent life, and that the potential mother*

*therefore has total moral right to do what she wishes with her
potential offspring, simply because, at this stage, the life is
seen as potential, rather than actual.*

▶ *That giving birth to children should be seen in terms of the
overall situation in which a woman finds herself. She should
be free to decide that her own personal development will be
stunted by continuing with the pregnancy, or that the financial
and social circumstances into which the child would be born
would be such, that perhaps the whole family might suffer as
a result.*

In part, this argument is utilitarian – weighing the loss of the
potential life now against the benefits to the mother and others.
In utilitarian terms, those who justify abortion generally use
an **act utilitarian** approach, whereas the anti-abortionists use a
rule utilitarian approach. Even where benefits in this particular
situation appear to go in favour of abortion, a rule utilitarian view
might be that the right to destroy life in one situation threatens life
everywhere, and that the greater good is achieved by giving all life
a chance to develop.

Arguments about abortion may therefore involve all the forms of
ethical justification so far outlined. Natural law is used to protect
the unborn child; utilitarianism in both forms is used to assess the
result of the abortion, personal development and the freedom of an
individual in a 'right to choose' argument.

Because women are so intimately involved with the process
of conception, pregnancy, birth and child-rearing, the ethical
discussion of abortion tends to highlight other issues in terms of
women's rights and their role in society.

EUTHANASIA

The word **euthanasia** means literally 'good death', and it is used in
situations when death is deliberately chosen. Euthanasia is not a
term that applies to situations where death happens by accident
(a person with a painful illness might be killed in a motor

accident), nor where death occurs as the secondary effect of, for example, failed medical treatment.

Euthanasia may be divided into four categories for purposes of ethics.

- **Suicide** *This is self-administered euthanasia. Suicide is not illegal (although it may be considered morally wrong), but helping someone to commit suicide is illegal.*
- **Voluntary euthanasia** *This is carried out at the request of the person who wishes to die when they are not able to commit suicide themselves, or for a person who is no longer able to ask to die but has left instructions that he or she wishes to be helped to die in certain circumstances.*
- **Involuntary euthanasia** *This is when someone is killed in order to prevent more suffering, and when, in spite of being able to ask to die, the person has not actually done so. Like a child's visit to the dentist, it is imposed 'for his or her own good' but possibly against the person's wishes.*
- **Non-voluntary euthanasia** *This is the killing of someone who is not in a position to ask to live or die (e.g. a person in a long-term coma following severe brain damage).*

In practice, you can divide euthanasia into 'active' and 'passive'. **Active euthanasia** involves an action taken to end life, e.g. the giving of a lethal injection. However good the motive, it is 'killing'. **Passive euthanasia** is 'allowing someone to die' by withholding treatment and letting nature take its course.

- *Under British law, a person has the right to refuse treatment as long as he or she is fully competent to make that decision.*
- *If a patient is not in a position to ask for or refuse treatment (e.g. if unconscious) then a doctor can decide to withhold treatment. He or she is not required to consult with the patient's relatives about this, although it is considered good medical practice to do so.*

> If a person dies as the result of treatment being stopped,
> relatives could be in a position to sue the doctor concerned.
> Because of this, a doctor can apply to a court of law to ask for
> a ruling on whether or not to discontinue treatment. The legal
> decision is a safeguard for the doctor.

It is often assumed that passive euthanasia, in the sense of simply
'allowing to die' by withholding treatment, is a less contentious
issue than actively taking steps to end a person's life. However,
some (such as James Rachels, in his book *Can Ethics Provide
Answers?*) have argued that ethically they are not so far apart,
and that if the first is permitted, there is a good case for the second
to be permitted as well. There is another important element
(presented by Rachels), namely that the process of natural death
(once treatment or life support has been removed) might well be
a long drawn-out business, whereas a simple administration of a
lethal drug is more likely to be the quick and painless alternative.
Accepting only passive euthanasia does not therefore represent an
'easy way out' in moral terms.

> In the Netherlands, euthanasia is available, although it is not
> strictly legal. Under guidelines drawn up by the Royal Dutch
> Medical Association, two doctors have to be involved and,
> having helped someone to die, they must inform the Dutch
> equivalent of the Director of Public Prosecutions that they
> have done so. It is accepted that no charges will be brought
> against them.
> In Australia's Northern Territory, 22 carefully worded
> questions, published in 1996 and designed to protect against
> subsequent civil, criminal or disciplinary action, take doctor
> and patient through to the decision about voluntary euthanasia.
> For example, the person requesting euthanasia must be of
> sound mind and must have thought about the implications for
> his or her family.
> In 1967 in the USA, a lawyer called Luis Kutner coined the
> term 'living will' for a document that sets out the conditions
> under which a person wishes to be allowed to die. Since

then, many millions of Americans have drawn up such a will,
and most states have passed laws that protect the rights of
someone who is dying to have his or her wishes followed.
The suggested wording for this was:

If I should have an incurable or irreversible condition that will cause
my death within a relatively short time, and am no longer able
to make decisions regarding my medical treatment, I direct my
attending physician ... to withhold or withdraw treatment that only
prolongs the process of dying and is not necessary to my comfort or
to alleviate pain.

Any justification of suicide and voluntary euthanasia is generally
made on the grounds that death is preferable to the suffering
that would be involved if the person continued to live – in
other words, it is based on expected results (relief from
anticipated pain). This may be related to the pain – physical
or emotional – that the individual suicide may be experiencing,
or it might be the suffering of other people that the suicide
seeks to avoid. For example, a person may sacrifice his or her
life in order to give others a better chance of survival, in a
situation where the means of supporting life are limited.
Equally, a person may be prepared to die in a suicide mission
in order to support a political cause. In these cases, too,
the basis in ethics is the expected results of the action.

Notice, however, that the suicide bomber or other person who
gives his or her life in order to achieve some political goal, is
in a very different situation from anyone contemplating suicide
or seeking euthanasia in the face of a serious illness. The one is
motivated by religious or political ideology – an ideology that takes
precedence over the life of that individual. The other depends on
the assumption that the individual life must be respected, even if
that life becomes intolerable. And such respect can be shown on
both sides of the euthanasia argument, either by allowing a person
to die sooner with dignity, or in offering better palliative care to
allow the final stage of life to be a positive experience.

An examination of the remains of 67 Roman gladiators, found in a cemetery in Turkey, showed that wounded men were carried from the arena and their sufferings ended quickly with a hammer blow to the head.

A traditional Catholic and natural law approach would argue that suicide goes against the idea of humanity as the 'faithful steward' of a life given by God. In other words, by seeking death one is avoiding the natural course of one's life, and the potential for making creative use of whatever happens, even if that involves suffering or personal distress. An exception to this might be the case of a religious person who is prepared to become a martyr, rather than renounce his or her faith. In this case, the law of double effect comes in again – the person does not choose to die but to maintain his or her integrity. The death penalty is a secondary result, not the intended end of that act of defiance.

The Oath of Hippocrates, originating from the fifth century BCE and taken (in one of a number of modern forms) by doctors, requires them to promise 'to give no deadly medicine to anyone if asked, nor suggest any such counsel'. The problem here is that many medical treatments and drugs are 'deadly' if given in sufficient quantity, and there is a balance to be struck, especially in the case of those suffering from terminal illnesses, between giving sufficient drugs to keep them pain free, and actually shortening their lives by doing so. In this case, the ethical principle used is 'the law of double effect' – you are responsible only for the intended result of your action, not for any secondary or unforeseen results. In this case, a doctor may feel justified in increasing the dose of a painkilling drug to the point at which the drug becomes lethal, simply because the alternative is to allow the patient to remain in intolerable pain. The intention is not to kill, simply to remove pain.

In the case of non-voluntary euthanasia, you need to decide when a life begins and when it ends. Is a person who has been in a coma for a number of years actually alive? He or she may have natural functions – breathe, have a heartbeat and some residual brain activity – but is that really what we mean by human life?

Right-to-life boy 'has intolerable existence'

Under that headline, an article in the *Independent*, 7 March 2006, described an application made in the High Court by doctors who argued that a 17-month-old boy was being kept alive by a ventilator, was in 'a wealth of discomfort and pain', and that the machine should therefore be turned off. He was suffering from an incurable degenerative muscle-wasting condition, was almost completely paralysed, but did not appear to be mentally impaired. The parents, however, argued that the boy enjoyed their visits, and that steps should be taken to prolong his life.

This was thought to be the first time that doctors had asked to turn a machine off in the case of someone who is not in a 'persistent vegetative state'. The problem was that nobody knows just how much the child was aware of, since he could not respond.

▶ Does the fact that the child is mentally sound make any difference to the ethical validity of what the doctors or parents want?
▶ Legally, the Court had to decide. But who morally should take ultimate responsibility for what happens – parents, doctors or the Court?

It was ruled that the machinery supporting the child's life should not be switched off. The judge said that, since the child was conscious, and since it had been argued that he could feel pain, it was equally possible that he might feel pleasure, and that he might understand the sights and sounds that his senses were picking up, as any other child of that age. On the other hand, it was accepted that, if the child's condition deteriorated, medics would not be required to resussitate hum. Baby MB died nine months later, in December 2006, aged two.

'Pro-life' campaigns, although generally focused on the issue of abortion, are relevant here. If you argue that human life begins at the moment of conception and ends at the moment of death, and that the person should be treated as a full human individual between those two moments then, whether you are dealing with an unborn child or an unconscious adult, that individual should be protected in exactly the same way as a conscious adult. In this respect abortion and euthanasia are often linked, and the ethical basis for this position is 'natural law' – it is not that the unborn child is going to be happier by being born, nor that the unconscious patient is going to experience benefit by being kept alive: it is simply that, by virtue of being a human individual, one should be allowed to fulfil one's natural life.

Voluntary euthanasia societies generally argue that euthanasia should be allowed if:

▶ *a person is diagnosed by two doctors as suffering from an incurable illness, likely to cause pain, distress, etc., and*
▶ *a person has made a written request for euthanasia (if the situation above should occur), at least 30 days beforehand.*

The moral basis for this position is respect for the human individual and the right of the individual to have his or her wishes followed.

Euthanasia illustrates the ethical division between natural law arguments and those based on **situation ethics**. In situation ethics, a person should do whatever love requires in a particular situation – and that may allow euthanasia, both voluntary and non-voluntary.

Underlying almost all of the points that have been made above, is the basic question of whether human life has an intrinsic value and, if so, how that value is defined: Quantity of life? Quality of life? Integrity of the individual? Contribution of the individual to society?

Helping to die?

In 2009, following a long campaign by Debbie Purdy to know if her husband would be prosecuted if he assisted her to take her own life, five Law Lords agreed that the law was unclear. The Director of Public Prosecutions had agreed to set out guidelines as to when someone should or should not be prosecuted for assisting a suicide, and it became clear that those guidelines would apply to England and Wales as well as those countries (e.g. Switzerland) where assisted suicide is legal.

This means that, although assisting a suicide will (for the immediate future at least) remain illegal in the UK, people will know under what circumstances they may do so without fear of prosecution.

Helping someone you love to die must be the most harrowing thing that anyone can be asked to do, except perhaps to stand by helplessly and see someone continue to suffer. It is the moral choice most hope they will never have to face.

Business ethics

Although since the time of Plato, there has been discussion of the different roles of people within society, and although concepts of justice and equality have economic implications, business ethics is a fairly recent addition to the range of topics covered in ethical debate.

There are various approaches to business ethics:

▶ *From the perspective of the individual, you can explore what constitutes a fair exchange. For example, is a person paid a fair wage for the work he or she is employed to do? Are goods being sold of a quality that the customer expects? Are the terms of a contract just? Is a business arrangement to the benefit of all concerned or does it reflect a fundamental injustice? What are my obligations to my employer? What, as an employer, are my obligations to my employees?*

▶ *At the next level of organization, you can explore the ethical behaviour of corporations. What responsibilities should a company have towards those it employs? How are decisions made within the company, and on what basis? Is the maximizing of profits the sole duty of a company, or should it be balanced by other factors?*

▶ *Then you can ask about the role of business within society as a whole. What are its obligations in terms of the environment, for example? Does a company have a responsibility to the society within which it is set (e.g. the role of multi-national businesses)? What affect on choices and values does free-market capitalism have? Should businesses be controlled by the state or limited in what they can do (e.g. should companies be allowed to achieve a monopoly position, thus controlling their own market)?*

▶ *Finally, there are the most general ethical questions about business and the markets, looking at how the production and distribution of goods, the making and sharing of profits, and the world of market manipulation, actually shapes the general lifestyle and ethical outlook of society. It is one thing to supply something that people need, but what is the morality of deliberately using advertising to persuade people that they want something that they really don't need? This leads to questions about the ethics of advertising – is it legal, decent and honest? Does it attempt to mislead in any way?*

At one extreme, a free-market view might claim that the only responsibility of a company is to make profits for its shareholders. If that company performs some social benefit (e.g. sponsoring a charitable event) it should do so only in order to enhance its public profile, or in some other way improve its standing and performance. The social action is not an end in itself, but only a means to an end.

Recently, however, there has been an increasing sense that corporations have wider responsibilities to those who own them, are employed by them, consume what they produce, live near them or are polluted by them. This wider circle of interest – sometimes referred to as 'stakeholders' – reflects all who are affected in one way or another by what a company does and is reinforced by litigation. It is becoming increasingly common for those who have bought faulty products or whose environment has been adversely affected by a company to take that company to court, seeking damages.

Example

Under American law, employers are liable for sexual harassment in the workplace. In one notable case, a multi-million dollar award was made against a law firm in San Francisco when a secretary who had been taken out to lunch by a senior lawyer accused him of brushing her breast on the pretence of dropping some sweets into the pocket of her blouse!

> Where such litigation is possible, companies have a special interest in maintaining good relationships between staff! One Los Angeles law firm specializing in labour law provides 'love contracts' for companies to use if members of their office staff embark on affairs with one another, to the effect that the relationship is fully consensual. Thus prevents either party from taking subsequent legal action.

The ethical arguments are sometimes utilitarian, weighing up who wins and who loses from a particular line of action; at other times they relate to rights and obligations, particularly in terms of employment law. But underlying many of the issues in business ethics is the second of Kant's ethical principles – that people should be treated as ends in themselves, never as means to some other end. Clearly it is very easy to see employees or customers simply as means to making a greater profit, which, according to Kant's principle, would be wrong. On the other hand, an organization that makes a profit for its shareholders, but at the same time sees its role as providing a service or commodity that is needed, may claim that general welfare is its end, and that the making of profits is the necessary means to bring this end about.

Waiters hit out at bad table manners as restaurants use tips to pay wages

Under this heading, an article in the *Observer*, on 20 December 2009, highlighted the plight of poorly paid waiters who had traditionally relied on tips to make up their income. Previously cash tips had gone straight to the individual waiter, unlike credit card tips, which had been processed through the payroll. Now some restaurants require cash tips to be used towards basic wages. It was claimed that some restaurants contributed far below the national minimum wage, topping up the rest from a fixed service charge added to every bill. Other restaurants claimed to pay 90 per cent of the service charge to staff on top of the minimum wage.

(Contd)

> ▶ Is it morally right to take what amounts to a gift for good
> service and use it as part of a waiter's wages?
> ▶ Is it prudent to run a business in a way that maximises profit at
> the risk of alienating employees?
>
> The first is a genuine moral question; the second is simply a
> matter of weighing up the long-term interests of the company.

WHO IS RESPONSIBLE?

It is a feature of modern society that, when anything goes wrong, someone is assumed to be to blame, even if the problem has been caused by, for example, unpredictable weather or freak trading conditions. If you are in charge of an institution, or the owner of a business, you may well find yourself challenged (by the media, if not by your board or shareholders) to 'consider your position' in the light of what has happened. This raises the following issues.

▶ *Is the chief executive of a company responsible for individual decisions taken by his or her staff?*
▶ *Are you morally responsible for all those things that are done in your name (or in the name of an institution you represent)?*
▶ *If you knew something was wrong, but took no action, you made a moral choice. You may be held responsible – not for the original wrong, but for your own inaction once you knew about it.*
▶ *If you were not told that anything was wrong could you be blamed for not knowing, and therefore not acting? Your responsibility in this case is to be well informed, and if you have not done everything within reason to find out what is happening you might be guilty of negligence.*

In a complex business, many people act together and no single individual may be pinpointed as responsible for what has gone wrong. In these circumstances, blame naturally attaches to those senior executives whose responsibility it was to control and guide what was done by those employed under them. Where there is executive failure, the board or chairman of a company may be blamed for a failure to monitor and control the executive.

Bad score!

Sport is inherently unpredictable; if it were not so, people would not bet on results. So why is it that in the world of football, a manager is blamed – often soon after taking up the post – when the team scores badly? Individual players are seldom sacked for failing to score or for letting in a goal, for the spectators can see the opportunities and threats being played out on the field; at most it is their longer-term career and reputation that suffers or gains.

Two teams face each other on the football field, the supporters of each team assume that someone will be to blame if their team does not win. In ancient Rome, gladiators paid the ultimate price for failure.

In a competitive commercial environment some companies have to fail in order for others to succeed – all cannot have prizes! Should business ethics be judged primarily in terms of commercial success?

In most circumstances the basis for moral blame is the actual or implied contracts that exist between shareholders, directors and executives. If a person is paid to take responsibility, he or she is liable if things go wrong. The question – argued out in many a television interview – is whether it is appropriate for a senior executive or chairman to resign if the causes of the problem of business failure could not reasonably be predicted.

Insight

In most other situations, saying that you couldn't help it, or did not understand the implications of what you did, are

(Contd)

regarded as mitigating against moral blame. In business or finance, where you are paid to fulfil your responsibilities rather than to be good, such arguments are not regarded as a valid excuse.

The competitive nature of economic and financial markets, and the interlocking factors that influence success or failure in business, make it problematic to consider whether (under any of the moral theories we have been considering) it is appropriate to treat success or failure itself as a moral issue. There are many other factors in business that are profoundly moral – treatment of customers and employees, fairness in business dealings, honesty, creating products that offer genuine benefits. Following moral principles and values in these areas may or may not lead to economic success – but following them should not be judged on the basis of success alone.

Insight

Do you run an honest, morally sound business, even if you risk economic failure by doing so? Or do you go for success, and cut a few moral corners (if necessary) on the way? Will people pay more for that organic or sustainably produced product? Will they go for the cheapest flight and not mind the ruthless competition that has made it possible? The balance here lies at the heart of business ethics.

Media issues

It is difficult to live in a developed country and not be influenced by the media, whether newspapers, journals, books, radio, television or the Internet. Both the content and style of what is presented have a profound effect on attitudes and assumptions and influence lifestyle. If it were not so, politicians would be less concerned about their media image and businesses less willing to pay for advertising. In this short section we can do little more than list some of the many ethical issues that are raised.

CONTENT

Facts are seldom allowed to speak for themselves: both in the selection of information put out by the media and in the language chosen and style of presentation used, there is an element of interpretation. Sometimes the particular viewpoint expressed in the evaluation and significance of what is described is obvious – in a party political broadcast, for example. Sometimes both sides of an argument are presented, in an attempt to maintain objectivity and fairness, but more often, the particular bias of a report has to be inferred.

Example

'A wretched law that threatens our free speech'

In its comment column, under this heading, the *Sunday Times* (in December 2009) opposed the use of Britain's libel laws on the part of a drug company to attempt to prevent a scientist from publishing evidence about the side effects of one of their drugs.

There are two separate things to note here:

▶ Because it heads a comment column, it is not wrong for the paper to refer to a law as 'wretched' because such a column sets out to make a particular case on behalf of the editors of the paper. If that same heading had been used within a news section, it might have been deemed to attempt to mislead the reader, by not attempting to present a balanced view of the law.
▶ The comment itself is about the balance between free speech (a key feature of liberty, as presented by J.S. Mill and others), public interest, and the ability of an individual or organization to resist the attempt to spread lies about them. A hostile media needs to be restrained by libel laws, but there may be a genuine public interest at stake.

Ethical issues here include the rights and responsibilities of the media in reporting events. The right to individual privacy, for example, needs to be balanced against the public interest in disclosure. Objectivity and balance in presentation is one ideal, but so is the need to give a genuine and freely admitted interpretation and evaluation of what is described. There is also the possibility of a genuine conflict of interest between government, the public and those who own or control the media.

> ## Insight
>
> In the law regarding purchases, there is a principle of *caveat emptor* (buyer beware) – if you go to buy something, it is your responsibility to make sure it is in good working order, unless it is covered by warrantee. The media needs a principle of *caveat lector* – that the reader/listener/viewer, needs to beware. Most media products come to you for a particular purpose and carrying a particular point of view. Where do you go for your news? BBC? CNN? Russia Today? Al Jazerra? Fox News?

Both David Hume and G.E. Moore argued that you cannot simply move from facts to values. When it comes to the media, the problem is to distinguish factual content from the value-laden packages by which it is delivered.

FREEDOM AND CENSORSHIP

Freedom from political control is regarded as essential if the media are to play a positive role within a democratic system.

If those who control the media are to take as their priority the overall interest of society, then they cannot unquestioningly accept the particular interpretation of events presented by any government, pressure group or individual. On the other hand, there is a danger that commercial media simply reflect the interests of those who own them but who are unaccountable to either government or public.

Censorship and propaganda have always been used as tools of government. Sometimes this has been done for what is perceived as the overall benefit of society (e.g. withholding information that might be of use to an enemy or terrorist group) or to boost morale. At other times it may be imposed in order to frustrate the critical evaluation of government or to silence the voice of opposition. The ethical issue here is to assess the overall public good, and this is generally done on a utilitarian basis.

Needs self-criticism?

In China, all newspapers are controlled by the government, and political criticism is therefore limited. In January 2006, a weekly supplement of the *China Youth Daily* was shut down and its editor was required to write a self-criticism (an admission of faults, commonly required by those condemned during the Cultural Revolution in China) and was told that the supplement would not be published until its ideology had been corrected.

Could censorship be justified in a 'rule utilitarian' argument, on the basis that social cohesion and benefits spring from a positive view of the political order? This would be the case if it could be shown that those publishing the 'offending' material represented only themselves, and did not represent a larger constituency.

It is often pointed out that those who investigate stories in the public interest, or who receive information in confidence, should be free from any compulsion to reveal their sources. Two reasons are generally given for this: that the source might be harmed if his or her identity were revealed, and that future investigations would be hampered if potential informants knew that their identity might become known.

Censorship also applies to material that is regarded as unsuitable for public consumption, on the grounds that its sexual or violent nature may tend to corrupt. There are two ways of approaching this ethically. One is to ask if there are certain things that should be opposed because they are inherently wrong (e.g. pornography showing violent or sexual abuse of children) and cannot be justified on the basis of individual preference. The other is to attempt a utilitarian assessment of the extent to which it is either desirable or possible for the state to police material of a pornographic nature, and whether its prohibition simply drives it underground.

Insight

Has a state any right to impose moral standards on its citizens? If so, on what grounds? The justification usually presented is utilitarian, namely that a democratic government represents what the majority of citizens want. But that argument always needs to be balanced against the benefits of freedom of speech.

The key classical argument when considering all matters of censorship is that given by J.S. Mill in his book *On Liberty* – a key text for anyone studying ethics. He argues that people should always be free to explore and express ideas, on the grounds that censorship does more harm than allowing someone to express their own views, however misguided. He sets out four reasons for not censoring free speech:

▶ *The opinion expressed might actually be true. To deny that is to assume that we are infallible.*
▶ *There may be some truth in a silenced opinion, and since we do not know everything, that contribution might have been useful.*
▶ *It is good to have our views challenged, even if they are right, in order to strengthen them.*
▶ *If views are not challenged, they tend to become dogma to which people subscribe, but without reason or genuine conviction.*

The one limitation he places of free speech is where it may incite a crowd to act with violence. That follows from his general 'harm' principle, but it does bring the whole issue full circle, for many regimes practice censorship precisely in order to maintain stability and prevent violent dissent. The question remains as to when it might be right to use free speech in order to provoke violent action – in other words, where it is judged that the resulting violence is the only (or best) way of overcoming an otherwise intolerable situation.

Insight

Of course, a whole new dimension to this debate arises as a result of the largely censor-free phenomenon of the Internet. On the web, news and views travel beyond national boundaries and beyond the control of governments. Censorship then becomes a matter for Internet Service Providers, in deciding whether a site should be taken down, or on a domestic level by 'parental controls', blocking sites that are considered likely to harm the young. In this new environment, liberty is the norm.

There are, of course, two layers to the moral (and possibly legal) responsibility for censorship of material on the internet. Thus, for example, in December 2009, the BBC was told that is might be legally obliged to censor contributions made by the public to its online discussion of issues raised by the Ugandan government's proposed legislation to make homosexuality a capital offence. Thus there is not only a matter of what one should or should not say (as an individual contributing to a debate), but also of what an organization controlling that website should or should not allow to be said.

IMPACT AND VALUES

Individuals are influenced by the images with which they are presented. If something is shown in a way that makes it appear quite ordinary (e.g. a television drama showing the taking of illicit drugs), there is a temptation to regard such behaviour as normal, even if it is known to be illegal. The content of what is shown in the media may therefore influence the attitudes and values of society as a whole. It could be argued that the media can trivialize important topics, and encourage unthinking acceptance of behaviour that should be a matter of ethical scrutiny.

A visual medium such as video or television requires less imagination than reading a book: what may be hinted at with words may be shown in graphic detail on the screen. It may be argued that this desensitizes people to the true significance of what they witness. On the other hand, it is widely believed that, since the Vietnam War, television has had a significant impact on the public perception of the gruesome reality of warfare.

Moral issues arise because of the values we hold. Facts alone do not make an ethical argument, and without values by which to judge actions good or bad, there would be no starting point for morality. But, by and large, we do not invent our own values, we inherit them from the society into which we are born, and those values are shaped by – among other things – the impact of the media. Hence, even if we set aside the moral issues that are considered by the media, or the ethical issues that guide the way in which they operate, it is clear that the media have a profound influence on the general moral sensitivity and values of society.

Insight

In other words, quite apart from the content, ownership and censorship of the media, the impact of the media on society and individuals is also ethically significant. It shapes what we see as the good life, or as acceptable behaviour and thereby influences our moral choices.

ADVERTISING

The Advertising Standards Authority receives complaints from members of the public who consider that an advertisement is not honest or legal, or if it offends in some way. The ethical issues concern whether an advertisement defrauds in some way, by promising something that the product cannot deliver, for example, or whether it is sexist, racist or in some other way contravenes accepted norms.

Of course, those who devise adverts try to catch people's attention by the images they use, and these images suggest more than can be said about the product in words – but are the images relevant to the product? One magnificent image was of a bronzed man lounging back in the stern of a sleek powerboat, slicing through blue water; everything to suggest a desirable life (or man, depending on your gender or proclivity). On closer inspection he is seen to be holding a bottle of water, label turned towards the camera. That label is reproduced in the corner of the photograph, with the words 'Serving suggestion'! Nothing illegal in that advert – but it suggests rather more than water is likely to offer you! But when does a hint or a suggested advantage become a deception? Perhaps it is all a matter of taste, of irony and of humour.

Fashion chain's TV fight takes a battering

An article on 25 February 2006 by Susie Mesure, Retail Correspondent for the *Independent*, outlined complaints made to the Advertising Standards Authority about the French Connection retail chain's television advertising campaign, which featured two women fighting, getting soaked with water and finally kissing. The sexual content of the advert is obvious, as is the modest amount of violence. In its defence, the fight was meant to symbolize a quote from the designer Yves Saint Laurent, who said 'Fashion fades, style is eternal' – so fashion and style, in the form of two women, battle it out. The subtlety and cultural reference is probably missed by most viewers, who – recalling French Connection UK's earlier, debatably dyslexic campaign – think, FCUK that!

COPYRIGHT

It is increasingly recognized that business is not just about physical goods and services. Intellectual property is equally important, whether it is the value in a song that is written, a computer game that is devised, a film, book, magazine or design. The value of these things goes beyond the physical object that you can buy, or the track or file that you can download. Hence the debates about copyright and intellectual property – which can be considered equally under the headings of **business ethics** and **media ethics.**

If things that are expensive to create in the first place are copied and shared for nothing, then the whole economic base that allowed them to be created will gradually be eroded. Things only get produced if someone pays for them, or if there is money to be made from them subsequently in some way. Selling books, CDs, software and so on is a way of paying back the cost of production and making a profit on the business.

Dan Brown stars in High Court tale of treachery and intrigue

In 2006, Dan Brown, author of the best-selling book *The Da Vinci Code*, was taken to court by the authors of *The Holy Blood and the Holy Grail*, published in 1982, for allegedly using the theory set out in their book as the basis for his novel.

In doing so, they raised an interesting intellectual property dilemma. Facts themselves are not copyright, so you can always quote a fact, no matter where you have first come across it. But a fictional narrative, or the actual words used to describe facts, remain the intellectual property of the author, and anyone wanting to quote them needs to get permission, and make clear the original source of that material.

The dilemma was this…

If the earlier book was a work of fiction, then its copyright could be protected. On the other hand, in order to be convincing, it had

Today, it is all too easy to make illegal copies of copyright material and, because it is easy, people assume that it does not matter. Why pay for something when it is freely available on the web? However, a basic utilitarian assessment of the ethics of copyright piracy shows that it cannot be in anyone's long-term interest. Arguments about theft, from whichever ethical perspective, apply equally to copyright theft in whatever medium.

In response to piracy, copyright owners, can seek to protect their intellectual property in three ways:

▶ *by taking legal action against those who infringe copyright*
▶ *by devising technical means of preventing illegal copying (e.g. software that will not work if installed more than an agreed number of times)*
▶ *by creating licensing schemes to allow people, for a reasonable payment, to make copies, where a copy or download is preferred to buying the physical goods themselves (e.g. downloading tracks for a fee, as an alternative to illegal file sharing).*

Following this last route, it is recognized that schools and colleges, for example, will need to make copies of printed material for students to use for their courses, or to put texts up on a college intranet or 'virtual learning environment' (VLE). Through getting a licence, such copying becomes legal, and a small payment goes to the publisher and author for each copy that is made.

Insight

Portions of this present book (but not the whole book) may be copied under licence, and although the author and

(Contd)

publisher receive rather less than if every student bought their own copy, it provides some compensation for this very convenient way of sharing information by photocopying, or scanning and posting material on a VLE.

Music, software, books, magazines, website material – there is a huge amount of intellectual property out there to be discovered and used, much of it not yet protected against illegal exploitation. Yet it has value, just as much as the physical objects that you might find within a home or workplace.

The problem lies in the ease with which material may be copied and used. You may not be prepared to break into a store and steal a book or CD, but what if you can get it simply by sitting at home and clicking a mouse? It does not change the nature of the act of theft, but it changes the ease with which you can steal and the range of goods that can be stolen, while at the same time appearing to minimize the chances of getting caught.

Now that is what creates a real moral dilemma...

THINGS TO REMEMBER

From this chapter, remember that ...

▶ *the best way to assess ethical theories is to apply them to real-life situations and see whether they deliver results that are acceptable*

▶ *environmental ethics may therefore consider the well-being of other species, not just humankind*

▶ *Peter Singer and others argue that being able to feel pain gives a creature the right for its welfare to be taken into consideration*

▶ *there is a fundamental problem with enforcement of global principles where nations remain autonomous*

▶ *the 'just war' theory sets out the basic criteria that justify going to war and for the conduct of war to be considered morally just*

▶ *terrorism lacks proper authority, and generally targets civilians, so it cannot be considered morally justified on the traditional 'just war' arguments*

▶ *medical ethics focus on the right of a patient to be treated as an autonomous human being (an 'end' not a 'means')*

▶ *questions of life and death may be discussed on a utilitarian basis (overall benefit/harm) or on the basis of natural law (it being unnatural to end life artificially)*

▶ *business ethics considers whether companies have responsibilities other than those to their shareholders and to make a profit*

▶ *media ethics and intellectual property issues are both global and challenging for existing ethical theories.*

Some conclusions

This book has attempted to present a general introduction to the major ethical theories, showing some of the strengths and weaknesses of each in turn, with examples of how they may be applied. Now, by way of conclusion, I want to draw together some of the key points and to give my own comments and evaluation.

The introduction was called 'The art of living'. This was intended to emphasize that the process of making moral choices, and the task of reflecting on the possible justification for them, is a creative and personal activity. Sometimes, when immersed in the details of a utilitarian argument, trying to assess consequences in a detached way, one can lose sight of this feature of moral choice. No matter how clearly the predicted results of an action are presented, people make their own decisions, often in what appears to be an irrational manner. They are responding to things that they value, memories of past actions, past hurts perhaps. They feel compelled by impulses, both conscious and unconscious, to do what they feel they must do. They are sometimes prepared to accept painful consequences, even admit that they are foolish – and yet the choice is made. The actual process of moral choice is by no means simple, and ethics (if it is to be not only a comment on how moral choices are actually made, but also a guide to how moral choices should be made, which is the implication of most ethical arguments) needs to reflect this.

Ethics – moral philosophy – is a rational activity. It studies moral choices, explores their implications and looks at how they may be justified. And therein lies its inherent weakness. Ethics tends to assume, just because it is a rational discipline, that a single theory may be found to explain the nature of moral thinking and give an overall view of life by which moral claims may be assessed. Its ideal is to find a definition of good and bad that will transcend individual preferences, and command universal acceptance. That is fine in theory, and yet it does not reflect the complexity of moral choice.

The problem was made more complicated by the narrow definition of meaning that dominated philosophy in the earlier part of the twentieth century. If a meaning of a statement is given only with reference to what can be empirically verified, or to the definitions of words, then there is little scope for the sort of creativity that is found in moral language. We saw in Chapter 3 how ethical thinkers have met this challenge and have come to recognize the variety of ways in which moral language is used – giving commands, registering preferences, expressing emotions.

Insight

Making moral choices is too fluid and complex an activity to be confined to a language appropriate to science rather than art. No wonder the logical positivists found it meaningless!

In the chapter on 'natural law', we saw how rational consideration of the final end and purpose of an object or an activity could be used as a touchstone for whether it was being used or abused: it is designed and intended for one 'right' purpose, and anything else is deemed to be wrong.

Insight

Natural law is clear cut, straightforward. It is a 'clean' theory, attempting to cut through the messiness of human experience. But it is also abstract, cerebral and linked to a philosophy that no longer commands universal acceptance.

When we moved on to utilitarianism, the argument was very different, but the impulse to systematize and quantify remained. The same drive that sought a rational explanation of final causes within the world now struggled with a definitive balance of happiness offered to the maximum number of people. But, again, this rational approach became more complicated because it needed to ask about what constituted happiness, and whether the gains should be immediate or long term, confined to the act or the general rule or the preferences to those involved. It became a quest for results – a quest which, as one event leads on to another, can never be completed.

Common sense tends to go along with utilitarianism: avoiding suffering and giving happiness are, after all, (on an emotional as well as a rational level) deeply embedded in human experience. And yet utilitarianism, in itself, does not seem to be enough. There are so many situations in the world – from the horrors of civil war, to the tragedy of drug abuse – for which, from a logical and utilitarian point of view, there can be no possible justification. Why do those involved not see it? Why do they not stop their spiral of violence and death? Why cannot they accept a utilitarian judgement on their actions, when all the evidence about the consequences of what they do is plain for all to see?

The answer to these questions is that choices are not always rational, and that sometimes they are made in the face of known consequences. The expected results of an action inform, but cannot define, a moral choice – they form part of a moral quandary; factors need to be weighed, and yet the weighing is not the whole of the experience of choice. To describe someone as 'cold and calculating' or 'hard headed' implies a narrow view of human choices and moral responsibility. Yet the most serious and socially committed utilitarian is still struggling in the grip of a calculation that may prove too challenging – as when one is expected to be absolutely even-handed in choosing to help either a stranger or a close relative, or to make massive changes in one's own situation in order to sustain a planet of limited resources.

Insight

The utilitarian approach accords with common sense and offers a rational and challenging ethics by which to live, and yet the feeling remains that there is more to the art of living than simply assessing results and acting accordingly. Utilitarianism sometimes seems just too neat or too unrealistic.

But what is this elusive 'more' that transforms an action based on calculated results into an act of creative living, of self-affirmation, of agonizing importance for the individual concerned? Kant approached this 'more' by seeing it as a categorical imperative – as something absolute, not depending on results. We might appear to be conditioned, but we experience ourselves as free. We might not know what the results of our action will be, yet we feel compelled to do it anyway.

Yet Kant offers the most generalized and theoretical of all frameworks for moral choice: that I should will that the maxim of my action become a universal law. Wanting everyone else to be free to make their decision according to the same principles that I choose to apply makes perfect sense. If I want to do something, I should allow everyone else to have that same choice. I should also make my decision as though I were legislating for a kingdom within which everyone is a free and autonomous agent. Yet I know that my choice is not, in actual fact, going to be enacted as a universal law, and that I am not legislating for others – and this remains in the back of my mind, even if I try to consider the implications of making it so. At the end of the day, I go ahead and make my choice as a unique individual.

Insight

Universalizing every moral principle, and acting only on those that can be universalized, is likely to produce a lowest common denominator of moral thinking – giving form but not content to what is considered right or wrong. It is hardly the stuff of which 'the art of living' is made.

Yet alongside this, Kant's second form of the categorical imperative – that everyone should be treated as ends and not only as means – touches another deeply held sense of what is right. Like the presupposition of utilitarianism, that we want to share benefit with all concerned, it touches the common sense base of moral discussion.

We looked at morality from the standpoint of personal development. And here there came a perspective that was closest to the idea of 'the art of living', for here was moral choice being used and justified in terms of its function of creating and expressing the human will.

There was another aspect to personal development, not based on
selfishness but on a consideration of those qualities or virtues that
make for human flourishing. Virtue ethics attempts to answer
the more fundamental question about what human nature is
about, and what it means to live well – questions which were also
explored earlier in connection with 'natural law'. And following
this we touched on existentialism, the philosophy that emphasizes
human freedom and responsibility in shaping the future.

We then moved on to explore the social and legal perspective
on morality, and then on the global or universal issues and the
special problems they raised. We do, of course, recognize that we
make agreements and take on responsibilities, and that is always
a feature of ethics – especially when considering the ethics of the
medical, legal and other professions.

Then we looked at the ways in which the world religions formulated
their values and moral principles. Without being able to explore
exactly what each religion would say about each moral issue, it was
at least clear that some worked on the basis of detailed legislation,
others on general rules, flexible social requirements, or on whether

an action was skilful in leading to spiritual development. The religions provide a wide measure of consensus on the general values that enhance human life, and each provided its own form of 'the art of living'.

And, in the light of all these ethical theories, we looked at two challenges to moral debate – scepticism and relativism – and noted how these have tended to undermine traditional ethical arguments, while recognizing that, in a multi-cultural, multi-faith world which includes such a wide range of philosophical and political views, consensus in ethics is unlikely.

Finally, we looked at a small selection of the many areas today for which there is an obvious need for ethical exploration and guidance, exploring briefly how the various moral theories set about framing moral guidelines to deal with them.

But does any of that actually help to improve ourselves and our world?

Moral progress: illusion or necessary hope?

We live in a world of change; everything evolves, nothing is fixed. Whether we look at the evolution of species or the changes happening in society, we try to make sense of change as though it were a story, and ask about the ending. Faced with change or development we tend to ask 'Where is it going?' Progress – as opposed to random or circular change – implies a direction and an end point.

History is always a story told from a particular perspective; facts in themselves do not make history. In the same way, descriptive ethics – the catalogue of who does what in what society and during what era – does not touch on the fundamental issues of normative ethics. It does not ask if society is 'better' now than in Greek, Roman or Medieval times. We may not burn witches, but do we still torture? Is the freedom to be openly homosexual a return to the enlightened times of the Greek city state, recovering from a temporary period of unfair repression? Is there a new world order emerging, or is universal communication merely giving the opportunity for people to exploit more widely?

> **Insight**
> If facts alone cannot make a normative moral argument, then facts alone cannot prove that there is moral progress.

Hence, any attempt to prove moral progress will hit the same problem that utilitarianism finds – that there is no end point at which all the evidence is in and we can make a definitive judgement. At that level, moral progress remains an illusion, never unambiguously proved or demonstrated.

And yet … If there were no sense of progress, of trying to improve a situation or cultivate a virtue, would the sense of right and wrong continue? Is having a conscience compatible with an absence of hope or any sense of what a better life could be?

> **Insight**
> The art of living as a human being involves thinking, creating, hoping, willing; it is always oriented towards the future. We may look back, but we live forwards.

Without any hope that morality makes sense, the very experience of morality becomes nonsense. In this sense, moral progress is a necessary hope – for without it, the rest of moral discussion loses its significance. There may be no evidence whatsoever that things are improving. But in the face of that bleakness, the moral impulse is to want to make it so – to construct a life according to our intuitions of what is right.

Progress is therefore a bit like freedom; analyse it empirically and it vanishes. I am utterly determined by events beyond my control, and yet I sense that I am free to choose what to do. **In the same way, I have no evidence of progress, but the experience of morality is of constructing a better situation and therefore of willing progress.**

So where does this leave us?

The moral choices people make are based on many things, but they are rooted in an understanding of the nature of the world, and the values that arise from that understanding. For some people this is well thought out and rational; for others it is provided by a religion and accepted ready made; others act instinctively, their understanding and valuation of the world working through their unconscious.

In the broadest sense, this is metaphysics: the quest to understand the meaning and value of the world as a whole. This is the process that lay behind the 'natural law' arguments, but it can be broader than the world view of Aristotle on which that theory was based.

The moment of moral choice is therefore informed by the way in which we generally understand and value life. Iris Murdoch expressed it in this way:

> *We act rightly 'When the time comes' not out of strength of will but out of a quality of our usual attachments and with the kind of energy and discernment which we have available. And to this the whole activity of our consciousness is relevant.*
>
> (Iris Murdoch, *The Sovereignty of Good*, 1970, p. 53)

To ask 'What should I do?' implies the question 'What is life for?' Life is constantly changing; nothing, not even our galaxy, remains fixed. We can try to run from this truth – craving absolutes that will justify our decisions for all time – but it is an illusion. Constant change is a reality, and it affects not just the world around us, but ourselves. We are not fixed as individuals, our minds shape the future; the choices we make today define the sort of people we become tomorrow.

We also have to accept that life, however much we shape it to suit our own ends, involves suffering and death. We can work to minimize suffering and promote happiness, but we cannot remove the fact that humans are limited and fragile creatures. Fallibility and failure are not just accidental features of life that should be quickly removed and forgotten; they are a feature of living in this sort of world, in which human aspirations outstrip human abilities.

Every choice we make is informed by many things – hopes, fears, the things we value and the understanding of life that we have gathered through education, the influence of others and personal experience. Whether we recognize this consciously or not, the act of making a moral choice sums up all that we have become.

Insight
This is why I sense that virtue ethics and existentialism, between them, hold the key to the future of moral thinking – since they add a personal dimension and impetus to the calculations and moral justifications offered by other ethical theories.

The relationship between ethical arguments and the moral life is rather like that between literary theory and the creative writer, or between musical theory and the act of composition. Writer and composer use all their feelings, intuitions, values and insights to produce a work of art that is unique. Later, the theorists and critics may analyse it, place it in within categories or the development of a particular style, or reveal likely influences.

Ethics is rather like that. It analyses moral choices and devises theories to show how they may be justified. It is a valuable process, a useful guide for future action, but it can never fully explain or adequately legislate for the process of creative living.

Taking it further

Further reading

Written particularly for students at A level, the following titles in the Access to Philosophy series (Hodder & Stoughton) give a broad introduction to aspects of ethics:

Thompson, Mel, *An Introduction to Philosophy and Ethics* (2nd edition, 2008)
Thompson, Mel, *Ethical Theory* (3rd edition, 2008)
Walker, Joe, *Environmental Ethics* (2000)
Wilcockson, Michael, *Sex and Relationships* (2000)
Wilcockson, Michael, *Issues of Life and Death* (2nd edition, 2008)
Wilcockson, Michael, *Medical Ethics* (2008)
Wilcockson, Michael, *Social Ethics* (2009)

Many of the classical texts mentioned in this book are available in paperback (see particularly the Penguin Classics series; of the more popular, there are several other versions). See for example:

Plato, *The Republic*
Aristotle, *The Nicomachean Ethics*
Machiavelli, Niccolò, *The Prince*
Hobbes, Thomas, *Leviathan*
Hume, David, *A Treatise on Human Nature*
Bentham, Jeremy, *An Introduction to the Principles of Morals and Legislation*
Kant, Immanuel, *Fundamental Principles in the Metaphysics of Morals* and *The Critique of Practical Reason*
Mill, J.S., *Utilitarianism* and *On Liberty*
Nietzsche, Friedrich, *Thus Spoke Zarathustra* and *Beyond Good and Evil*

Moore, G.E., *Principia Ethica*

For those wanting a short introduction to a number of classical texts, including those relevant to a study of ethics, see *Philosophy: the Classics* by Nigel Warburton (2nd edition, Routledge, 2001).

A Companion to Ethics (Blackwell, 1993) edited by Peter Singer, remains one of the best general introductions to the subject, covering both ethical theories and their application along with articles giving a broad range of perspectives on ethics. There is also a section on 'Right and Wrong' in Nigel Warburton's *Philosophy: Basic Readings* (2nd edition, Routledge, 2005).

For an Eastern perspective on ethics
Thompson, Mel, *Teach Yourself Eastern Philosophy* (Hodder Headline, 2003)

Thompson, Mel and Appelbaum, D. (eds), *World Philosophy* (Vega, 2002)

Other useful books include
Mackie, J.L., *Ethics: inventing right and wrong* (Penguin, 1990)

Murdoch, Iris, *Metaphysics as a Guide to Morals* (OUP, 1992)

Sandel, Michael, *Justice* (Allan Land 2009)

Singer, Peter *The Life You Can Save: Acting Now to End World Poverty* (Picador, 2009)

Singer, Peter, *Practical Ethics* (Cambridge, 1996)

Sterba, J.P. (ed.), *Ethics: the big questions* (Blackwell, 1998)

Rachels, James, *Can Ethics Provide Answers? and other Essays in Moral Philosophy* (Rowan and Littlefield, 1997)

Warnock, Mary, *An Intelligent Person's Guide to Ethics* (Duckworth, 1998)

Alternatively, search for 'Ethics' on the Amazon website and browse more than 67,000 results. Top of the list comes *A Very Short Introduction to Ethics* by Simon Blackburn (whose little book *Being Good* is also popular), along with Peter Vardy's *The Puzzle of Ethics*. Peter Singer rightly features prominently in the lists, as do classic texts, social work ethics, business ethics and a host of other titles. There is no doubt that publications on ethical issues, like the issues themselves, are alive and kicking!

Websites

There are a huge number of sites covering all aspects of ethics – from academic departments offering notes on ethical theories, to single-issue campaign groups. Searching for 'ethics' via an internet search engine is likely to produce literally millions of sites, but the search can easily by narrowed by specifying particular issues, terms or theories.

The web is constantly changing, but – at the time of writing – the following are just a few of the sites you might find useful in following up issues discussed in this book:

www.bbc.co.uk/ethics/index.shtml gives a summary of a whole range of issues and arguments, and is very clearly set out. This is a useful resource for students wanting a concise summary on a topic.

For a huge, authoritative encyclopedia of philosophy: http://plato.stanford.edu/contents.html. But be aware that keying 'ethics' alone into the search engine on this site is going to produce a vast collection of references. Home in on what you want and be aware of alternative terms – e.g. for 'utilitarianism' the direct reference in the index may be 'consequentialism'.

Easier to use is www.iep.utm.edu/ the website for the Internet Encyclopedia of Philosophy. Key 'Ethics' into the search box and you will find a huge range of articles.

For a whole range of short essays on ethics, clearly written, try www.moralmoments.com, the website of Joel Marks, the Professor Emeritus of Philosophy, University of New Haven

For information on my other books on philosophy and ethics, or other useful websites, to see additional material of interest to students and teachers, or to contact me with your views, suggestions or questions, log on to: www.philosophyandethics.com

Glossary

a posteriori Used of an argument that depends on sense experience.

a priori Used of an argument that arises prior to, or is not based on, a consideration of evidence from sense experience.

absolutist Used of moral arguments that suggest that it is possible, in theory, to find moral principles that can be applied universally.

agapeism Moral theory based on the application of love to each situation.

ahimsa The principle of non-violence; used in Jain, Buddhist and Hindu philosophy.

altruism The unselfish consideration of others.

amoral An action that, with respect to the person who performs it, is done without reference to any moral system.

axiological ethics The study of the values that give rise to moral choices, and on which those choices are based.

cardinal virtues Prudence, justice, fortitude and temperance; Stoic principles of the moral life, found in Plato and Aristotle and used also by Aquinas.

categorical imperative Used particularly by Kant, this refers to a sense of absolute moral obligation (compare with 'hypothetical imperative'). In Kant, it takes two particular forms: that an action is right only if it is possible for the person acting to be prepared to accept the basis of that action as a universal law; that persons should be treated as ends, and not simply as means.

consequentialist ethics Ethical theories based on results (e.g. utilitarianism).

deontological questions Questions about a person's rights and duties.

descriptive ethics This term refers to the description of the social behaviour that may raise ethical issues.

determinism Philosophical view to the effect that every act is totally conditional and therefore that agents are not free.

Dharma This is a Sanskrit word used for 'reality' or 'truth', in the sense of the way in which the world is organized. It is used in both Hindu and Buddhist ethics. For Hindus it means right or appropriate action or duty (i.e. duty that is in line with fundamental reality); for Buddhists it refers to the teaching of the Buddha.

double effect, the law of The principle that an action may be considered right, even if a secondary effect of that action is harmful, or could be considered wrong.

egoism Theories that place the human ego as of primary concern.

emotivism The ethical theory that moral assertions are in fact the expression of emotions, i.e. to say something is wrong means that you dislike it.

Existentialism A philosophy based on the recognition of freedom and responsibility for giving meaning and direction to human life

hedonism The view that the quest for happiness is fundamental to morality.

humanism A cultural movement stemming from the rediscovery of the classical works of Greek philosophy. Humanist ethics emphasizes the dignity of humankind and the centrality of human reason as opposed to the unquestioning acceptance of tradition.

intuitionism The view that 'good' cannot be further defined (in other words, it cannot be explained by more basic concepts) but only known through intuition.

karma 'Action' in Sanskrit; used of the idea that actions (good or bad) have an effect on the person who performs them. It is found in slightly different forms in Hinduism, Buddhism and Jainism.

logical positivism A philosophical view that accepted as meaningful only those statements that could be verified with reference to sense experience (and therefore argued that most ethical statements were meaningless).

logos The Greek term for 'word', used by the Stoics for the fundamental rationality in the universe and therefore the basis of a 'natural law' approach to ethics.

meta-ethics Second-order statements, explaining the nature and function of ethical language.

metaphysical ethics An approach that relates morality to an overall view of the nature of reality.

natural law The ethical theory based on the idea of the 'final cause' or purpose of things, which defines their proper use.

naturalistic fallacy The common error (pointed out by Hume and G.E. Moore) of trying to derive an 'ought' from an 'is'.

non-cognitive Used of a view that moral claims are related to the emotions and preferences of people who use them, rather than to any objective fact.

normative ethics A study of the moral norms or principles.

preference utilitarianism The utilitarian theory based on the satisfaction of the preferences of the individuals concerned.

prescriptivism The theory that ethical assertions prescribe courses of action, i.e. to say something is 'good' is to recommend that you should do it.

relativism, ethical The view that there are no absolutes, but that right and wrong are relative to each social, historical or cultural context.

situation ethics The theory argued by Fletcher in the 1960s that Christian morality should be based on doing whatever is most loving, even at the expense of traditional moral rules.

teleological ethics Used of any ethical theory based on the expected end or purpose (telos) of an action.

utilitarianism A theory that evaluates morality according to its aim of achieving 'the greatest good for the greatest number'.

virtue ethics A moral theory based on the development and promotion of qualities and virtues that embody the good life.

Index

Credits

Notes

Notes

Notes